FINDING THE WORDS

FINDING THE WORDS

WRITERS ON INSPIRATION, DESIRE, WAR, CELEBRITY, EXILE, AND BREAKING THE RULES

EDITED BY JARED BLAND

EMBLEM

McCLELLAND & STEWART

Library and Archives Canada Cataloguing in Publication

Finding the words : writers on inspiration, desire, war, celebrity, exile, and breaking the rules / edited by Jared Bland.

ISBN 978-0-7710-1369-0

1. Canadian essays (English) – 21st century. I. Bland, Jared

PS8373.1.F56 2011   C814'.608   C2010-906742-8

Library of Congress Control Number: 2010940060

We acknowledge the financial support of the Government of Canada through the Book Publishing Industry Development Program and that of the Government of Ontario through the Ontario Media Development Corporation's Ontario Book Initiative. We further acknowledge the support of the Canada Council for the Arts and the Ontario Arts Council for our publishing program.

Typeset in Calisto by M&S, Toronto
Printed and bound in Canada

ANCIENT FOREST
FRIENDLY

This book is printed on acid-free paper that is 100% recycled, ancient-forest friendly (100% post-consumer waste).

McClelland & Stewart Ltd.
75 Sherbourne Street
Toronto, Ontario
M5A 2P9
www.mcclelland.com

1 2 3 4 5   15 14 13 12 11

CONTENTS

——

Miguel Syjuco | Visitation
286

INTRODUCTION

———

JARED BLAND

When I was thirteen years old, I said something extremely rude to my father. It was a summer day in central Illinois, which meant it was exceedingly hot and humid, the sort of weather that clings like a particularly thick sweater. We were on the path that wrapped around the back of our house, and as soon as I said what I said he turned on me. His rage was radiant, and I knew that he was doing all he could not to strike me. Instead he pushed me off the path and through a landscaped bed of plants and flowers, until my back was pressed against the brick wall of our house. With his large hand pinning my shoulder to the bricks, he leaned in so that our faces were mere inches apart.

"Do not say anything like that in my presence ever again," he said.

I must have muttered something pathetic. His palm slid up off my shoulder, so that he pinned the fabric of my shirt against the flats of the bricks and grooves of the mortar.

And then he let go. He just let go, turned around, and walked away. I never looked at him quite the same way again, which isn't to say I loved him less, nor even liked him less. But something passed between us, my transgression manifest, and on that day our relationship underwent one of the innumerable adjustments

1

that define a lifetime of knowing another person. His words exist still in my mind – I can hear them echoing between my ears. Few things said to me have ever had greater effect.

But here's the thing: I can't even remember what I said to him in the first place.

———

One might conclude that my inability to remember is a result of wilful forgetting or some other form of repression. I prefer not to think so, partly because I remember everything else of that day with such vividness – when I finally left the flower bed, I looked down and could see the darkening imprint of my heel left like a bruise on the leaf of a hosta plant – and partly because I believe that this moment highlights one of the things that is so unique, so incredible, and so challenging about language and its power over us.

I remember with piercing clarity each word my father spoke to me that day. If I tried, I could probably remember more words said that day, and certainly many others said in the years that followed, especially between him and me. This is nothing un-usual, of course. Many fathers and sons have the sort of relation-ship marked by these big, ugly moments, and it's quite natural to remember such moments as being lit with an especially bright light. But nor is it unusual to forget vast quantities of what we say or hear, even when recalling such formative incidents. This is the essential mystery of the way words function in our lives: they are at once capable of altering the course of the world we inhabit and changing the amount of sugar in our coffee. Language exists for us as something sublime – and, for some, even divine – as well as something incredibly banal. Is there anything else that is so defining yet disposable, so immortal yet instantly forgettable?

And this is more complicated still for writers, who are, after all, the artists whose raw material is most omnipresent in their lives. (A pianist plays notes to make art, but must use the words "window seat" or "gluten-free alternative" to make an airline reservation; a painter, it is true, could write a letter in acrylic, but he cannot speak to his child in watercolours.)

That unique fact makes language an incredibly rich subject for an anthology, and to capture it as broadly as possible we invited novelists, journalists, songwriters, memoirists, philosophers, and essayists to write about the idea of finding the words. And as material began to arrive from writers across the country and from around the world, we were gratified to find this evocative theme had led our contributors to produce such multifaceted meditations on the nature of creativity, language, power, and storytelling, pieces that reflected the varied and unique experiences, obsessions, and inspirations of each writer. Many of the pieces are wonderfully intimate; they open the doors to their authors' creative lives and invite the reader in to learn about how a certain character was shaped, how a given book was composed. Some essays deal with the intersection of language and the writers' own lives – revealing the quiet desperation that comes from the silence of a small prairie town, or the incredible wealth of stories that exists behind prison doors. Some grant the reader access to a previously unknown corner of the world through the remarkable lens of a South African intellectual or a Malaysian expat in Beijing or a streetwise wannabe gangster in mid-century Montreal. But as diverse as they are, each of these pieces reflects in a particular way on the role words play in all our lives – on what it means to be a citizen of a world both united and divided by the lines language draws.

These essays all have something else in common as well. The writers in this collection have all generously donated their time, effort, and talent to this anthology in support of PEN Canada, an organization dedicated to defending the freedom of expression in Canada and around the world. None of these pieces has before appeared in book form, and all but a small handful were composed especially for this anthology. Cartoonist Seth has also generously donated his cover design and illustration to the project. To ensure that as much of the anthology's cover price will go directly to PEN Canada, McClelland & Stewart is contributing all of its resources in the publication of the book, and Random House of Canada is contributing its warehousing and shipping costs. Friesens is also providing its printing services at a significant discount.

Across the country, writers, readers, and supporters are eager to join together to do the important work of defending free expression and lobbying for the liberation of writers imprisoned around the world. We hope our theme – these variations on the idea of finding the words – can pay tribute to these men and women whose cases remind us that the freedom of expression we enjoy in this country does not exist in many corners of the globe. While we use language every day – sometimes gloriously, sometimes frivolously – we cannot forget that being able to do so is an essential right that must be defended.

Jared Bland
August 17, 2010
Toronto

FINDING THE WORDS

—

HEATHER O'NEILL

A Story Without Words

1

My dad was the youngest of nine children. My grandmother's first husband, with whom she had four children, never returned from the First World War. They buried a little Canadian flag and his favourite hat in the backyard. Later, there were rumours that he had indeed come back and had changed his name and was living a few streets away from his family. The way my father tells it, he would be spotted on Saint Catherine Street dressed in a fur coat, swinging a cane around his finger, with his head thrown back, laughing.

My grandmother's second husband – my grandfather – had a big laugh. He would stand on a table and sing. His name was Oscar, but he liked to be called Louis Louis. He gambled all his money away, but my grandmother said that they were never, ever hungry when he was around. He died when my father was only three years old. My grandmother was left to raise the nine children on her own in 1930, the beginning of the Great Depression. Fathers were a bit of a mystery to my dad. They were legendary creatures that you stopped believing in after a certain age, like Santa Claus and the Tooth Fairy.

One of my father's brothers was run over by a horse-drawn beer carriage. The beer company offered to pay the costs of the funeral if the family didn't press charges. My father and his brothers walked down the street in new little black suits. The whole neighbourhood came out to admire the little boys in their tailored suits.

It was an age in which children died all the time. There was a booming business in little white coffins back then. People were always at funerals. They had to rush home from work and school to go to funerals. My father's mother was always dressed in black because she was always in mourning. Her cheeks were always as pink as roses from standing out in the cold at the graveyard every weekend. That was why she appeared so lovely to men. And her eyes were enormous from crying. Life was much, much more unfair back then. They cried all the time back then. They had proper things to cry about.

My grandmother made my father light candles in the church for all the little babies who had gone to heaven. He imagined heaven was filled with babies with ribbons in their little curls, clutching dolls in their round fists. The babies stood up shaking the bars of their cribs, crying in heaven. The babies wanted angels to pick them up and rock them the way their mothers had. But angels were very busy. Angels had to listen to all the petitions and prayers from insensitive people who would call on them to win a baseball game.

The priests would always ask my grandmother how she was coping, but she would hurry away. The only people she told her children not to talk to were priests. Eventually, they took two of my dad's older brothers away and put them in orphanages when my grandmother wasn't looking. The priests were always taking children away. They would get money from the government for every child they collected. The way my dad tells it, there were priests in their long black coats, hiding behind garbage cans with big butterfly nets waiting to swoop up unsuspecting babies.

There was no point in trying to get your children back once they believed in God. They looked down on you and thought that you were mad. They insisted that you put your nickels in the collection plate.

In terror of the priests and death, my grandmother returned for a time to Prince Edward Island, where she was from. She had moved to Montreal looking for dashing men and wondrous fortune and she returned with nothing but hungry boys. My dad doesn't have many memories of Prince Edward Island. He says that a goose fell madly in love with him. It followed him everywhere he went. The goose was incredibly demanding. He could never love the goose the way it needed to be loved. Who can really love anybody the way that person needs to be loved? It's hard enough now; it was impossible during the Depression.

He and his mother spent the days going to big houses trying to get work, or charity. One old lady they were visiting handed my dad a plate of lemon cookies. He devoured them greedily. Afterwards, as they were walking home, his mother asked why he couldn't have at least saved one cookie for her. He says he never felt so bad in all his life.

His mother decided to return to Montreal. The goose wept and wept when it heard the news. What could my father say? He never knew what happened to the goose. That's the way things were back then. You lost one another so easily.

Back in Montreal, his mother found a job as a janitor. She worked every day washing the floors of Baron Byng high school on St. Urbain Street. One winter someone stole her coat. She couldn't afford a new one, so she had to run to work every day. She never had anything new. She didn't have any magic tricks for any of her boys. She couldn't pull coins out of anyone's ears.

She had to yell all the time just to be able to get all the scolding done. She had to start yelling before she even opened her eyes in the morning. Who knows if she imagined anything? If she had time to sit around thinking about Prince Charming and frogs that begged to be kissed? The boys just stayed out of her way and hung out on the street corners and in the alleys of Montreal like cats sent out to roam.

2

Then my father started school with the other neighbourhood boys his age. On the first day of kindergarten, the teacher called out Patrice and Charles and Raymond. No one answered. They all thought that their names were Buddy and Itchy and Blackie and Pepe LePuke. His mother never packed him a lunch. Once his teacher gave him a sandwich to eat in the coat closet, so that the other children couldn't see and he wouldn't be embarrassed. Another time she asked him why he didn't tie his shoelaces. He told her that no one had taught him. No one taught him anything.

Over the next four years at school, my dad wasn't able to learn to read. The grade three teacher called his mother in and told her that he had trouble reading. His mother was humiliated. Single mothers are always easily humiliated. They identify too much with their children. They are too proud of their accomplishments and too ashamed of their failures. They are terrible for their children. She was mortified and didn't want to be called into the school ever again. She decided that he shouldn't go back to school at all. That was her way of solving the problem.

So my dad left school in grade three. After that, he was always looking for a way to make enough money to get something to eat. He sometimes sold roses that he'd dug out of the graveyard garbage bin on the street corner. He tried selling newspapers but he would get beat up mercilessly by the older boys who worked the busy street corners. Finally he was left sitting on his pile of newspapers by the river with only the mice hopping by. Mice are not big newspaper readers.

He used to go with his cousin Marie to sing in a rich woman's house. The woman would invite her friends over to watch the sweet poor children sing. They would sing little French songs. He would get dizzy from singing while hungry. She would always give them fancy treats to eat that they were crazy about. Candied apples and bags filled with cookies. They would eat them on the street corner feeling horribly guilty because they knew that they should be saving some for their mothers.

One day the woman gave my dad a whole quarter as a reward for fainting at the end of his rendition of "Le Petit Navire." When he saw the quarter in his palm, my dad could think of only one thing: he was going to go see *Snow White and the Seven Dwarfs*.

He needed more than money to get into the movie, though. There had been a great fire in a movie theatre in Montreal several years before. Loads of little children were trampled to death or died of smoke inhalation. The mayor or the prime minister or the judges or the politicians decided that children couldn't go to the theatre by themselves anymore. They had to be accompanied by an adult.

He stood outside the movie theatre, approaching adults going in. He asked if they would pretend that he was their child. Finally a man agreed to be his father, if just for a second, at St. Peter's Gate. It was the first movie my dad had ever seen. My dad says it was so beautiful that he almost wept. It was like being in a garden of flowers that whispered, "I love you." Butterflies were everywhere. He never wanted the movie to end. He didn't want to grow up and be burned out by the world like his mother.

He wanted to feel and feel and feel. He always wanted to feel the way he did while watching *Snow White*.

3

One day my dad looked over a fence in an alleyway and saw a pretty little girl sitting in a backyard. She had a big basket of potatoes and a pot of water at her feet. She was pretending that the potatoes were her babies. She would pick up a potato and kiss it and beg it to stop crying. She would tell the potato that it was time to undress and get into bed. Then she would peel the potato and put it gently in the pot of water.

My dad climbed over the fence and introduced himself. The girl said her name was Sally and asked if he wanted to play Bluebeard. They would pretend to get married and then he would chase her around the yard threatening to kill her.

My dad had never heard of Bluebeard. He was worried that the little girl might be completely mad. His eldest brother had warned him about girls who are off their rockers. They lured you into their houses with sweet words and then locked you in and never let you leave. They forced you to have loads and loads of babies and then put a spell on you that made all the hair fall off your head.

Sally explained that Bluebeard was just a story in a book. She went into her house and came out with an enormous book filled with fairy tales. They sat next to each other on her back step as she read him the story of Bluebeard. He felt so happy and little and protected listening to the story. No one had ever read to him before. He wished that he could read. All the stories that you would know! How boring this world was! He begged Sally to read him another one.

Sally turned the page and read him the story of Puss in Boots. It's the story of a very clever cat who gets the job done. The cat is an accountant, a foreign diplomat, and an investor. He is wicked when he needs to be wicked.

After reading half the stories in the book, Sally lost her voice. She asked my dad to read her one. But he couldn't because he still didn't know how to read. He had left school seven years earlier and hadn't been able to figure out a single word since.

My dad stood by and watched all his other friends read words: comic books, movie marquees, labels of clothes, newspaper headlines, street schedules, bus directions, the fortunes in fortune cookies, Valentine's Day cards. You realize how much there is to read when you cannot read a thing. So many things are just beyond your grasp, like looking at a pile of sweets behind a window, like not being able to run in a dream. Everything is like a lottery ticket and you can't scratch the gold off.

<h1 style="text-align:center">4</h1>

My dad's family moved every year. Their apartments were always cold and falling apart and they always expected the next one to be a little bit better. But during the first night in a new house, they could still hear bugs crawling around under the wallpaper and they knew it was no different.

One year they moved a little farther away, to a place in Chinatown. My dad met a group of gangsters that were hanging out there at the time. The gangsters called the kids over and introduced themselves. Whenever he described them to me when I was a kid, I would imagine the fox in the top hat and the cat in the waistcoat who stopped Pinocchio on his way to school, to entice him into a life onstage. It is easier to romanticize criminals from back then. They wore suits and fedoras on the sides of their heads. They had the reputations of rock stars. They had names like Lucien La Boeuf and One-Eyed Maurice.

It seemed that being a criminal was a legitimate profession. For some people, there was no choice but to steal. It was nothing to be a bank robber. In elementary school, when the teacher asked what the children wanted to be when they grew up, at least three or four would say bank robber. There were so many bank robbers. They would come out at night with the alley cats. They would be riding the all-night bus. The diners would be filled with men with black masks on. There would be loads of them up on the rooftops, sitting there worried about the competition.

One of the gangsters my dad met was Johnny Young. Johnny Young was a magician like Harry Houdini. Except that whereas Houdini liked the limelight, Johnny Young flourished in the shadows. He was the reason you put more and more locks on your doors. People covered their houses in locks, as if their homes were impenetrable vaults. Whereas Houdini made a show of getting out of such contraptions, Johnny Young made a spectacle of getting into them.

Johnny Young was always coming off some magnificent heist. He unrolled Persian carpets and bluebirds flew out of them into the air and horses galloped off the designs and down the street. He had paintings of the Virgin Mary that actually wept. He had teacups made of porcelain so fine that they closed up at night, the way sleeping flowers do. Johnny Young was like Marco Polo returning with amazing wares that no one had ever seen before, that were meant for only rich people to lay their eyes on.

Johnny Young had a French girlfriend who was a singer. She would start singing and then everyone started singing along with her. She walked like a baby bouncing on someone's lap.

Even her curls seemed to enjoy being on her head. My dad couldn't imagine his mother having ever, ever looked like that.

Johnny Young and his gang were funny and clever. Especially compared with the other adults my dad met, who were always about to drop dead from exhaustion. The gang members were like aristocrats because they didn't have to work nine-to-five jobs. My dad decided that a life of crime might be for him.

5

The summertime drives everyone in Montreal a little crazy. You take off your fur hat and you can't help but feel light-headed. Walking without your boots, you feel like a dancer. Everybody seems naked without their coats. All the girls on the bus have such a shy sweet way about them, as if you'd been married the day before and are waking up next to them for the first time.

My dad was walking around with a friend of his. My dad can't remember his name. It was either Karl, Étienne, Réjean, Philippe, Pierre, or Normand. I'm partial to the name Normand.

My dad and Normand were walking down an alley. There were cats everywhere. Some meowed in French and some meowed in English, depending on which language their family spoke at home. There were dogs too. They walked without leashes back then. They said, "Hello, Governor," under their breath and went on their way. There were flowers growing through the fences, reaching out at you like the hands of patients in asylums. There were little girls with pieces of chalk writing terrible and libellous things on the walls about boys who didn't love them.

My dad and Normand weren't looking for trouble. But it was very important to always keep an eye open for opportunities for crime that might arise unexpectedly. You had to spot them, like spotting the paper doors on Advent calendars that chocolates were hidden behind.

When they passed behind a bakery, the boys knew at once that it was their lucky day. The back windows of the bakery were wide open because it was such a hot day. The bakers had placed six huge pies on the windowsill to cool off. My dad and Normand quickly stacked the pies on top of each other and ran off. They were so excited! To have your heart beat like that and not have it kill you! That was youth.

They climbed up a fire escape and onto the roof of a building. They sat down cross-legged up in the sky and began cutting slices out of the pies with a pocket knife. Eating made them happy. All their dreams for the moment had come true. There were strawberry, apple, and rhubarb pies. They were so full that they thought that they would never be hungry again. They had never imagined there was a point that you could reach where you had had enough pie and didn't want any more.

They sat on the roof feeling satisfied. They were so high up that clouds were right around their shoulders. My dad and Normand took some of the clouds in their hands. They moulded them like clay. They made them into rabbits and elephants and then put them back in the sky. People lying on their backs in the grass in the park pointed out that there seemed to be more forms in the clouds that day.

My dad and Normand looked down below at the street. The people seemed so tiny. You could put them in a dollhouse and have them cook and clean up and kiss one another, and whatever else you wanted them to do. They decided to throw the rest of the pies over the side of the building and onto the heads of passersby.

As soon as they heard the sounds of people yelling, they scrambled up and started running over the rooftops. They clambered all the way down the block. They noticed another open window. They climbed in to see what fortunes this one would lead to.

The place ended up being a suit factory. Even though they were boys, they had no trouble finding suits their own size. Men were smaller back then. Some men were as small as five-year-old boys. They would take off their hats to show waitresses their completely bald heads to prove that they were of drinking age.

They went back to my dad's house with their new suits under their arms, eager to try them on. His mother would be working for hours and hours, so she wouldn't be in their way. They scrubbed themselves clean, greased their hair to the sides, and changed into their new duds. For the *pièce de résistance*, they went outside, pulled up some dandelions, and stuck them in their buttonholes. Then they set off. They wanted everyone to see them in their fantastic new outfits. This was their moment to shine. They were multimillionaires.

They walked down De la Gauchetière Street, trying to pass themselves off as rich gentlemen. Their idea of how rich gentlemen behaved was an amalgamation of illustrations they'd seen in picture books, the voices of men advertising toothpaste on the radio, and villainous caped puppets that performed in the park. They knew to act fancy free as if they didn't have a care in the world and to put a skip in their step. They also knew to talk loudly and in British accents.

"It was a jolly good outing we had!" my dad exclaimed.

"A perfect day for plundering," Normand agreed. "We did have ourselves some jolly laughs."

"That's a boy, old chap."

"That's a decent sort of bloke."

"I'll spend a fortnight in Scotland Yards."

"If you please, sir! If you please!"

"Cheerio, I say! Cheerio!"

"Yes. Yes. Well done!"

Johnny Young spotted them right away from the window of the café he was sitting in. He knew crime had been committed, the way that leopards are able to detect a small animal moving about in the dark. When Johnny Young walked out of the café and stood directly in their paths, my dad and Normand started making up a story about a new job or a wedding. Johnny Young screwed up his eyes, as if listening to their lies were like listening to an out-of-tune piano.

Johnny got them to admit they'd stolen the suits. He also got the two boys to take him and his cronies back to the factory. My dad climbed up the fire escape and opened the doors for everyone to get inside. They all got arrested.

6

My dad was held in Bordeaux Jail for a year, awaiting trial. He wept every night. He sometimes wished that he were dead. He fantasized about a huge funeral procession for him on St. Catherine Street. All the little girls would wear black coats and throw flowers at his coffin as it passed. They would weep because they would never be able to marry him.

My dad was terrified of everything. He was terrified of being in jail. He was terrified of going to court. He was terrified that all the lawyers would yell at him. He was terrified that all the people who had had pies land on their heads were also going to show up. Then the judge would lose all respect for him. Maybe the trial would be written about in the newspaper. He wouldn't even be able to know what it said because he couldn't read.

He told himself the stories that Sally had told him. He told them to himself over and over again. He started adding himself into the stories. Puss in Boots would come to visit him in prison in a three-piece suit. Puss would say that he would serve as my dad's attorney. He would be able to get him out of this mess.

These times – if you've ever been desperate – are when you rely on your imagination. It is the only thing that keeps you from going mad. It leads you out of the darkness, like will-o'-the-wisps that lure you to adventures far from home.

My dad sometimes imagined going to the ball where Cinderella met Prince Charming. He would tell Cinderella all his funny jokes. She would find the prince so stiff compared to him. Cinderella would like him better because they were from the same neighbourhood. He would tell her how his mother scrubbed floors, too.

Other times he imagined that he was able to play the flute like the Pied Piper of Hamelin. All the little girls would follow him to the St. Lawrence River, just as the rats had followed the piper. The girls would take off their dresses and go swimming in their slips and underwear in the river.

My dad imagined that he had a son like Tom Thumb. The boy was so tiny that he would do laps in a teacup. He couldn't play ball. If someone threw a ball at him, it would kill him. Everyone would say to my dad, "How marvellous. How did you ever manage to have such a very, very tiny boy?"

In this land of stories, my dad was king. He wore a golden crown. He had little girls bite his cupcakes for him to make sure that they weren't poisoned. They would fall ill and die and it was a tragedy. He had horses that spoke and geese that were his confidants.

My dad was finally called to court. The court was filled with strangers, including a very angry-looking factory owner.

When the judge walked into the courtroom, he took one look at my dad standing there, shorter and younger and more miserable than the rest of the cons, and declared, "Get this child out of my courtroom."

7

It was years before my dad learned to read. He always kept his illiteracy a secret. Secrets are an incarnation of fear, and fear is irrational. Since it's irrational, it can be as tall as it wants, or as small as it wants. Whatever it needs to be in order to take over your life. It is like living with a wife that you despise: even when she just taps the spoon against her teacup, it makes the noise of a traffic jam. If you don't share a secret soon enough, it begins to have a life of its own. It will get a restraining order so that it can live independently of you and you can never touch it.

When my dad was eighteen, he met a woman that he trusted. He told her that he couldn't read. She said that she would teach him.

She was so patient and gentle that the letters didn't run away like deer the minute my dad laid eyes on them. They didn't play hide-and-go-seek, or run down the corridor naked, like a kid escaping from a bath. They didn't crowd together like children trapped in a burning theatre. They were no longer like knots in a shoelace that were impossible to untangle.

Instead, each sentence was like a bird's nest with eggs in it. There was suddenly sense in all that scribble scrabble. It was spring and the eggs would hatch and the birds would sing. They would sing loudly, great long compositions. They could not be made to keep quiet.

And my dad smiled and the woman clapped her hands.

And her name was Heather. When I was born, he named me after her.

And the factory owner had a son who also grew up to be a writer. And his name was Leonard Cohen. But that is another Montreal story.

LINDEN MacINTYRE

On Mediocrity, Consensus, and Success

Recently I won a prize for writing a novel. It was a significant prize, the Scotiabank Giller, arguably the prize most coveted by Canadian fiction writers, from the heights of accomplishment all the way down to the earliest flickers of lonely aspiration. The Giller is a signature moment in the autumn literary harvest, and not just because it delivers a hefty monetary salute ($50,000). The prize acknowledges an arrival. Like any arrival, anywhere, it is a euphoric moment when heavy baggage is set down, drinks are poured, food proffered. In the din of celebration, the literary celebrati set aside their most venal impulses for at least a few hours of generosity and hospitality.

I have been writing for a living for close to fifty years but never really considered myself a Writer. I have, for all that time, been part of a profession called "journalism," but neither have I even been able to comfortably adopt the designation "journalist." When I started out in that field we were all "reporters." The job title "journalist" was widely regarded as an affectation by foreigners and delusional poseurs. (The actual word for a poseur in those more candid times was "wanker.") I am of a generation and a disposition that resists ostentatious labelling and logos. But on November 10, 2009, I became – as a consequence of what I then called "an accident of consensus" – a Writer.

There was a glow, the typical emotional aftermath of a cathartic release. This glow, though superficial, was enough to defeat a lingering suspicion of unworthiness and a genuine uneasiness that was being caused by the confident assertions of others that "this is going to change your life." I have outlasted most juvenile delusions about the long-term value of unplanned alterations in a life. I was more optimistic about the possibility that this development would change the prospects of a book I cared about. That was good. The rest was debatable.

I'm told that at the climactic moment, when the distinguished Giller patron, Jack Rabinovitch, announced my name, a senior publishing executive snatched a BlackBerry from a tuxedo pocket and authorized what would become an avalanche of books: my books, soon to dominate the entrances and windows of bookstores everywhere in Canada. A BlackBerry in my own pocket buzzed as I stumbled to the podium and fumbled for some words of gratitude. The message buzzing in my pocket was from my friend Rick Mercer, who was in the crowd. I would later be touched by his simple electronic message and how perfectly it captured my own reaction to the moment: "Holy fuck. You won the Giller!!!"

Prizes were far from my mind in early August 2009, as I drove through Nova Scotia contemplating the possible impact of a novel that was about to be released after a gestation of some years. The novel was about a priest caught up in the suppression of potential scandals inside his church. The scandals related to a topic I believed most Catholics didn't want to hear about: sexual abuse of children by clergymen. It was something that happened and had been dealt with, if in a mostly superficial way. Some outrageous cases had been prosecuted, some offenders sent to jail; it was, in the minds of many, over. I anticipated criticism, if not outright censure, for picking at a still-infected scab, raking up old controversy for mercenary reasons.

Then, just above the threshold of anxiety I heard the name of a local bishop, Raymond Lahey, on the car radio. I listened. It was a news report. The bishop was publicly apologizing for ... what? Sexual abuse by priests? Going back through time for decades?

I almost had to stop the car to properly absorb the news. Furthermore, this enlightened man was offering a financial compensation package for the victims – a sum in the range of fifteen million dollars, a vast amount of money in a diocese that had been economically ravaged in recent years. The money would be coming from the meagre bank accounts of poor parishes; in other words, the pockets of the faithful, most of whom wouldn't have recognized a pedophile if he was sitting at their kitchen table – but would probably have murdered him if they'd had the tiniest suspicion. Now they'd be asked to dig deep in empty pockets to pay for criminal transgressions they hardly understood. It was a dark moment in the history of the diocese, but by some miracle of timing, my book suddenly seemed to be astute, prophetic even.

A few weeks later the same bishop, Raymond Lahey, announced his retirement from the episcopacy. He was sixty-nine years old, with some unquestionably good work behind him. It made sense. But then, just days after that announcement, the bishop was arrested and charged with criminal possession of child pornography.

This was too much. Mercenary considerations (book sales) notwithstanding, I was now alarmed by the possibility that relentlessly unfolding real events could hijack a carefully constructed literary work and turn it into a peculiarly postmodern kind of "journalism" – the prose equivalent of reality TV. If there was any serious intent behind the writing of the book, it was to elevate the public consciousness about some deeper issues in an institution that still matters to a lot of people: the loneliness of priesthood; the paradox of being personally isolated while occupationally engaging in the most intimate aspects of other people's lives; the consequences of abuse of trust and power; the ease with which even good people compromise their principles at the cost of personal integrity.

There was a danger now that all my nuanced purposes would vanish in a daily torrent of dirty detail – that the book would be degraded to mere vulgarity by the inadequacy of instant reportage. It would be shunned by the literary world as another mediocre commentary on transient phenomena, the kiss of death for any serious Writer.

It's a word that I've been afraid of for many years: *mediocre*, meaning "neither good nor bad . . . just barely adequate." "Mediocrity," in the opinion of serious writers, is the opposite of "excellence." It is a fate, like atrophy and death, awaiting most of us, but one we struggle to transcend.

In the fall of 1989, I was in Prague, in what was then Czechoslovakia, working on a television documentary about unfolding political events and the role of creative people – writers, musicians, theatrical performers – in what was being called a "velvet revolution." We attended a conference of writers because of the possibility that the leading writer of the day, Vaclav Havel, would turn up. There was an optimistic rumour that he would emerge from hiding (he was being hunted by the authorities) to inspire his fellow citizens and literary peers. In fact, he did appear. And I know that he inspired the crowd, though I can't remember what he said. What I do remember is my conversation later with a woman, a well-known writer, who was at the gathering, a conversation that has haunted me.

I had asked her, in the deliberate tone of naïveté that is a common journalistic pose, to explain why Havel was on the run, at risk of imprisonment or worse, while here was a room full of other writers, many of them outspoken critics of the system, who were allowed to meet openly at a time of national unrest.

"Why," I asked, "do they publish you, let you and others like you meet openly to talk about your work, while Havel's writings are suppressed and he's in hiding?" I've saved a transcript of our brief exchange.

"I have been allowed to write," she said, "because I'm mediocre."

"What," I asked, "has the government got against excellence?"

"Excellence would not tolerate the mediocrity and the stupidity of the leadership," said she.

Her point was clear. Havel was a threat because he had been able to rise above a mediocre herd of people through his writing, and this made his ideas accessible and persuasive, and thus very dangerous. The ideas themselves weren't especially original. They were about fundamental human rights, the responsibilities of power, and the duties of the powerful who, in truth, are all servants of the people. But driven by the eloquence of Vaclav Havel, these ideas were inflammatory and influential.

I have recently arrived at the opinion that the writer with whom I spoke in Prague in 1989, though provocatively brave, was wrong. I have decided that she profoundly underestimated the potential that resides in mediocrity. I have, in time, come to the realization that the bureaucrats who ran her country at the time, in their obsession with a handful of outstanding talents like Vaclav Havel, had utterly misunderstood the existential peril of failing to recognize their true adversary.

The danger to the status quo, as would be shown dramatically within days of that conversation, was in a growing consensus among mediocre people that it was time for things to change. Havel was a symbol not of intellectual prowess or literary talent, but of something infinitely more potent. He represented courage. And when ordinary people realize that almost everyone is capable of courage, human circumstances change dramatically. Historical transformations begin with a consensus among mediocre people that they are capable of achieving, and entitled to possess, something better than that which they have.

Barbarians toppled the Roman Empire; peasants transformed Europe; farmers and small merchants snatched control of the American continent away from dynastic and commercial royalty; mediocre artists and blue-collar workers and students and populists drove Communism out of Europe.

Power lies in consensus. In the crucible of consensus, ordinary ideas become inspirational; common leadership acquires charisma; the mob, inspired, becomes an agency of human progress; mediocrity becomes . . . success.

Before the announcement of the Giller Prize, my book was modestly successful as a result of sensational publicity involving priests and bishops and sexual deviance. After the Prize, the book became exceptionally successful. It was hard to believe it was the same book. Not a word had changed, but it was perceived differently. As people learned that a small jury of distinguished authors had selected it from a stack of nearly a hundred other worthy books and awarded it a prize, a growing number of people arrived at the fortuitous consensus that it was worth reading.

Almost overnight, it became prominent on lists of what was currently most popular in bookstores and libraries. On some lists it was number one, on others number two. The weekly rankings of popularity generated more popularity. In one week alone, I was told, Canadian bookstores sold eight thousand copies of my book. I had written other books – books that I thought were just as worthy of attention – but none of them had come close, in their lifetimes, to the success this novel achieved in *one week*. I found it difficult to resist a perilous conceit: that my book was exceptionally good. It was at that point that I began to reflect on the power of consensus, the complex nature of success, and the ambiguous relationship between popularity and excellence.

Weeks passed. A new year began, and with it a new decade. The book's popularity continued as weeks turned into months. In time, its popularity became a kind of drug. I felt a palpable uneasiness, not unlike a hangover, during the intervals between the publication of the weekly lists. In time, an appearance on even the most obscure list would be sufficient for the necessary ego jolt. And that was when I realized that in the interest of my own mental health, I had to find a basis for an objective and sustainable evaluation of my book and, increasingly, myself.

I found it, eventually, with the assistance of another author, Dan Brown, whose enormous popularity in recent years surpassed my own.

Dan Brown's book *The Lost Symbol* had been my book's constant companion during the many weeks it was on the bestseller lists – Brown's book usually ranked just ahead of mine, usually in first place. It actually became a cause for celebration when, in the last week of January, my book moved ahead of his on the list that many people seemed to take most seriously, in the *Globe and Mail*. By the next week, in a correction that should have been predictable, Dan Brown resumed his place ahead of mine and, perhaps energized by his brief slippage, stayed there.

I haven't read *The Lost Symbol* for the simple reason that I have been too busy reading other things. But I have read reviews that were, without exception, cruel. *The Lost Symbol*, in the almost universal view of literary critics, was of a quality a grade or so below mediocrity.

But the book was a bestseller. As a matter of fact, it was more than that. It was a better-seller than the book I had written, which was itself a book catapulted into popularity by breaking news and by the Prize, if not by excellence of prose and insight. The key to understanding the true nature of success – the code, if you will – could be uncovered by no greater project than an objective reading of *The Lost Symbol*. Dan Brown would show me the intrinsic value of our popularity, and, hopefully, the integrity and durability of our success.

By April, I had noted that my novel had vanished from the list compiled for the *Globe and Mail*. Dan Brown's book held firm considerably longer.

I resolved to buy and finally read Brown's book. Only then could I, with confidence, establish any certainty about the nature of success and excellence and mediocrity and the relevance of such ephemera to Writing. But I keep wavering, stopped by some idiopathic paralysis just before I reach the cash desk, perhaps afraid that truth can be a greater burden than delusion.

MARINA ENDICOTT

How to Talk About Mayerthorpe

We weren't there when the men were murdered. We were eight years gone, in 2005, when four RCMP constables were killed in Mayerthorpe. A CBC producer called to ask me about earlier events behind the story. Not as the wife of an RCMP member, but because years before I'd been the editor of the *Freelancer*, Mayerthorpe's weekly newspaper. I couldn't tell him a thing. There's a blue cloud in my mind over that time; I am unable to remember anything except one day when Roszko stormed into the newspaper building in a rage, demanding to buy a half-page ad, in which he wanted to defend himself from some imagined slight. I went back into my office and the advertising manager dealt with him. I was unable to meet his crazy, suffering eyes. When he appeared in town, I crossed the street to avoid him, and not just because I knew he hated us all; I had an animal reluctance to let him overlook my baby.

I had the sense not to tell the CBC producer that story. I stammered, I fell silent; I told him there was nothing I could say. He hung up, angry, probably assuming that I was protecting the police.

But I knew nothing anyway. Compromised by my job as newspaper editor, I was never allowed to know anything that was going on. Some other wife would call to let me know if something really bad had happened, so I could brace myself; by that bush telegraph I sometimes had an inkling of why Peter hadn't come home for thirty-seven hours on his twenty-second straight shift on duty, but he was pathologically careful not to tell me anything, ever. Anyway, he had gone almost entirely silent by that time.

If I can't remember what happened, how can I tell the truth about it?

Even back then, before Mayerthorpe became a household name, words had failed me. When we first arrived, I tried to write about the experience of being with a new RCMP recruit.

Peter was stationed at Mayerthorpe straight out of Depot. He'd asked for a posting within 150 km of a major city, and Mayerthorpe just qualified. We drove out there the day before he was to report for duty, and drove up and down the single paved street. It was the ugliest town I'd ever seen.

We registered at the Haven Inn, in a plain room off the upstairs balcony, and then Peter went to report for duty. If I stood out there leaning against the metal railing, I could see the detachment. I had no experience of police, or of living in such a small town, or of the Alberta countryside.

Peter was put on the night shift with his trainer, Rick. That first night they came to take me for dinner, tires scraping the gravel outside our room, Peter calling up to the balcony like a uniformed Romeo. He opened the car's back door for me when I ran down, and closed it after me, and then I realized that there was no inner handle. No handholds, no seatbelt, nothing to hold on to or hit anyone with – plexiglass separating me from the men, with a special homemade adaptor that Rick had added at his wife's request, so the sliding divider couldn't be slid over far enough to hit the driver on the head.

I swayed in the lonesome blackness back there, listening hard for what they said up front, the two men with the rifle between them, all the strange equipment and the terrible smell. When we arrived at the highway restaurant I had to wait for Peter to let me out. His prisoner.

How this happened, by the way, how we ended up there: Peter was a poet and journalist when we met; I was a dramaturge, beginning to write fiction. When he told me, a couple of weeks later, that he had applied to the RCMP, I laughed and laughed. But he was serious. He was always being mistaken for a policeman. I think he succumbed to a feeling that this was his destiny, and to a strong desire to take action in the world, to do something worthwhile. To serve. Plus, his dad (a retired Staff Sergeant) told him that if he wanted a quiet place to get some writing done, a rural detachment would be an easy job.

When he finished the ferocious six months' training in Regina, we set off for Mayerthorpe, northwest of Edmonton along the Alaska Highway. The detachment contained a large Stoney reserve, Alexis; the highway was two-lane then, known for bad accidents; the countryside they policed spread a hundred kilometres each way, and contained the usual sprinkling of violent and crazy people. Ordinary detachment stuff.

We drove the single paved street in a daze, that first afternoon. You could not get the *Globe and Mail* there. There was no Internet, not even cable TV. Cell phones didn't exist.

Outside of town, the country is beautiful. We ended up renting a long-empty house on Brown Smoole's farm about ten kilometres out of town, and shared the place with a herd of chuckwagon ponies led by a licorice-black stallion. We paid the horrific electricity bills for the waterer and the yard light, and I chased the mice out of the stove and tried to write, while Peter fell into the black abyss of rural police work.

The last year we were in Mayerthorpe, 1997, I tried again to write about the RCMP: two mornings a week I gave the children, one and three by then, to a babysitter and sat in the ice-cold kitchen of an abandoned farmhouse (lent to me by Jean Zwicky, mother of the poet Jan Zwicky, and a good friend in an unexpected quarter), working on a novel about the wives of RCMP members and how they deal with fear. Jean would start a fire in the woodstove an hour before I arrived on those mornings; I'd sit and type in my parka until the room warmed up. In six months I had written enough to satisfy the requirements of the Alberta Foundation for the Arts grant I'd been given. Sounds romantic, sounds novelish.

But it was all crap. An illustrative excerpt:

Lesia was always loyal, careful, positive. Blue shadows under her eyes from worrying. How could someone that nervous be a nurse?

"It gets easier. It gets easier. Nothing bad has happened, we've been lucky. Touch wood! I don't think about it now. Of course, I'm at the hospital when he comes in with bad cases, I see a lot of the things he's dealing with, that helps. I know how hard it is for him. And I'd be right there if anything did happen, they wouldn't have to come and get me! I'd be right there with the bandages!"

Her laugh was sickeningly nervous, it was hard to keep on talking to her. For both our sakes, I changed the subject. Maybe seeing injuries all the time made it worse for her.

At first, remnants of our old life still clung to us – from time to time either Peter or I would be asked to write something.

I had a story in the *Journey Prize Anthology* in 1993; his book of poetry, *Purity of Arms*, which he'd been working on when we met, came out that fall; he wrote a couple of new poems. Only two, in the five years we lived in Mayerthorpe. Here's part of one, talking about how impossible it is to talk about the work:

> Explaining once, not the work, but at least the speed, 200
> on a night highway when the headlights can't guarantee a thing,
> they just can't see enough. How the dome lights spin
> red and blue in the rearview mirror, catch roadsigns
> . already gone.
> Another night, static on the radio, no place in particular to go
> wandering home on gravel, windows down and shooting stars
> shattering my windshield, I honour this storm of broken planets
> with the dome lights and watch my passing colour
> crash into hayfields.
> In those memories I still believed there was a way
> to be that brilliant against the night and never to burn up.

I struggled with the final section of my first novel for a year and a half, then threw the whole thing out and took the job as editor of the *Freelancer* – where I reported on the rural munici-pality council, high school sports teams, highway disasters, and the Ag Fair, and wrote editorials. All of which I did badly, un-derstanding neither journalism nor the place itself.

There was no way to talk about this life, in fiction or non-fiction. Even in letters to friends it was impossible to describe the place or the work – it was like we spoke Attic Greek, for all they understood. Some of our friends knew the *place* well enough, having lived rural themselves, but even with them there was no shared vocabulary for the exigencies of police service.

Which I only observed at second hand. So it shouldn't be

me writing this anyway. It seems like there's some work I haven't done yet, some thinking that would convert experience into conveyable truth. Perhaps that work is getting my own whining voice out of the story. Boiling down, boiling the self out of it.

Last year in Perth, Barry Lopez (talking specifically about his wife's memoir, *Live Through This*) said that autobiography is the recounting of what happened; memoir requires the courage to look at one's self in that time. For me it seems the opposite: to get to memoir, I am having to peel my eye off myself.

Maybe that's right. Mayerthorpe was a thing that happened, but not to me. When I think about the four young men who were killed, I am ashamed of my weakness and grief.

After a couple of years there, I took a stab at a radio play, thinking I might be able to make some coin out of all this misery.

(In a hospital corridor, talking to a dream surgeon.)

SURGEON: He'll never be the same. This has damaged him too far. His heart is broken. He's going to have an uncertain temper, always. His spirit is exhausted, his vision is blurred, his hearing rings, and he'll have a bad taste in his mouth for the rest of his life.

Alice? Here, have mine.

(ALICE blows her nose. The surgeon consoles her.)

SURGEON: He's still brave and kind, he's been able to save some lives and some sadness. He's healed a number of people by the compassion he's given them, and the value in which he places them. A great host of people

whose lives are better will rise up in heaven and thank
him . . .

(String music swells, cuts off with a squawk.)

ALICE: I don't care about them. I don't care about all the bad
          guys either. I want everyone to go home. Let anarchy
          rule.

Lots of sobbing in that one, boy. It didn't sell.

Nothing worked. I couldn't write anything else, either. It
was like we had a gag order imposed on us. It got ridiculous
when Peter was commissioned to write a piece on rural policing
for the *National Post*. Here's a taste:

After accident scenes there are day dreams of broken
bodies opening their eyes, wide and surprised. Frustrated
with me because I failed to find the pulse in the armpit.
Long after sweeping glass off the highway, a quick prickle
of fear, and I convince myself that there might have been
life under all that blood and brain. No doubt this is some
kind of denial of responsibility, rejection of the assigned
task. I belong in Craiglockhart with the mute and the
paralyzed.

The piece never appeared. He did finally get a kill fee for it
(and the money was very welcome at the time). Eventually, a few
years later, Peter wrote an episode of a TV series called *The Beat*,
not about Mayerthorpe, which was turned into the pilot and
won an AMPIA award for best drama. Which he couldn't bear to
watch, and still has never seen.

—

Ten years later, far from Mayerthorpe, I finally inched toward writing about it, in poems. I ought to have known poetry would end up as the only option. On our first drive to town, getting close, Peter remembered Jan Zwicky's line about "the brown Sangudo hill" and realized that she must have travelled this road before us. It's in her collection *Songs for Relinquishing the Earth*.

> Sangudo, of the long hill and the river flats;
> of the long shadows in the river valley; Sangudo,
> of the early evening, in the summertime,
> on the way out Highway 43 after
> a day in the city: how ugly
> I used to think your name . . .

In the end, all my thinking about that RCMP wives novel boiled down to a poem. Boiling down is a good phrase; not that any novel can be cut and cut till it becomes a poem, but that this material never was a novel. It reminds me of the process of felting: you take a loose-knit sweater, wash it in scalding water until it's had the shit kicked out of it and shrinks to half its size, then matt it with an emery block and dry it at the highest heat. You end up with felted wool, a tight, dense, thick fabric that practically holds water. It's not that it's a good poem, but it's closer to the truth than anything else I've written has been. I'm still in there commenting, you'll notice.

HOW

> One said: *I'm not scared*
> *any more. It goes away.*
> Looked sideways out the back
> to where her husband laid his whip
> across the horse, whipping and shouting.

One talks to hers while he's at work.
He calls pretty often. We've been married sixteen years.
Shot at twice, one partner killed,
his moonface gleams in headlights
drowsing under an overpass.

One poor woman,
slip-eyed, nervy:
It gets easier.
It gets easier. No.
I don't think about it now.

Another, a peaceful smiler:
Well I just know
he's in God's hands, I'm
just never afraid at all.
(Maybe that is true.)

The last wife shook, laughed, shuddered,
laughed – fright spilling over her lower lids:
Oh nobody nobody ever talks, I'm
sick that something will happen. The whole time
he's on shift I plan his funeral.

Don't speak.

The sergeant coming up the walk
two of them together
that's how you know.

Mayerthorpe, 1996

Talking to Andrew Wreggit, who was then writing the made-for-TV movie about Mayerthorpe, Peter said, "A normal day might contain the ongoing Roszko issues but would also be punctuated by car accidents, domestics, disturbances on the Reserve, impaired drivers, and so on. We were very busy because we often worked alone. On a regular basis we did things without backup because our partner might be off sick, on leave, on a course or whatever. We did what we could, in the fashion of sticking a finger in the dike. The Roszko thing was like a purple thundercloud on the horizon taking a long time to work its way east. You know it's there, all night you see the flashes, but in the meantime there's too much else to be done."

After avoiding it for thirteen years, I drove out to Mayerthorpe last week. I thought I might arrive where we started and know the place for the first time, like Eliot promises.

It is a very ugly town.

I drove through it and out again, out to the refuge of Jean Zwicky's farmhouse, now given to the land trust; past the spot on the highway where I once saw six men scrambling to catch an escaped pig; the place where my baby son and I watched fox kits play in the long grass, where a tall young moose stepped over a fence without even jumping. Past the low-lying bit of road where, once in a while, I'd see a heron lift out of the creek, and be able to live for a few more days. That Quonset, from a distance. Peter not there.

The day those men were killed, Peter was at work, at meetings up in Edmonton. He called before anyone knew exactly what had happened, to reassure me that he had not been in Mayerthorpe.

But he was, we were.

DAVID BEZMOZGIS

Requiem For My Grandfather, Jakov Milner, Zionist

When the war started, on July 12, 2006, my grandfather was bed-ridden and had been so for nearly two months. My mother, aunt, and uncle had resolved to keep him in his own apartment for as long as they could. With great difficulty, they had sought out and hired a Ukrainian woman named Nadja who was in Canada illegally to earn money to send home to her children and grandchildren. She slept on a pullout couch in my grandfather's living room, fed him, washed him, and changed his diaper. Toronto Social Services helped by providing forty-two hours of nursing care each week. My mother and aunt visited him daily. On Sundays my uncle went over and gave him a shave. The rest of us – me, my wife, my cousins – came to see him on Friday nights. We stood by his bed, kissed his forehead, made feeble attempts at conversation, and tried not to cry. From week to week, we watched as he grew progressively frailer. He spoke very little, then not at all. In his room he had no radio or television. Outside his window there was a good view of a large park; on the wall facing him was a souvenir plaque depicting old Jerusalem; and above his head was a framed photograph of him and my late grandmother, taken in honour of their fiftieth wedding anniversary. He showed no interest in any of these things. Mostly, he lay silently with his eyes closed. When we would nervously inquire, Nadja would say, "No, he is not sleeping. He is just lying like that."

More than a year earlier, my grandfather had been diagnosed with malignant melanoma. The cancer had started as a tiny black spot on the small toe of his right foot. We thought little of it at first. My grandfather blamed it on an infection. Instead of going to see a chiropodist, he had tried to save money and have a man in his building trim his toenails. The man had done a poor job and cut his toe. When, after an exceedingly long time, the toe refused to heal, my grandfather re-diagnosed it as some type of fungus. Whatever it was, it looked horrible, and my mother took him to see various doctors. Their opinions diverged. Then they all went on vacation. By the time they returned, my grandfather discovered a lump in his groin. I was in the examining room with him and my mother when the oncologist insisted that we inform my grandfather of the test results. The doctor didn't speak Russian or Yiddish and so couldn't perform the task himself. My grandfather sat waiting on the examining table where, moments earlier, he had finished buttoning his woollen long underwear. My mother and I looked at each other, unsure of how to proceed. We were both furious at the doctor for making us say what we didn't want to say. "*Dedushka*, the doctor says you have a bad disease." The doctor gave him six months. On the drive home, my grandfather sat miserably in the back seat. When I got out of the car I saw that he was in tears. "I am a guest," he said.

But six months later, my grandfather was still alive. He had managed to survive a number of falls, a few cardiac scares, and the amputation of two toes. When I was married in October 2005 – almost a year after the grim diagnosis – my grandfather delivered the ceremonial blessing over the bread. That December, we celebrated his ninetieth birthday. The following April, although he was very unsteady on his feet and easily fatigued, he still managed to lead much of the first seder.

After this, his decline became more pronounced. In late May, when my wife and I left for our belated honeymoon to Israel, he was already confined to his bed. As we said goodbye to him, we knew it could be for the last time. From Israel, I called daily to hear if his condition had changed. "Everything is as before," was my mother's unvarying response.

When we returned after two weeks, we found him much reduced but still capable of studying the photographs we had taken on our trip. By this point, there was very little that seemed to engage him. His illness had caused him to become almost completely divorced from the world. To talk to him about our lives – which still involved innumerable preoccupations and future plans – felt absurd and callous. My mother and aunt rarely ventured beyond asking him if he was in pain, or if he wished to have his posture adjusted. The only reliable topic was Israel. My grandfather was a lifelong Zionist and Israel was his enduring passion. In his youth, in Latvia, he had been the leader of his local Betar group and, if not for the Soviet annexation and the war, he would have almost certainly emigrated to Palestine. After the war, even under the Soviet regime, he continued to nurture his Zionist aspirations. In 1979, when our family emigrated from Riga, his aspirations were realized. My parents and I, along with my aunt's family, settled in Toronto, but my grandparents and uncle went to Israel, and lived for seven years outside of Haifa, in Kiryat Bialik and Kiryat Motzkin. My grandfather loved the country, considered it his home, and believed uncompromisingly in its robustness and security. When the decision was made to reunite the family in Canada, he accepted it with some reluctance. But even though he physically relocated to Canada, he didn't concern himself with Canadian culture or politics. He arrived at the age of seventy and never learned to speak English. He went to synagogue, rarely strayed too far from his apartment

building, and socialized with elderly immigrants from the dispa-
rate corners of the Soviet Union, Yiddish speakers like himself.
Beyond this, he read newspapers in Russian and Yiddish, primarily to keep apprised of what was happening in Israel.

It is impossible for me to separate my grandfather's death from
the war. In my mind, the two tragedies are wedded together, or at
least proceed in parallel. My grandfather seemed to relinquish
his last hold on life when the rockets started falling on Kiryat
Shmona and Haifa. It was around this time that he started to slip
in and out of lucidity. What had before been a resigned or wilful
silence became something remote and otherworldly. Three
times a day, either Nadja or a nurse would succeed in penetrat-
ing his stupor to give him food – which he accepted obediently
or instinctively, like a baby bird. Otherwise he drifted. We would
stand at his bedside and watch his chest rise and fall with surprising regularity. Occasionally, and totally unpredictably, he would
emerge from his stupor for a morning or an afternoon and regard
us with comprehension and clarity. In these rare moments we
peppered him with dull questions but said not a word about
Israel, the war, the catastrophe that flickered non-stop on television in the other room. We didn't want to upset him, but by keeping the war from him I felt that we had severed his last meaningful
connection to the world. Now that we could no longer talk to
him about Israel, we could no longer talk to him at all.

For the first two weeks of the war my grandfather remained
in this limbic state. As the war exerted a greater claim on our attention, he hovered spectrally in the background. Whenever I
spoke to my mother to ask after his condition, the conversation
inevitably deviated onto the subject of the war. I spent hours
each day comparing the coverage in the *New York Times*, *Haaretz*,
the *Globe and Mail*, and even on Al Jazeera – hoping in this way

to approach even-handedness and truth. Although I feared terribly for Israel and was incensed by editorials that distorted facts and were latently if not overtly anti-Semitic, I tried, for the sake of my mother's edification, to bring to her attention certain subtleties and complexities: in other words, examples of Arabs who did not cry out for the blood of Jews. I didn't convince her, but I felt obliged to offer a rebuttal to sentiments I considered ill-informed and impetuous – though not necessarily wrong. It was impossible to say what was right or wrong. Human history was a lesson in brutality. Jewish history was a string of massacres, interrupted now and again by a theory, a poem, or a clever transaction. There was always cause for alarm, but there was also room for philosophy. On our trip to Israel (taken one short month before the start of hostilities) my wife and I had met any number of people who assumed a philosophical stance. The very first Israeli we met, a cab driver who picked us up from Ben Gurion airport, a veteran of two wars, summed up Israel's predicament like this: "Some countries have earthquakes, some countries have hurricanes, we have Arabs."

We spent two extraordinarily pleasant weeks in the country. I had been once before, when I was seven, to visit my grandparents in Kiryat Motzkin. My wife, a convert to Judaism, had never been. We stayed in Tel Aviv and Jerusalem and then headed north in a rented Mazda. We hiked in the Golan Heights and Banyas near the Lebanese border. We stopped overnight in Tiberias, Tzfat, and Acco – all places later targeted by Hezbollah rockets.

On July 25, two weeks after the war started, Nadja called in a panic to say that my grandfather was refusing to eat. She had panicked like this once before, a month earlier, when he had uncharacteristically refused his breakfast. That time, by the afternoon, he had resumed eating again. We subsequently learned that the reason for Nadja's panic was that she had secured another job, with longer-term prospects, and was looking for a decorous way to take her leave. She knew that if my grandfather did not eat we would be obliged to transfer him to the palliative care ward at Baycrest, a Jewish geriatric hospital, and she would be free to accept other employment. But once my grandfather started eating again, Nadja found herself in a bind. For reasons that remain ambiguous, she reconsidered, became emotional, spoke lovingly about my grandfather's stoicism, and promised to "stay until the end." On July 25, it appeared that the end had arrived. My grandfather had refused to eat the previous night and again in the morning. My mother and aunt went to see him, and my aunt tried to force his mouth open and deposit a spoonful of mush. He resisted and clamped his jaw shut. When my mother described the scene to me she said of her sister, "It was like she believed she could save him with a spoonful of kasha."

My grandfather didn't eat again. The next day, we hired an ambulance which took him to Baycrest, where he lay in a semi-conscious state for nine days. He died on a Friday evening, on the fourth of August, 2006. When the nurse called, my wife and I were at my mother's house, rushing through dinner, preparing to visit him in the hospital. On television, Anderson Cooper, raffishly dressed, was detailing another nightmare. My mother didn't need to say anything for us to grasp what had happened. We drove with my aunt to Baycrest, and performed, with self-conscious exactitude, the motions required to reach my grandfather's room. At which point the death became stark, and my mother and aunt began to wail dreadfully and hysterically, calling again and again for their father with a sorrow that felt distinctly primal and Jewish. Seeing this, I remembered the devastating conclusion of the Isaac Babel story "Crossing the Zbrucz," where a Jewish woman, considering the body of her father, murdered by Poles, demands of the narrator: "Where in the whole world could you find another father like my father?"

Some minutes later, when we had all calmed down, I regarded my grandfather's pale and wasted body, and commented on how he no longer looked like himself.

"Why doesn't he look like himself?" my aunt asked, offended. "He looks just like himself. See, even his brows are black."

Of all of us, my aunt had been the most tenacious about keeping my grandfather alive. She hadn't shied away from any task, no matter how gruesome or unpleasant. She wanted to keep him with us in any condition and at any cost. There was something irrational and totemic about her approach: so long as his heart beat, she still had a father.

We buried my grandfather on Sunday afternoon, the sixth of August. The funeral home and the cemetery were both uncommonly busy that day, owing in part to the fact that no funerals were permitted on the Sabbath, and perhaps also because nobody could be buried on Tisha B'Av, a fast day that had fallen on the day before my grandfather died. There was a backlog of the dead, and everyone seemed to be impatient and in a hurry – the funeral director, the limousine driver, the gravediggers. Competing funeral processions nearly caused a traffic jam on the way to the cemetery and, once there, four, five, or six burials took place simultaneously and in uneasy proximity, each one encroaching upon the singularity of someone else's death. We laid my grandfather down into the plot beside my grandmother's, with the blank headstone that had been awaiting a date for seven years. My mother said, "Now they will be together." Which, if it offered her some consolation, offered me none. So much of what I'd loved and what had loved me had been put into those graves.

After the funeral we retreated to the common room in my grandfather's building, which we had reserved to host the mourners. My wife and my uncle's wife had prepared the room, covering the long tables with white tablecloths, setting out plates of salads, herring, fruit, and bread. According to custom, we also provided bottles of vodka so that people could toast to my grandfather's memory. The room filled up with middle-aged and elderly Jews, mostly Russian. Also present were two Lubavitcher rabbis, one of whom, Rabbi Z., had known my family for decades, and had presided over the funerals of my grandmother, my father, and now my grandfather. He was an incredibly charismatic man who had, for many years, and nearly single-handedly, shepherded Toronto's Russian Jewish Community – quite possibly the most fractious, fickle, querulous congregation in the world. He was renowned for having an impeccable memory, with a capability to recall not only the name of any Russian Jew he encountered but also the names and interconnections of all of their relatives. ("David, Mendel's son, may he rest in peace, your wife is Hannah, your mother is Sara, her sister is Musia, whose eldest daughter is Katya, who has that little boy and is pregnant again, praise G-d.")

Out of deference to the rabbi, the seating arrangement in the room was divided – though not altogether perfectly – according to sex. Women either sat at their own tables, or segregated themselves from the men on one side of a given table. The rabbi sat at a table at the far end of the room, surrounded by men, all of whom drank liberally from a large bottle of vodka. The talk in the room, and particularly at the rabbi's table, centred less on my grandfather than on Israel.

By every estimation, the war was in its final stages. The Americans and the French were brokering a ceasefire, which seemed imminent. In anticipation of this, the Israel Defense

Forces had massed troops on the Lebanese border and were preparing to press north to the Litani River, to secure as much territory as possible before the ceasefire took effect. Meanwhile, rockets continued to rain down on northern Israel in undiminished numbers. The situation was frustrating, terrifying, and exhausting. I didn't like talking about it in general, and particularly not immediately after burying my grandfather, but my aunt's husband, who had been sitting at the rabbi's table, came over to me and, with drunken enthusiasm, declared how surprised and impressed he was with the rabbi's take on the war. He insisted that I follow him back to the table so that I could sample the rabbi's wisdom myself. From my uncle's excitement it wasn't hard to derive the substance of the rabbi's position, but my uncle was bent on dragging me over – as if he felt that I specifically would benefit from such wisdom. As we approached, I heard the other men at the table – men whom I had known nearly all my life, who had attended my bar mitzvah, my wedding, and my father's funeral – vigorously, and somewhat drunkenly, decrying what they perceived to be Israel's anemic approach to the conflict.

"Rabbi Z.," my uncle said eagerly, "I want David to hear what you think Israel should do."

To everyone's gratification, the rabbi repeated that he thought Israel should bomb Lebanon out of existence. That way it would be possible to start with a clean slate.

"What do you do with a field when you need to plant a new crop?" the rabbi asked rhetorically. "First you plough it under."

The rabbi grinned; the men at the table grinned. Inherent in their grinning was the invitation to grin. Also to participate in the fantasy: instead of menacing and chaotic Arabs, there was now (look!) a vast ploughed field – orderly, peaceful, and serene. Impossible not to like. Its appeal wasn't sadistic; it was utopian. Nobody was glorifying carnage, they just wanted the problem to go away. One moment the Arabs were here, the next they were gone. What happened between "here" and "gone" was instantaneous, magical. There were no gory scenes and no consequences, moral or otherwise. Israel, a tiny country of six million, simply cancelled Lebanon and would do the same to any other country that posed a threat. It would keep bombing until Israel was finally surrounded on all sides by bucolic fields. There would be no more Arabs or anti-Semites and we would spend our days eating matzah ball soup and dancing the horah. The idea was idiotic, and not worth discussing. It was also, in my opinion, un-Jewish. I didn't expect my uncle or the other Russian men – products of Soviet education, unschooled in even the most elementary points of Jewish law – to understand that such indiscriminate killing conflicted with Jewish morality, but I was disappointed in the rabbi, who had never struck me as irresponsible, or as a fool. However, I said nothing since I wasn't interested in a debate or a confrontation. I wanted only to mourn my grandfather and not have my grief compromised by hostile feelings. That this proved impossible is something that I regret to this day.

Following the reception in the common room, my family and some of the mourners retreated to my grandfather's one-bedroom apartment, where my mother and her siblings would be sitting shiva. It was early evening, and we chatted for the two or three hours before the prayer service, which was to take place, on this first night, in my grandfather's apartment. We moved awkwardly among my grandfather's things, the possessions which he had fussed over and organized in his meticulous way. What little he had in the way of valuables, we would have no trouble dividing up. I stood to inherit two items that were dear to me: a checkers set, which he and I had often played, and also a chess set

– individual wooden pieces stored in a blue cotton bag – which
he had used in the trenches as a Red Army soldier during the
Second World War. Other than this, my grandfather also had
an accumulation of what most people would consider clutter.
He hated to throw anything out, and always assumed that the
day might come when he would be asked to produce an old
Israeli utility bill, or that some job would require a handful of
bent and rusty screws, or that a use would be found for the
broken heel from a shoe my aunt had owned decades ago in the
Soviet Union. All of these things he wrapped neatly, secreted
away in boxes and cupboards, and kept catalogued minutely in
his head. Now, without him, they remained, flatly oblivious to
the fact that they were orphaned, worthless, and would soon
be discarded.

At sundown, men started to trickle in for the evening service. Most of them were members of the one-room synagogue
located on the building's ground floor. The building had been
established by the B'nai B'rith and was – so far as I knew – populated exclusively by elderly Jews. Until he had been debilitated
by his illness, my grandfather had been a stalwart member of the
building's congregation and attended services every Friday evening and Saturday morning. Five men from the congregation –
one or two fewer than promised – arrived at the appointed hour.
Including myself, my uncles, and an unsuspecting friend of the
family, we counted nine men until, fifteen minutes after sundown, Rabbi Z. burst through the door, thus completing the
minyan and allowing us to commence prayers. For the duration
of the service, the women were relegated to the balcony, where,
safely out of sight, they could talk and enjoy the warm summer
evening. The men, meanwhile, filled the living room. Those who
knew how to pray followed the service. Others, like my uncles
and our family friend, absently flipped pages and gazed about.

Rabbi Z. prayed, called out the page numbers, strode affably around, and invited the unobservant to fulfill the *mitzvah* of putting on *tefillin* – a set of which he carried with him at all times in his briefcase. ("You never know when you will meet a Jew who needs to lay *tefillin*.")

In the break between the evening and nighttime services, Rabbi Z. delivered a sermon on the subject he perceived to be most relevant – not death or mourning, but Israel. Unlike his earlier pronouncement, however, his sermon began reasonably, and was grounded in Jewish law. The question at its heart was: When is a Jew permitted to kill? The example he cited involved a Jew pursued by a knife-wielding assailant. In such an instance, the Jew is not permitted to kill his assailant. He is directed to impede his path, cripple him, wound him in the legs, so that the assailant can no longer do him harm. To do anything beyond that, to take the man's life, the Torah regards as excessive, criminal, and forbidden. But what if the assailant is armed with a gun? Of course, though there were no guns in biblical times, the Torah – wherein all truths reside – nevertheless provides an answer. Assuming one's assailant is armed not with a knife but with a bow and arrow, how must one proceed? Simply wounding him in the legs will not eliminate the threat. In such an instance, one is not only permitted, but commanded to kill the assailant. This is because a man's life is not his own; rather, it is a gift from God and therefore cannot be treated negligently. One must go to any length to protect life. From this, Rabbi Z. indicated, it was possible to extrapolate concerning Israel, Hezbollah, Lebanon, and the Katyusha rockets. He didn't delve into nuances or specifics, and nobody urged him to. But, after prayers, when the old men and the mourners had departed, the rabbi remained behind and resumed the disquisition. By then the only people in the apartment were me, my wife, my mother, my aunt, my uncles, the rabbi, and one of the rabbi's sons, himself a rabbi, who had come to join the prayers and to offer his condolences.

The hour was very late, but the rabbi seemed prepared to speak deep into the night. Though tired, my family could not refuse the rabbi's personal attention – he was, after all, a very busy man, a father of fourteen, and spiritually responsible for a community numbering some thirty thousand. We didn't know if he allotted this much time to every grieving family, and so we also felt flattered and honoured. As it was, the talk didn't immediately turn to Israel; the rabbi had known my grandfather for many years and reminisced about him. My aunt, with a mixture of fury and dismay, asked – as she did after every familial death – how it was that God allowed bad things to happen to good people, and then accepted the standard response about the mystery of His ways. My uncle inquired about the rabbi's progress raising money for a permanent centre for Toronto's Russian Jewish community, and the rabbi told a fundraising joke about a chicken and a cow who pass a restaurant advertising "Steak and Eggs."

"Look at our contribution to the world," sneers the chicken.

"What for you is a contribution," replies the cow, "for me is a total commitment."

Somewhere, thereabouts, the subject of the war resurfaced. I don't remember what initiated it, but I recall the immediate tension in the room, the sense of ideological antagonism, and the factionalism. The thrust of what the rabbi said aimed to repudiate the idea of a secular Jewish state. Democracy, the rabbi said, was a foreign idea. A Greek invention. Anathema to the Torah because it did not adequately sanctify individual Jewish life. It was preoccupied with public opinion and votes. This moral confusion was why Israel had fared so terribly against Hezbollah. "If you know that a terrorist is hiding in a civilian building, should you not bomb that building? Or should you instead risk the lives of Jewish soldiers? On this point the Torah is clear."

I said, no longer knowing what exactly I believed, that I wasn't sure it was clear.

"After the Six Day War," the rabbi said, "Ariel Sharon came to see the Lubavitcher Rebbe. Six hundred Israeli soldiers had been killed during the war, four hundred of them in the battle for Jerusalem.* The Rebbe asked Ariel Sharon why the casualties had been so high in Jerusalem. Sharon said, 'Because there were many ancient sites. Old synagogues, King David's Tomb. The Jordanians took refuge in these and we did not want to destroy them.' The Rebbe answered, 'Is this how you explained it to four hundred Jewish mothers? You worry about protecting Jewish lives, I'll worry about King David's Tomb.'"

The rabbi looked at me to see if I intended to challenge this logic. I had no such intention, particularly since I admired the audacity of blowing up King David's Tomb or blasting a hole through the Wailing Wall to save a solitary Israeli paratrooper. This was a version of Judaism I could endorse. Less easy to endorse was a Judaism that sanctioned the killing of civilians if a terrorist sought refuge in their building. And yet I could see how my qualms might be impractical, if not completely inimical to the reality of war. I also did not want to bear the responsibility for the deaths of the young soldiers whose brief obituaries I studied in the pages of *Haaretz*. The fact was that I could envision any number of ways to agonize over such a decision.

---

* The actual number of Israeli war casualties was 338 on the Egyptian front; 300 on the Jordanian front (including Jerusalem and the West Bank); and 141 on the Syrian front. Derek Hopwood, *Egypt: Politics and Society 1945–90* (London: Routledge, 1991), 71, as cited by Wikipedia contributors, "Six Day War," *Wikipedia, The Free Encyclopedia*, http://en.wikivisual.com/index.php/Six_Day_War

My aunt, it turned out, could not. She had been sitting across from the rabbi, listening with growing consternation to what he said. When she couldn't stand it any longer, she exclaimed, "Oh, just kill them all!"

This set off the pathetic and inevitable chain reaction. There were real feelings involved – fury, disgust, indignation – but I can see our exchange rendered as if in cartoon panels.

In the first panel, I rise from my chair and declare, "That's genocide!"

In the next panel, my mother looks at me wearily and says, "Okay, so your aunt is a bad person."

In the final panel, we're still in my grandfather's living room, except now my family's faces have been replaced with the faces of monsters.

As for how I look to them: I am a naïve fool, unacquainted with hard truths, not to be taken seriously. If matters were left up to me, the Jews would perish in a second Holocaust.

We had quarrelled along these lines before, but never had our differences felt so intractable, divisive, or acute. I couldn't remember a time when I had felt such absolute loathing for my family. They seemed to me to be worse than strangers. They were morally bankrupt, hypocritical, and cowardly. They were precisely the kind of people I detested: the kind who lined the boulevard, waved the flag, and saluted the parading army – and later, silently or jubilantly, countenanced all the usual homicidal shit. If I had a conscience or principles, I would disassociate myself from them completely. That they were my family, and that we shared common bonds, should be of no consequence. They were corrupt and the thought of spending the next week in the same room with them was revolting.

It should have ended there, but that night my wife and I drove my mother back to her house. We had promised to stay with her so that she wouldn't be alone on the day she buried her father. In the car, we observed a brittle silence most of the way home. We should have observed it all the way, but at some point my mother decided that she couldn't let the matter rest. In response, I told her that if she cared so much about Israel she should at least donate some money. I knew that, no matter how righteous I felt, it was a shameful and impertinent thing to say to my widowed mother. But I said it. And I was immediately punished. Once the subject of donation was raised, my wife, overcome by some corrective impulse, decided to announce that she *had* donated money. To UNICEF. For Lebanese relief.

"You gave money to Lebanon?" my mother asked, aghast.

"For the Lebanese children," my wife countered, misguided in her assumption that my mother might appreciate the distinction and see something noble in the gesture.

The car was plunged immediately back into a dismal silence that lasted all the way home.

I'd known about my wife's donation, and frankly hadn't approved. The day I had donated $100 to an Israeli soldiers' fund, she had told me that she had donated $150 for Lebanese aid. I couldn't help but feel a sense of betrayal, not least because the Lebanese would be getting $50 more of our money than the Israeli soldiers. But I'd tried to understand my wife's rationale. She had been motivated by sympathy, by humanitarian principles. I reminded myself that she had grown up in California, the daughter of loving American parents. As a girl she'd surfed and ridden horses. Until she'd become involved with me and my family she'd been a normal person, unafflicted by persecution complexes and immigrant neuroses. Try as she might, she hadn't yet cured herself of being essentially a well-adjusted and healthy human being. I recognized this for what it was but I knew that my mother would see it as an unpardonable sin. Despite warm relations, countless demonstrations of loyalty, even the fact that my wife had held my father's hand when he died, my mother continued to harbour suspicions. In her heart of hearts, she wasn't fully reconciled to having a convert for a daughter-in-law, and she remained alert to the least sign of falseness. The UNICEF donation was such a sign. It proved that my wife was an imposter. Forget the weekly business with the Sabbath candles, the kosher wedding, the synagogue choir – that was all superficial, an act. My wife was not a real Jew, since no real Jew would ever give money to Arabs.

It was past midnight when we reached my mother's house. In a black mood, my mother went inside, while my wife and I trailed our dog through the quiet suburban streets. We lingered for some time, reluctant to return and share a roof with my mother. But we were also aggravated with each other. I thought that her decision to tell my mother about her donation was petulant and ill-advised. She was angry with me for trying to stifle her and for trying to insulate my family from conflicting perspectives.

"How can they, of all people, think this way?" my wife asked. "They are in mourning themselves. They know how it feels to lose someone they love."

"They know how it feels to lose their father," I said. "A Jew, a Zionist, and a war veteran who fought the Nazis. Don't be so surprised. You have to think how they think."

It was yet another pointless conversation in a string of pointless conversations. We succeeded only in proving that even in agreement there was still room for disagreement. We could talk like this forever and still resolve nothing.

This was where we found ourselves on the night we buried my grandfather. A man whom we had all loved and respected had died, but we were caught in a tangle of bitter feelings, where one feeling bled into another and made it impossible to mourn, to comfort each other, or to reflect about Israel or the war. All of it amounted to a profound desecration of my grandfather's memory. I imagined him looking down upon us in despair and lamenting, *Everything I cared for in my life is either destroying itself or being destroyed.*

ANNABEL LYON

Alexander

I wanted to write a novel about Aristotle, not Alexander; at first, the boy was just along for the ride. In early drafts he was a supporting actor, no more. My real passion, or so I thought, was the philosopher who was his tutor. Here was a subtle, adult mind; a once-in-a-thousand-years genius; a character of Wagnerian scope. All I knew about the kid was that I wanted him to be annoying.

There's a reverent literary tradition around Alexander, beginning with his first biographers (Arrian, Plutarch), through the so-called "Alexander Romances" of Medieval times (where he often had superpowers), right up to the present (most recently with Oliver Stone's 2004 biopic, *Alexander*, featuring Irish heartthrob Colin Farrell).

But years as a teacher have taught me that teenagers with brains and talent are often the most arrogant, insecure, and impossible students of all. I wanted to create a character who would both defy expectations and be immediately recognizable to anyone who's ever had to deal with an exceptionally bright, difficult teenager. I pictured the young Alexander as an annoying narcissist who needed to be taken down a few notches. Just the job for my fictional Aristotle, whose brilliance I much preferred (in the beginning, anyway) to Alexander's brawn.

But I struggled. Early readers told me they believed Alexander as an annoying teenager but couldn't see the seeds of the man who would conquer the world. The more I thought about him, the more he bothered me. I knew he needed to be more than just a smart aleck, but I still couldn't buy into the tradition of the sexy, hotheaded military genius.

The penny finally dropped when I read William Finnegan's "The Last Tour," about an Iraq war veteran suffering from post-traumatic stress disorder, in the September 29, 2008 issue of *The New Yorker*. I was struck by the symptoms Finnegan described: headaches, nightmares, alcoholism, loss of touch with reality, and, most of all, the paradoxical desire to be at home when you're at war and at war when you're home. These symptoms fit the later Alexander, an alcoholic given to fits of blinding violence immediately followed by crippling depressions, who left home at nineteen and never returned.

The ancient biographer Plutarch writes that after a night of drinking with a long-time companion named Clitus, who had scolded the king for accepting obeisance from his soldiers in the Eastern manner, "Alexander, snatching a spear from one of the soldiers, met Clitus as he was coming forward and was putting by the curtain that hung before the door, and ran him through the body. He fell at once with a cry and a groan. Upon which the king's anger immediately vanishing, he came perfectly to himself, and when he saw his friends about him all in a profound silence, he pulled the spear out of the dead body, and would have thrust it into his own throat, if the guards had not held his hands, and by main force carried him away into his chamber, where all that night and the next day he wept bitterly, till being quite spent with lamenting and exclaiming, he lay as it were speechless, only fetching deep sighs."

Now here's Lieutenant-General Roméo Dallaire, describing his reaction to the Rwandan genocide in *Shake Hands with the Devil*: "I wanted to scream, to vomit, to hit something, to break free of my body, to end this terrible scene." And: "I see-sawed from rage to tears and back again, with brief interregnums of numbed-out staring." And: "The news sent me spinning into a tirade against every nation and body who could have assisted us in preventing this. . . . My ranting was beyond the bounds of decorum, and rendered my own staff and the French liaison officers noticeably ill at ease. When I stopped, the orders group headed quietly off to their duties. . . . I remained alone for a time, staring at the big map of Rwanda tacked to the wall. I had to recognize that I was exhibiting the signs and symptoms that caused me to send others to Nairobi for a rest. I could rarely sleep, and could not bear to eat anything other than peanut butter from [my wife's] last care package. I was moody and overtaken at the most inopportune times by spontaneous daydreaming."

The king in his chamber; the general in his headquarters. Insomnia, nightmares, violence, depression, shame, silence. I had found the language I needed to capture the weight and the horror of military leadership in a time of war.

One could argue that Alexander's and Dallaire's contrasting levels of moral responsibility should preclude any such comparison. Dallaire didn't set out to conquer the world, and Alexander didn't set out to keep its peace. But the more I thought about the boyhood that must have preceded Alexander's tormented life, the more I wondered if the trauma might have begun very early indeed. His parents, by all accounts, hated each other. His father took numerous wives and produced half-siblings often enough to keep the young prince's expectations about his future off-balance. His mother was suspected of witchcraft. Alexander was trained as a child soldier, leading troops into battle when he was only sixteen.

Child soldiers exist today, and we know what damage and trauma they suffer (when we allow ourselves to think about them at all). An ancient child would have suffered no less. Once I understood that, I understood how to proceed with the character I now cared and feared for as much as anyone in the novel.

STEPHANIE NOLEN

To Tell Her Story

I filled a first notebook, and then a second. Three days into a planned three-week trip, I filled a third, my "emergency note-book," the one I had doubted I'd need but had thrown in my backpack just in case – writing in tiny letters, two layers per line on the page, words packed all the way to the edge, from the metal coils at the top to the very bottom, on the inside and outside of the covers. Then I used the back of my plane tickets, the mostly white pages of a magazine I had nicked from the plane, and, eventually, a label I peeled off a shampoo bottle and the covers of three boxes of matches.

In Kibombo, in the east of the war-shattered Democratic Republic of Congo, there was no paper for sale. But I had to keep writing.

It was 2004. I had hitched a ride on a UN flight into the heart of the Congo and set off on a motorbike down a narrow dirt track from the town of Kindu. I was on assignment for the *Globe and Mail*, and I wanted to write about rape – about how every party in Congo's unending war has used mass rape as a weapon, how tens of thousands, maybe hundreds of thousands, of women have been raped repeatedly, then left to suffer without so much as a gauze square for their wounds, physical or otherwise. The rape had been going on for years, and yet rarely attracted attention beyond the occasional despairing report from a human rights organization.

I had struggled to plan the trip – there were no surviving roads in the vast area I hoped to cover, no regular air service, no telecoms network, and only the most scattered, nominal presence of the United Nations or the government. And everyone I had spoken to had said the same thing: there was no point seeking out women to talk about rape, because they wouldn't. The shame was immense. Raped women were viewed as "spoiled," ruined, less than human. To talk about it – especially with a foreigner – would be almost as bad as a second rape, they had said. UN peacekeepers, aid workers, Congolese politicians, and social workers all told me the same thing: You won't find anyone to tell you her story. No one will talk about rape.

And so as I set off through the forest, where clouds of tiny blue and yellow butterflies rose in the path of the motorbike like mosaics come to life, I was preoccupied and anxious about how I could possibly report on the subject. (And, of course, with how I could avoid getting killed in the middle of a lawless zone the size of Europe.) Two days of driving, through which I clung to the back of the cheerful young motorcycle driver who shot our bike across spindly tree branches laid in place of bridges, and we came to Kibombo near nightfall. He deposited me at the entry of the only brick building in the town, the shell of a Catholic church and adjoining rectory, and the caretaker ushered me through its crumbling hallways to a Spartan room, where he left his lone candle stub for me. I used my earrings as hooks to hang a mosquito net, then lay in the trough of a concave mattress wondering what on earth I would do next.

But as the night settled thick over Kibombo, the caretaker came back and knocked softly on the door. "*Mademoiselle*," he called. "*Des visiteurs sont venues.*"

I took the candle stub back to the front door of the parish hall, and in its flicker I could make out a group of Congolese women, hair in stiff braids, hips wrapped in faded cotton, feet bare. I stopped and looked at the women, puzzled. They looked back, eyes fixed at a point just below my own. The caretaker nudged me towards the front room, empty but for a few crude wooden benches and a small solar lantern on the floor. "Go and sit," he said. So I did. And the women followed me, their thick callused soles making a shushing sound on the floor.

We sat in silence for a few moments, until the oldest one met my eyes, squared her shoulders, and said, "We heard that you wanted to know about what happened to us."

Word had got out, apparently, in just the short time I was in Kibombo: a white woman was at the parish, and she had come to hear about the rapes.

So these eight women waited until the dark obscured their destination, and then came to find me. And one after the other, they talked.

Shami Alubu, twenty-one, was raped with sticks and with gun barrels by the members of a gang of Mai Mai, a paramilitary force, while her seven-month-old son, Florent, sobbed hysterically on the floor nearby. Anifa, fifty-four, was raped by ten government soldiers while her husband was held at gunpoint across the small room. Léonie, fifty-two, was raped while held atop the body of her father-in-law, and Onya, sixteen and tiny, was raped repeatedly for months, held by rebels at a camp in the forest.

They talked until long after the lantern faded out, after the stubs of candle were gone. I wrote it all down. When the sky began to lighten to grey, they slipped out the door.

All the next day, in ones and twos, more women came to the parish. Another big group came that evening. My hands were seizing up from hours upon hours of writing down their words. The women seemed to wonder at those words even as they spoke them. "He put a bayonet inside me." "They came every day, five or six of them." "They made my sons watch."

When I emerged from the rectory on the third day to get back on the motorbike and head farther east, there was a lineup of women waiting outside in the warm morning sun. Apparently their eagerness to talk outweighed the shame of identifying themselves as rape survivors (although by then I was not sure if there were *any* women in Kibombo who were not rape survivors). I held up my hands in apology, said I had to leave, to cover the road to the next town before nightfall. They stepped back, grumbling in a polite, Congolese sort of way.

The next town, and the three after it, were much the same. Two weeks later I flew home to Johannesburg and sat down in my sunny office, the pile of notebooks and paper scraps covered in tiny writing piled in front of me, feeling sick all over again.

I remembered how every woman who came to see me watched me write down what happened to her, staring intently as my hands around the pen formed each of the succession of words that described what they did to her. What was it in this act of recording, something none of them could do themselves, that drew them, that made them willing to relive the brutality for a stranger?

No doubt they hoped that I – the first foreigner most of them had ever spoken with – would somehow help, although I tried to make clear, with my usual awkward, hasty speech, that I could promise them nothing, no money, no medical treatment, no ongoing support – nothing save that I would tell their stories to the outside world, and perhaps that might bring some attention to the ongoing horror in which they lived. They met the news with a sort of resigned air, as if they had hardly dared to expect better of me. But it didn't matter. They would talk anyway.

I wrote, that fall, about the wreckage of Congo, and I went back, and went back, over the next five years. Very slowly, more attention has come to Congo's war, and to its sadistic weapon of choice, although rebukes from Hilary Clinton and hand-wringing from the UN and promises from the government in Kinshasa have done exactly nothing to slow the rapes. On every trip, in every village, there are always women who seek me out to tell me what was done to them.

There is no dignity in living for six years with wads of old fabric stuffed between your legs to sop up the blood that leaks every day from your crushed cervix, because you live two hundred kilometres from a doctor, who has neither equipment nor skill to help you in any case. There is no dignity in bathing down the river from the other women each evening, so they do not see the pulpy mess of your genitals, the mark the soldiers left on you, so you can all maintain the polite fiction that no one knows. And there is no dignity in passing them each morning, the men who attacked you, lolling in the shade at their checkpoint, their heavy boots untied and laces trailing in the sand, all of them leering at you because they remember what they did to you in your yard, or maybe just because they leer that way at every woman, or maybe because they did it to every woman.

But there was endless dignity, that night in the dim light inside the *paroisse*. They gave me their words. I could give them nothing but the sight of those words being recorded. But the women knew: they could make it a story, the story of something that happened. It was their story, of what happened to them, and in that, if in nothing else, there is control, and there is power.

ELIZABETH HAY

Between Books

A few years ago, in early May, I went to a friend's magnolia and martini party on the other side of the Rideau Canal. First I had a great big martini, then I had a medium-sized martini, then I had a baby-sized martini (rather like Goldilocks, except that instead of running off into the woods I would totter home). In the garden, the magnolia was a mass of white blossom, and my friend bloomed too, sexy and voluptuous. Nevertheless, the man in her life had recently told her that he wanted a woman ten years younger. Now she was between men, as I was between books.

My friend took up painting to regain her balance. I made a little journey by train. The solitude of writing is nothing compared to the emptiness of being between books, or of waiting to hear an editor's reaction to the book you've just completed. A quiet train ride restores the soul.

On this occasion, a story angel sat beside me. He was a small, elderly man in a brown suit, and when he returned from the lavatory he upended his plastic cup of beer attempting to sit down. The little spill dampened one corner of the seat and caused him to remark what a comedown travelling first class was, if you compared it to the past. He pressed his point by saying that he had worked on a train as a pantry man and waiter when he was seventeen, on the Newfie Bullet, in fact. The dining car, he said, had linen tablecloths and real silver. It sat twenty-four and you had to move the diners through fast, because others would be waiting.

He went on, telling me all the details I could have wished for. A good waiter carried four cups of tea with one hand, despite the movement of the train, by spreading his fingers on two saucers and then balancing another two cups and saucers on top of the two he had in his grip. Shifts were long, sixteen to eighteen hours, and he was responsible for doing the dishes and making sure all the bread was cut and looking after the ice cream. Always vanilla, it came in a big cardboard and metal tub, which he dropped into a deep hole in the counter, then he packed the tub around with layers of ice and rock salt: the rock salt he put into a canvas bag and knocked into small pieces with a mallet. In the morning, he said, you couldn't dig a spoon into it, the ice cream was so hard. The salt was the same salt they used in the fishery: it came from Spain, where they let seawater evaporate into sea salt. The coal that powered the train and heated the cooking stove came from Wales. To make a steak you placed it in a sort of toaster rack and held it over the coals (but few ordered steak since it cost $3.75).

He was a retired judge, it turned out, who had red wine with his meal, and so did I. "The French are careful," he said, watching me, "to drink a glass of water with every glass of wine." (I've done so ever since.)

Another of his jobs was serving Jell-O, and he served it with his hands; a perfect serving was a fistful. This detail, in particular, I thought my mother would enjoy. Also, his sleeping arrangements. At night they took down the tables and slept in the dining car on a couple of cots, or stretched out on chairs, and the chef woke them in the morning by flinging all the pots and pans into the air and letting them fall with a crash and a clatter.

When the train pulled into Toronto, I lost my brief and glorious companion. He got off and I continued on to London, where my parents lived. Now I had the glory of the world outside my window. Did I know that soon I wouldn't have reason to make this particular journey anymore, the one that Margaret Avison wrote poems about, teaching me the beauty of the word "tawny": tawny grasses from the train window?

I pulled out my notebook and began to jot down everything my retired judge had told me, glad to be putting words on paper again. The hardest thing about being between books is that you lose what's been keeping you company. You also lose faith in what you've written and lose hope about what you'll write in the future.

As a boy he did everything with his mother, he had told me, since his father was never around. He was thirteen when she died, the same year Newfoundland joined Confederation, but she died before she had a chance to vote in favour. In favour, because if Newfoundland joined Canada, she would be able to get a divorce. The night she died, she was feeling so much better that she suggested they go to the pictures. "Look," she said. "The fluid's gone from my legs." And it was true. Her huge swollen legs weren't swollen anymore because the fluid had travelled up to her lungs. She drowned in her own fluid.

He said, "You've heard of the seven fat years and the seven lean years? Well, those were my seven lean years."

After a mother dies, everything changes. Not the father, he said. But the mother. The whole family dispersed, and his brother, who was three at the time, never recovered.

It's a pretty run from Toronto to London, at least from time to time, something you forget when you travel by car. There's a sudden view as you cross a bridge of the river curving below and an old-looking town of stone perched on the steep riverbank. It looks European, graceful amidst the greenery. And then the glimpse is gone.

Did he say his name? I don't think so. But he told me that he went west when he was twenty-three. In Saskatchewan his van broke down and the mechanic wouldn't take his money (he had only one dollar and seventy-three cents, since he had sent his money on ahead to Alberta), but insisted upon giving him ten dollars. "You may be needing this."

He paid the man back later on. But they lasted only six months in Alberta, he and his wife and their one-year-old son, they were so incredibly homesick.

Some things remain the same. Homesickness is one. Certain hurts that begin in childhood are another. I was thinking, as the train approached London, of my own mother, by then in her eighties. The last time we had spoken, she was riddled with the wounding remarks of a friend, suffering much as an eight-year-old would suffer, but with a clearer sense of her own failure to rise above it. "Here comes Jean in her sweaters," the so-called friend would say every time they met. To find my mother's sore spot like that, needling her about her clothes: hand-knit, and so dressed because she wouldn't turn up the heat. Behind my mother's overreaction, if it *was* overreaction, were eighty-some years of sensitivity about poverty, cheapness, appearance.

Every little thing bothers me, too. My insides are primitive, a dark cabin heated by a woodstove. Either hot or overheating or cold. Some people seem to have sophisticated internal thermostats that regulate all such things.

I slept in my father's study downstairs to get away from the beaten path to the bathroom, and from his alarm clock, which went off at 7 a.m., as it had every day of his working life. His study had a wall of books and I pulled one off the shelf and took it to bed with me. *Finding the Trail of Life* by Rufus Jones: "Poetry and art and religion, which are as old as smiling and weeping."

In the morning, my father told me something I had never known about his own mother, how she was the first in her circle to have a camera, she even had a darkroom in the basement. "A darkroom," I said. "Are you sure?" He was sure. Uncle Harold, her brother, would have provided the equipment, and Uncle Hugh the know-how.

"And my father," he said dismissively, "would have been useless."

The pain you feel from these men who loved their mothers is the same. It enters into your bones, their profound disappointment in their fathers, which bolstered their deep love for their mothers. Uncle Hugh wasn't an uncle; he was a family friend, and in my father's opinion much more suited to his mother than his father ever was. He even suspected a hidden love between them, or at least a cherishing of his mother on the part of Uncle Hugh.

On the way home, two days later, I stopped in Toronto to meet with my editor. She gave my manuscript back to me and on the train I read her comments, instantly and deeply ashamed of the book's shortcomings, which now seemed obvious. It would take more work, more clarity. This is what comes, I thought, of importing old scenes from my life into the lives of my characters: too much doesn't fit.

I was no longer between books, in other words. I was back rewriting, rewriting.

At home at my desk I made a notation, a change to the first page, and fell into reading page after page. It needed more changes of direction – more sudden sights of things looming up – more angles. There was a sameness, a soft sameness to my telling. Then, despite the heavy rain, I went outside to mail a letter and pick up a book at the library and breathe some fresh air. Soon my pant legs were soaked through. I kept the letter dry by holding it up high under a wide umbrella. From the mailbox, I continued down Bank Street towards the library, and it occurred to me to step into the bookstore. Michelle was there behind the counter, small, slender, poetic, whimsical Michelle of the dazzling smile. She spoke of feeling a new dizziness lately when examining parts of her past: her parents' divorce, her mother's death; events she used to think had left her unscathed.

Someone else came in from the rain and Michelle went to attend to her. I made my selection of books, choosing two. I took them to the counter and Michelle asked if there were any books I had read as a child for comfort. I couldn't think of any offhand. I couldn't think of any books I had read as a child that were *not* a comfort. "Did you?" I said.

"Yes. The *Winnie the Pooh* books." She still read them sometimes.

I said I loved Milne's poem about the king who just wanted a little bit of butter for his bread. Yes! Her face became radiant and expressive. And she began to recite it: "'The King asked the Queen, and the Queen asked the dairy maid.'"

I said I also loved the one – how does it go? – about the boy who loses his mother.

"Yes!" she cried again and searched her memory. "'James James Morrison Morrison duddy de duddy Dupree, took great care of his mother, though he was only three.'"

"And he *loses* her," I said. "And she's so beautiful. You see her from the back, tall and elegant."

"And do you remember the dormouse with his geraniums red and delphiniums blue?"

"It rings a distant bell," I said.

"About the dormouse who lived in a bed of geraniums red and delphiniums blue until the doctor comes round and changes them to chrysanthemums yellow and white. I felt so sorry for the dormouse. The poems weren't all light and happy," she said. "I've always remembered geraniums red and delphiniums blue."

"You're a poet, Michelle."

And she was. She was also a scamp. I reached into my wallet when she rang up the books. "Will you take a fifty?" I said.

She took it. "But how will you pay for your books?" she said.

We bid our fond goodbyes and I went back out into the rain and turned towards the library, and as I walked I said to myself, "James James Morrison Morrison Weatherby George Dupree" – the full name came back – so I turned around and walked back through the puddles and opened the bookstore door and called out, "Michelle! It's James James Morrison Morrison *Weatherby George* Dupree."

And then I continued on to the library and the subject of a future book slipped its hand into mine. I would write about boys and their mothers. The thought gave me such happiness and such courage – the energy to go on with the labour of finishing a manuscript that would always be less that I had hoped – because the next book was waiting and it would be better. It would be simpler and truer. It would be my reward. I believed this, even though I knew that as soon as I began to work on the fabled next book, I would have the same problems I have always had.

At home I wrote down my encounter with Michelle against the day that I would have forgotten the pleasure it gave me. And I found my battered copy of Milne and read the heartbreaking poem about the doctor who destroyed the dormouse's view "of delphiniums (blue) and geraniums (red)," struck by the poem's brilliance and sadness, and utterly grateful to Michelle.

Every so often you catch these glimpses, as if from a train window, of promised lands of memory and pattern and wit and meaning. They have been there all along. They disappear from view as you trudge forward on your own feet, and then they reappear from time to time. I made a note about boys and their mothers, and wrote "next book" in the margin and circled it for easy reference.

TASH AW

Lulu

I met Lulu on a cold morning in March, on the way to Mutianyu. There were five of us in the back of the minibus, huddled into our puffer jackets against the cold draughts whistling through the windows that could neither close tightly nor open widely enough to let out the driver's thick fog of cigarette smoke. Four friends and I had hired a cheap minivan to take us up to the quieter reaches of the Great Wall for the day, to the villages that (we were told) remained mired in the nineteenth century, a mere two hours from Beijing. We all spoke Chinese; most of us had lived in China at some point or another. We did not know that the driver was going to come with a *tour guide.*

"And now we have just passed the area of the famous Summer Palace," Lulu announced with a wave of her red leather-gloved hand, "though you cannot see it – it's far over there."

"Really," one of our party said. Someone else was feigning sleep; the other two were concentrating on their mobile phones, sending extended texts, or at least pretending to. But Lulu's too-bright patter didn't cease. Did we know that the Empress Dowager had two hundred dishes cooked every day for her breakfast? Did we know that China was bigger than all the countries of Europe, Eastern and Western, put together, and that Xinjiang Province was bigger than France, Spain, and Britain combined? Beijing people are very hardy, descended from Mongols. Look at that group of young art students. Things are changing so fast in China today. Did we know that Mutianyu village is twinned with Shelburne Falls in the U.S.A.?

I was the only one paying attention, for in spite of her air of Beijing chic – the sleek quilted jacket, the Vuitton tote bag, the slinky Japanese jeans, the long Zhang Ziyi–style hairdo – there was something about her that wasn't quite right. Maybe it was the garish enthusiasm for all things Chinese, or perhaps it was the over-careful colour coordination of her accessories (an almost identical shade of red, to go with the stripe on her Burberry scarf). I suppose it was more to do with the way she spoke, her crystalline pronunciation and flaunting of hip Beijing slang – a complete contrast to her laugh: warm, earthy, un-studied. It was the kind of laughter that was out of place in this barren northern landscape; it came from a hot country thou-sands of miles away. That was when I knew. She was a foreigner, an imposter. She was just like me.

I had been in China for a few weeks, dividing my time between Shanghai and Beijing. I had come to research a novel, but my subject was proving elusive, as subjects always do. I had learnt about modern Chinese history at school in Malaysia and contin-ued to read about it, but it was not so much the documented changes I was searching for; rather, I was after the nebulous human stories that flutter on the edge of history, the type of thing that sociologists might try to collate and record several years hence, when the people in those stories are no longer with us and the stories themselves are cold, perfectly dissected.

For the past decade, every time I went back to Malaysia or Singapore, I would ask after various people only to be told that they had gone to China in search of work. At first it seemed only to be low-skilled workers – construction workers or waiters who had gone to try their luck in the booming restaurant scene in Shanghai and Beijing. Some went because they wanted to, others because they had to. My closest cousin worked in a semi-conductor factory in Singapore that moved its operations to Hangzhou. The company gave him the choice to move or be made redundant. He chose to move. Button factories, bra manu-facturers, water cooler distributers – these were the kinds of em-ployers that were attracting Southeast Asians to China. The more affluent did not feel pressure to move. The economic growth en-joyed by countries such as Malaysia, Singapore, and Thailand throughout the '80s and '90s had been fired by the rise of a young bourgeoisie, who, having created a comfortable material habitat, weren't budging. When they did move, it was to the great capitals of the West – London and New York, in particular, or else Canada or Australia, where the streets and the politics are clean.

But in the last four or five years a marked change has emerged in the pattern of these tales of emigration. Investment bankers, lawyers, and PR gurus have moved, with alarming haste, to China. So, too, have people who work for UN bodies and a whole host of NGOS. Painters, journalists, writers, dancers, Michelin-starred chefs, fashion stylists, yoga instructors, holistic lifestyle coaches – everyone has gone to China. Desperation is no longer the reason that these people are leaving their sunny home-lands. Nor is it a simple desire for money, for many of them al-ready have enough to live decently. It is something deeper than that, something that before going to China I couldn't quite fathom. Once there, however, these earnest questions of who does what, where, and why began to seem irrelevant. I had crassly been look-ing for "economic migrants," but in China they seemed impossi-ble to define. Caught up in the frenetic pace of life in Shanghai, I quickly became embroiled in the daily grind of how to feed myself, how to travel from one place to another, how to meet friends. Virtually every foreigner I met qualified, theoretically, as an economic migrant; everyone was just doing what I was doing – trying to survive and, if possible, have a good time. By the time I met Lulu, I had given up all thoughts of research. Like every other foreigner, I was just searching for companionship.

"This is a typical Qing Dynasty village," Lulu said as we walked amongst the small low stone and plaster houses of Mutianyu. Through open doorways we could see dirt floors and charcoal braziers, but in one or two houses the dirt had given way to ceramic floor tiles. The same poster of Liu Xiang winning Olympic gold in Athens hung in several front rooms, as if someone had made a bulk delivery of it.

"Until just a few years ago, there were still women with bound feet in this village," Lulu continued. "Imagine that!"

Our party had dispersed. My roommate was crouching by a doorway chatting to a young mother and her child; others were walking up the hill ahead of us, where the village faded into the countryside and the trails led into the dry scrubby hills crowned, eventually, by the Great Wall. Already, there were views over the rocky valleys, the harsh tawny landscape.

"Huh, no one's listening," said Lulu. "Maybe you can't understand Chinese. I can speak English instead."

"Maybe it's the weather," I said. "Too cold to listen."

She looked at me with a frown, and under her makeup I could see that her eyes were tired. She sat down on a stone step, drawing her knees up to her chin; suddenly, she looked just like the kids I had grown up with.

"May I ask you something?" I ventured. "Are you from Malaysia?"

She looked at me suspiciously for a long time before replying. "Yes – but I have a proper visa, you know."

———

She was born in Alor Setar, a quiet town in the far north of Malaysia, where her parents ran a sundry shop, but when she was nine the shop closed (an event for which she gave no explanation) and her family moved to Taiping, a once prosperous town of parks and avenues planted with rain trees in the tin mining region of Perak, not far from where my own family comes from. There they lived with an aunt who could not walk, having had both legs amputated following an earlier botched operation. Lulu spent her free time caring for her aunt or helping out on the family farm, a smallholding that grew pomelos. She left school at sixteen and moved north to Penang, then south to Kuala Lumpur in search of work. She had been, among other things, a waitress, a babysitter, and a ticket vendor at the old Coliseum cinema.

We discovered that we had many things in common from Malaysia and from our youth – she was two years older than me, the right age for shared reminiscences. And so, as foreigners do when they find someone from their past, we spent many hours over the next few days talking about home – about childhood trips to the coast at Teluk Anson, about the bend in the great muddy river at Parit and open-air suppers late at night in small-town Malaysia. Now and then she would break into song, perfectly hitting the notes of a Cantopop hit of the eighties. We exchanged jokey insults in Chinese-Malaysian slang that placed us squarely in the same generation and, for comic and sentimental effect, now and then slipped into the Hokkien dialect of our parents, which she still spoke fluently (but I never did). These were the kinds of things that Malaysians talked about when they were lonely in a cold country – the reassuring minutiae of one's youth. But there were, underneath the nostalgia, many things that bonded us, things that did not have to be articulated, for they were so much a part of the landscape of our childhood.

We were born in a region still coming to grips with the notions of independence and democracy; unrest was a way of life. In 1969, the year Lulu was born, there had been bloody race riots all over Malaysia, and the people of my generation grew up with the threat of violence hanging thinly in the air. A few years prior to that, of course, was Suharto's frenzied massacre of Communists and their sympathizers as he seized power in September 1965, a prolonged campaign of slaughter that symbolized the traumas of nation-building in Southeast Asia and set the tone of social politics for the next two decades. My father, an engineer, travelled extensively in Southeast Asia for work, and as a small child I would hear mumblings of rushed departures from Bangkok or Manila, or missed flights due to "problems," or "a lot of students in the streets"; we became accustomed to newspaper photos of tanks and soldiers in streets of cities that looked very much like ours.

The common thread that ran through this violence was something else that linked Lulu and me – something that resonated deeply within us and charged our presence in China with a particular undercurrent. Historically, the most visible targets of political bullying have been the ethnic Chinese communities. Southeast Asian violence is indiscriminate and widespread, but the scapegoats are often, to one degree or another, people of Chinese descent, particularly when the root of the violence is dissatisfaction with the economy, as witnessed in Jakarta during the monetary crisis of 1997. In a region where racially divisive politics seem to have constitutional status, most people have long since reached an uneasy truce with this bizarre quasi-apartheid, but divisions remain deep, and it takes little to incite underlying tensions. King Rama VI of Thailand once called these long-settled Chinese communities of Southeast Asia the "Jews of the East," and it takes little to discern elements of the pogrom in anti-Chinese violence over the years. And because free travel to China simply wasn't possible until late in the twentieth century, China became more than a country of cultural and ancestral roots for many Southeast Asian Chinese. In the overseas Chinese imagination, China became idealized, I think, as a place of security and hope.

These were some of the things that Lulu and I understood without ever needing to discuss them, things that had brought us together in a country that was at once foreign and familiar. When I met Lulu I had blithely assumed that we were in the same boat, stragglers in China. But as I would very soon find out, China has a way of confounding one's cozy impressions of life.

"Of course I miss my parents and my sister and they miss me too, I guess – but I send them money every month so they don't complain," she explained as we strolled through the World Park on the outskirts of Beijing (*You'll love it,* she'd said. *All the most famous places in the world in one place – everywhere you've ever dreamed of visiting!*).

"How long has it been since you've seen them?"

"Not long," she shrugged, "about three years, I think."

We walked past the Eiffel Tower, the arch of its legs framing a view of the Arc de Triomphe beyond. There were squares and circles of neatly clipped lawn and box hedging, filled with brightly coloured flowers dusted with the chalky grey Beijing pollution that fell on every surface.

"Have you ever been to Paris?" she asked. "I bet you have. Is it really like this in Paris? I mean, does the Eiffel Tower really look like that?"

"Yes, I guess so."

We walked on, past Notre Dame cathedral; the Leaning Tower of Pisa rose into view in the distance, cocked at a jaunty angle, and out of the corner of my eye I spotted a Dutch windmill.

"When I was young I dreamed of going to Europe," Lulu said. "I think it must be very beautiful. And clean, not like Asia."

"London's *way* dirtier than KL," I said. "But why don't you come and see for yourself?"

"Maybe one day."

"Why not soon? Next spring. I'll be back in the U.K. You can come and stay with me. You can take my bedroom, I'll crash on the sofa."

"Um, maybe."

She stopped to take a picture of Michelangelo's perfectly sculpted David. If it had not been for the oddly slick lustre of his skin and – maybe I was just imagining this – the slight Chineseness of his eyes, he could easily have passed for his Florentine twin.

"You're not afraid of travelling all that distance, are you?"

She half-laughed, half-snorted. "Of course not. I just don't have the time. I mean – you know what life is like in Beijing. I'm just so busy all the time. To take a few weeks off to go travelling . . . well, I just can't afford that."

"But there's more to life than making money," I said. "You need to broaden your horizons, see new things, new places. Money is important, but not as important as culture and learning and education."

Even through her huge black sunglasses I could tell she was frowning. "Yes, but money's the most important thing," she said. "Anyway, there's loads to do in China. I'm always doing interesting things and meeting cool people. I can see the whole world without even leaving China." She lifted her arms and swept them in a semicircle, gesturing around her. "Europe was just a dream from my childhood. I'm an adult now, I don't *need* to go there."

"Okay, forget Europe. What about just going somewhere else – I don't know, India or Nepal?"

"Too dirty."

"Or South America?"

"Too far."

"Or just anywhere else, for God's sake."

"What for?"

"I don't know – to live. To educate yourself. To experience different cultures. You can't just work all the time. It's all money, money, money with you."

"It's alright for you to say that," she said. "You and your lot."

"My lot?"

She shrugged. "Well . . . you and I are not exactly from the same kind of background, are we?"

We walked on in silence, past the Pyramids of Giza and the Sphinx that I could have sworn was smirking. I was strangely hurt by her comment and wanted to say that it wasn't accurate. I wanted to take issue with it, have a blazing argument with her amidst the statues of Easter Island. But the moment passed, and we spent the rest of the afternoon taking pictures of each other in front of various locations – the Sydney Opera House, Tower Bridge, the Taj Mahal. Places she was sure I had visited, she pointed out matter-of-factly. We were civil to each other, but something had passed between us that signalled a shift in our nascent friendship, a divide.

From then on, I became hypersensitive to perceived barbs in offhand things she said. We continued to see each other frequently, though no longer on a daily basis. Our meals and outings were as jolly as ever, particularly when there were other people present, but now and then she would say something that (I imagined) involved a change in tone, an accusation. Once, she collected me from my studio apartment and, while waiting for me to lace up my shoes, idly thumbed through a copy of *Le Père Goriot* that was lying on my desk. "I don't know how you people find the time to read such long books," she said. She picked up some other novels and flicked through the pages, adding, "It must be nice to be able to read French." I didn't want to ask her whom she meant by *you people;* whoever they were, I was one of them, and she wasn't. I was soon to leave Beijing for good, and already I knew I would miss Lulu's company; I didn't want to get embroiled in petty arguments, for ultimately, we understood each other. When we talked about my impending departure, she said she was sad I was leaving. She would have to find someone else to hang out with, she joked; but then she added, "It's alright for you, you can just pack up and leave whenever you want."

One afternoon we met at the Noodle Bar, which, in its aggressively pared-down concrete-and-cedarwood aesthetic, perfectly represented modern Beijing cool. She liked this place, she said; it looked half-finished, as if someone ran out of paint, like in a cheap coffee shop in Puchong. I was relating a story to her – of how I had been singled out from a mass of Chinese commuters emerging from the subway by a man flogging fake Rolexes. What was it that gave me away as a foreigner? The way I walked? My wavy receding hair? Lulu was laughing – her full-throated, un-Chinese laugh that cheered up any room. "No, sweetie, it's the awful clothes you wear."

We watched a chef behind the bar roll out long flaccid rolls of noodle dough, massaging, pummelling, twisting. "Do you think you'll stay in Beijing for long?" I asked.

"As long as the money's good. I have to support my parents back home, you know."

I nodded. "Yes, I know. But what about other stuff? Things outside work and money."

"Like what?" she asked as our noodles arrived.

"I don't know – planning for the future. Stability. A home. Friends – like real friends, not temporary ones."

Lulu shrugged her shoulders. "You're nuts."

"I guess what I'm trying to say is: do you really feel you belong here?"

"Mm-hmm," she said, head inclined over the rising steam of her bowl of noodles, "of course I do." She sat with her coat on – a lightweight canary yellow mac that set off her immaculately straight dark hair. In a city that is still overwhelmingly grey, women like Lulu are like flashes of colour in a cold desert landscape, a reminder of the growth of Beijing bling. She was right, she did fit in.

"Don't you feel you belong?" she asked, turning her head slightly to toss her hair to one side before lifting some noodles to her mouth in a single graceful movement. I wasn't sure I'd ever seen anyone look elegant while slurping noodles. "Apart from your little encounter with Mr. Fake Rolex, what's there to stress out about? You're Chinese, and you're surrounded by Chinese. It's reassuring, no?"

I became self-consciously aware of my dirty old trekking shoes and distinctly un-bling Gore-Tex outdoor jacket; everyone around me was sleekly dressed in figure-hugging clothes that seemed to protect them adequately from the cold *and* make them look like film stars. It was a problem I had had since arriving in China, this sensation that I looked out of place, and that people could tell, just by looking at me, that I was foreign, just as that man in the subway could. It wasn't what I had expected to feel surrounded by twenty million other people who shared my ethnicity.

As she complained to the waiter (half-scolding, half-flirting) about the quality of that day's noodles, Lulu even sounded like a Beijinger. She had gently assimilated the northern "er" suffixes and picked up elements of modern slang so successfully that she sounded like someone from Beijing who was trying to sound standard, neutral. My own accent remained obviously southern – foreign.

"I don't know," I replied. "I'm just very aware that I'm a *waiguo ren*. And besides, I don't really want to belong."

Lulu snorted and rolled her eyes. "What nonsense."

"Well, I might be ethnically Chinese, but I'm Malaysian," I insisted, trying to sound matter-of-fact rather than defensive. "It makes a difference. I have different roots, a totally different background. Don't get me wrong, I do love being here – but I'll never really belong here."

She looked up at me, her chopsticks pointing like little javelins in my direction before she lowered them again. "Is that so?" The tone of her voice changed, tauter now, no longer warm. "Then where do you belong?"

I hesitated for a moment, trying to think of what might or might not upset her. "Well, that's complicated of course, as you well know," I started. "But I guess, in spite of everything, Malaysia is always my point of reference."

"Your point of reference," she repeated, imitating my accent and laying her chopsticks down on the table with a sharp clack, "is a country that treats you as a second-class citizen. But let's not even get started on that. Let's just talk about China. Look around you, darling. People come here from all over the world to make a new life. No one cares where you're from. You can just come here, be whoever you want to be – and you're accepted. It's safe. No one hates you. Everything is possible. You're so small-minded and . . . arrogant."

"Arrogant? It's *they* who don't accept *me*."

"Have you ever asked yourself if you accept them? It's your problem, not theirs, honey. You're the one making the judgment, not them. You're the one who doesn't want to be accepted because you think you're superior."

"That is not true." I pushed away my half-eaten bowl of noodles; Lulu was toying with her food, lifting up thick strands of noodles before letting them fall again. Now and then she would smooth back her hair and I would catch a glimpse of her earrings, which she had told me were from an expensive Italian shop in Wangfujing. All of a sudden she seemed ridiculous – a girl from small-town Malaysia who had reinvented herself as a Beijing glamour queen, and yet she worked odd jobs as a tour guide and florist, and her next big thing was going to be managing an office for a small Taiwanese trading firm that imported bottled peach-flavoured green tea. What was the point? The sacrifice, the leaving behind of home and family – for this? It's an illusion, Lulu, I wanted to say. It isn't worth it.

"Why are you pretending to be someone you're not, Lulu?"

"Pretending?" she said, smoothing away strands of hair from her face. "Who am I supposed to be? What kind of person should I be?" She had picked up her chopsticks but now threw them down on the counter again, clattering them across the smooth wooden surface the way a petulant child would. People were looking at us now, but I couldn't let go of the argument. That word, *arrogant,* implied many things – the kind of things I had felt from previous exchanges we'd had – and I wanted to dare her to articulate them. A chasm opened up between us; maybe it had always been there, but we'd somehow managed to ignore it. I thought of the experiences we'd shared. We'd walked through the hutongs singing Leslie Cheung love songs at the top of our voices and cooked Malaysian curries for her friends and giggled our way through a performance of *Uncle Vanya* by a Singaporean amateur dramatic company. We shared a childhood, a history, a language – a whole lifetime, it seemed; but now, suddenly, I saw that our friendship had, like so many other things in China, been an illusion, and a fleeting one at that. She had been my best friend

for three weeks, but now she was disappearing. She had something against me; she hadn't really liked me at all.

"What you are," I said, "is a forty-year-old Malaysian
woman, not a mainland Chinese Barbie doll imitation trying
desperately to fit in to a country that isn't yours. How many
close Chinese friends have you got?"

She lifted her hand and beckoned for the bill. "Whatever. I
knew it from the start. You people are all the same. Arrogant."

"Hang on, what do you mean, 'you people'? I just want to
remind you where you're from, Lulu. You've forgotten where
you're from."

"Sure," she said, "thanks. Remind me where I'm from. It's
okay for you people. You *love* remembering where you're from.
Because you're from happy, lovely, educated families. That's why
you don't ever want to fit into anywhere else. That's why you
keep reminding yourself where you're from. That's why you're
so arrogant. You just look down on everyone else."

"I do *not* do that. I can't understand what you're saying."

"Huh. Don't pretend you don't understand. You look down
on me, I know you do. You just want to drag me down again.
Put me back where I belong. *Kampung* girl from Kedah looked
down on by rich big-city kid like you. Things never change.
You're all the same."

She fumbled in her Vuitton handbag for her Gucci wallet.
Things fell to the floor – a crumpled bit of tissue, a key ring – but
I didn't pick them up.

"Don't worry," I said, "I'll settle it."

"Nope," she said brightly. "My treat. It's only noodles,
after all." She left a hundred-yuan note on the little wooden tray
– far too much for the bill – and then she was off. The heavy
wooden doors opened briefly to let in a flash of pale sunshine
before closing again. I bent down to pick up the key ring. It was

something I'd seen before, a little blue Japanese manga cat that waved its hand every time you pulled the little chain attached to its belly.

I had other friends in Beijing – British, French, American, a few local Chinese – but I didn't look forward to seeing them the way I had looked forward to seeing Lulu. With them, there could be no presumed humour; they could not reduce me to inappropriate giggling fits with a slight flicker of their eyebrows and a barely whispered Malay vulgarity. They could not share an instant understanding of the futility of our situation – a bunch of foreigners trying to establish ourselves in a country that had no real need for us. In spite of her flawlessly reconstructed Beijing persona, Lulu had realized this in the way the Swiss hotel manager and German petrochemical engineer did not. They believed that their expertise would make a difference, that it would be a gift, but Lulu knew that China was already ahead of us. It was using us; we were convenient. It was the most ancient country in the world but it was also the most modern, and in this synthesis there was no place for people who stuck to rigid ways of behaviour, for the points of reference changed with such speed that all preconceived notions would be obsolete on arrival. Lulu knew, too, that China would be a place of temporary refuge, that one day she would move on to somewhere calmer and more settled. She was here to see what she could make of herself, to test herself against the speed of China's change. She felt empowered by her relationship with China, though not necessarily by China itself. And it was this understanding that I had found intoxicating, and that I now missed.

What she had said of me was, of course, true. I had known it even before we had argued in the trendy noodle bar. I had known it all my life. For in Asia, as much as we politicize racial differences, it is not colour that truly divides; it is class. In Malaysia, as elsewhere, friends are bound by tribal divisions that transcend race. A rich ethnic Chinese will be much closer friends with an ethnic Malay who went to school with him and grew up next door than he will be with another ethnic Chinese who grew up in a deprived outer suburb.

In the West, where I spend at least half of each year, it is convenient to see Asia in terms of the haves and the have-nots, the super-rich and the grindingly poor, with no one in between. The gap between the billionaires and the street kids is getting larger all the time, it is reasonably held, but what is less easy to accommodate is the rapidly growing middle class, which is itself beginning to stratify into layers of great complexity. Europeans do not, sadly, have the monopoly on class systems; Asians are just as adept at recreating them even where none existed before.

My sadness at losing Lulu as a friend in Beijing was compounded by my accompanying awareness that Asia has become markedly polarized over the past few decades, at a time when its increasing wealth should have brought about the opposite effect. Last year's riots in Bangkok are just the latest proof of this – they were openly about class differences, about disempowerment and abuse and the lopsided nature of material advancement. And what saddened me most was that I had been personally implicated in the failure of this system.

In many ways, my own family's trajectory modestly but accurately represents the growth of the Southeast Asian middle class. Both my grandfathers came to Malaysia as young children; both grandmothers were Malaysian-born Chinese. Not one of them had any money and only one of them had had proper schooling. One of them might have been illiterate, but I never found out for certain. One set of grandparents ran a village shop (another connection to Lulu), and the other ran a village school and a coffee shop. They were fairly typical of rural Chinese in the 1940s – poor but optimistic. My own parents were the lucky ones of their families – they did well at school, got scholarships, and went to university in Kuala Lumpur. Both got jobs in solid technical vocations. In just one generation, in the heady innocent years post-Independence, my family had become middle class, just as my country had.

But just as my parents were the lucky ones, there were also the unlucky ones, like some of my uncles and aunts, who still live in rural Malaysia. These are the people who are neither living on the streets nor working in air-conditioned offices in the booming metropolises, and who are slowly being left behind as Asia's glitter becomes ever brighter. I have always thought that I was part of this world, this huge mass of people who struggle in vain, for this is, after all, where my roots lie. But at the same time I am reluctant to meet my cousins, self-conscious, almost ashamed of my big-city vowels and the clothes I wear, of my iPod and my stories of travelling the world. Most of the time I am able to ignore these differences, but every so often I meet someone like Lulu who reminds me that my life does not, in fact, involve any real struggle.

For Lulu and my cousins and millions of other Southeast Asians, China is the new America, a place where reinvention is not just possible but celebrated, where pretense and illusion are part of personal drive and ambition rather than dishonesty. It represents a chance finally to have something when previously they have had little. Their idea of the future is vague. It doesn't involve the meticulous planning of things like career progression, family life, mortgage, and school fees. Rather, there is a frightening, intoxicating sense of the limitlessness of possibility, in which personal sacrifice becomes irrelevant. Being close to this phenomenon is an immensely exhilarating and seductive sensation. Every time I go to China I want to throw myself into this whirlpool of promise, but when I am not there I start to recoil from it, and, in my London flat, my chaotic Chinese optimism begins to turn slowly into calm, ordered European pessimism.

I sent Lulu a couple of text messages after our half-finished lunch at the half-finished Noodle Bar. I was sorry, I said, *but you know what Malaysians are like, we are hot-tempered but five minutes later we are all smiles again, LOL. Why don't we go to Café Sambal and eat expensive Malaysian food?* I put two smileys at the end of each message and even rang once. She never replied. I considered going round to the apartment she shared with two Hong Kong Chinese girls, but decided not to. Just before I left Beijing I emailed her, wanting to drop her a line to say I had her cat key ring. *I'll keep it just in case,* I wrote. *He (she?) looks v cute! Drop me a line sometime,* I added at the end.

EMMA DONOGHUE

Finding Jack's Voice: Some Thoughts
on Children and Language

When my son was five, I wrote a novel called *Room* in the voice of a five-year-old boy. Put like that, it sounds easy, even opportunistic: a simple transcription of my son's quirky language. But although having him around helped me immensely in creating Jack (the boy in the novel), the process was anything but simple. It made me think as I had never had to before about how children talk, and what it says about them (and, of course, us).

Over the course of a decade of writing fiction and plays set in the past, I have developed a habit of compiling a mini-dictionary for the time and place in which each work is set: seventeenth-century rural Ireland, for instance, or mid-nineteenth-century middle-class London. Historical slang lists (increasingly available on the Internet) are useful sources, but I find I have to put my own guide together one idiom at a time, to make the words my own. I throw out any that are so bizarre they would stop my readers in their tracks, or that sound too self-consciously "period," and I adapt some to my needs. When writing a novel about an eighteenth-century prostitute, for instance, I could find no generic term for "the client" equivalent to today's "john," so I borrowed one from the criminal underworld: "cully," meaning one who is tricked.

Then, paradoxically, I always set my homemade "dictionary" aside. I refer back to it only to check that the dialogue I'm inventing does not sound anachronistic, or to find flavourful idioms to salt that dialogue. I want to give readers the impression that what they are reading might plausibly have been said back then. So what I end up with is roughly halfway between the language of the present and the past; it's a cultural translation that strives to retain some foreignness, a bridging of the gap.

I did exactly the same thing with the English of contemporary North American five-year-olds when I was writing *Room*. The first decision I made was that my narrator would sound like a five-year-old child, within each sentence, but that he would not tell his stories in the maddening way that small kids do. Ever ask a five-year-old how his day at school went? You'll get anything but a straight answer. Either a monosyllable ("Fine"), if you're lucky, or a crazy, repetitious monologue so full of references to Transformers or Pokémon that you won't be able to tell today from last year, fiction from fact. Only a child's own parents, I believe, are motivated enough to play the game of Twenty Questions that making sense of his account may require: *You know the thing, the thing there does be with the other thing but not the big big thing?* It was a tricky balance; I wanted the (adult) reader of *Room* to have the conviction of verisimilitude, of reading the unadorned, odd segues and non sequiturs of a five-year-old, yet I was afraid they would throw the book aside in frustration if Jack took as long to explain himself as my son would.

So I did grant my narrator the gift of coherence – which I thought was plausible enough, because his situation is so unique: Jack has been raised from birth in a single room, where he is locked in with his intelligent and devoted young mother, who talks to him all the time. But Jack is not particularly precocious otherwise. (I get irritated by the number of novelists these days who use child-prodigy narrators – adults in dewy-eyed disguise.) I wanted every line of Jack's to sound like something a boy of five might think.

I began by listening closely to my son, and charting all the irregularities in his spoken English. I already knew that mistakes are what give children's language its flavour. One of the most useful warnings I ever read in a parenting book was a passage in Penelope Leach's classic, *Babyhood* (1974), where she records a series of exchanges between a mother and a child to show that correcting children's grammatical mistakes does nothing to speed up their acquisition of correct grammar; like their bodies, their speech has its own timetable and it can't be rushed.

But what astonished me was how much my son's spoken English could diverge from the adult norm, without affecting his ability to make himself understood easily enough. I chose just a few of these characteristic mistakes to give Jack – the verbal habits that were intriguing without being too confusing – so that his narration would convey the mindset of a five-year-old without making the reader trip up on every second word. And I found myself mulling over what the language of children tells us about the difference between them – as a tribe – and us.

Children learn immersively, fearlessly, without embarrassment. They don't perfect the word "horse" before moving on to "zebra"; they take a wild stab at both, coming out with *hos* and *zeba* or confounding them into one *heba.* Sometimes their guesses say more than the correct versions: "Planet Earth" becomes *Planet Us.*

They are logical. Like little George Bernard Shaws, they endeavour to reform English, especially by giving verbs a consistent past tense: *I finded, I singed, I winned.* They persist for years until, resigned to the stupidity of adults, they start using our verbs in the irregular way we do.

Children adopt the idioms characteristic of the technology they take for granted, such as a DVD player: *turn on* for "wake up," or *pause* for "stop."

Their native religion is animism. They have a play drive the way adults have a sex drive or a death drive; needing to play, with whatever comes to hand, they automatically turn objects into characters, common nouns into proper nouns. *Forkie's going to sleep on Plate now.* Anything can have feelings, even agency. *Is the pan hurting? Rain is melting me!*

Children's prepositions are random and their conjunctions are AWOL and they say *and and and* a lot and they really do and all their punctuation sounds like commas and this is why, their world is not structured by predictable relations such as cause and effect and it's just one damn thing after another and all a kid can do is try to stick the bits together and hope it'll all make some kind of sense later. Actually, children would all prefer to speak German, in which hybrid concepts can simply be compounded like magnetic train sets: *It's a gorilla shark whale snail.*

Their favourite grammatical modes include:

- the possessive (*my cookie, mines, my one for my own self, not yours*),
- the negative (*I won't ever never not eat no spinach no way*),
- the emphatic (because they *really really feel the worsterest a very enormous really lot much often*, and they *actually really real for true real* want to convince you of the factuality of their wildest fantasies),

and, but only when they are old enough to notice the taboos, which in the case of my laid-back son was not until about five,

- the genito-scatalogical (*you poopy penis poo!*).

Since children live in the eternal moment, their sense of time past and time future is vertiginous: *My tummy's always hurting sometimes all the days, Why you never gived me a brownie not ever, I'm not going to talk to you for a million of years.*

Similarly, geography (beyond the end of their street) is a bewildering abstraction to them: *Is Canada in Toronto or Outer Space?*

But then, their ignorance rarely bothers them. If they don't know a word, they figure out a way to say what they mean: "curled up" can be rendered as *sleeping in circles,* "a draw" becomes *first-at-the-same-time.* (Any parent reading this will be able to think of different examples, because even though it's possible to generalize about the grammar of children, each child comes up with his or her own dazzling neologisms every day, in a spirit of inventive necessity.)

Children's speech is not primarily functional. If much of the language of adults is "phatic communion" (the one term I remember from a linguistics course at university, meaning "small talk" that performs a social task such as politeness rather than transmitting information), then much of children's language could be described as self-pleasuring. *Eenie meenie minie monie itsy witsy ba-baa black sheep Dora Dora Dora splora,* my son used to chant in the back of the car.

Finally, they are natural poets. Shunning simile – because *like* implies only an orderly comparison between two things – they rush straight to the more magical, transformative power of metaphor: *Sock's a snake!*

One of the few facts that has stuck in my head from that same linguistics course is that babies babble in the sounds of all tongues, at first, but as the adults around them fail to respond to most of those sounds, the babies – ever pragmatic – stop making them. Then the toddler narrows, focuses, specializes in the sounds of one or two mother tongues. (When I was a child, I was devastated by the chapter in P.L. Travers's *Mary Poppins*

[1934] revealing that babies are born understanding the language of animals but forget it by their first birthday.) Every educator knows that education means a "leading out," but let's be honest: it's also a narrowing down.

One of the banal ironies of parenthood is that we hurry our kids up, then try vainly to slow them down. We do everything we can to educate our children out of their gorgeous childishness. We tell them about the Nazis, then wish they were still innocently ignorant. Like robins urging their fledglings out of the nest, we are driven by a sense that we'd better get our kids ready for the world before the world hits them. And it's the same with language: we self-consciously model proper usage and gently correct them a hundred times a day so that they will end up speaking like us (but without the swear words, we hope), then we trade nostalgic stories of the fabulously weird things they used to say.

My slightly melancholic conclusion is that parents who are writers are more aware than most of the perversity of this process. Our kids are verbal eccentrics whom we work on rendering ordinary: we teach them thousands of words, but mostly conventional ways of combining them. We do this so that they'll be able to ask directions of a police officer or get good marks for "verbal presentation," so that one day they'll ace a job interview. And in the meantime, at our desks, we try to put words together on the page in strange and original ways, longing to capture even a fraction of the Edenic freshness with which our kids used to play with words when they knew no better.

RICHARD POPLAK

Affricates

On the strip of asphalt that connects the city of Kimberley with
South Africa's deep, unknowable interior, I watch an oncoming
Toyota swerve to avoid a weaving truck. It is a sharp winter's
morning; the car mounts the gravel shoulder, slides broadside for
several metres and, after a terrible suspended second, flips over
once and a second time, sending glass and plastic and fuel across
the simmering tarmac. The episode unfolds, as all accidents do,
in reality's anteroom, bathed in an oneiric half-light.

The Toyota lies like a wounded beast, leaking viscous
fluids, whining. I leap out of my own car and run toward the
wreckage, repeating an absurd little mantra: "No dead babies.
No dead babies." A woman opens the passenger door skywards,
and stands blinking in the sunlight. She is enormously over-
weight, all but uninjured. There are, apparently, no dead babies.
"*Asseblief,*" she says as I approach, "*asseblief kan jy my broer bel?*"
Please, please will you phone my brother?

The scene settles, and a South African tableau unfolds: her
question, asked in a moment of shock and panic, flays open the
land on which we stand. The authorities mean nothing here; kin
is the law. New South Africa, new Toyota, newly paved roads:
meaningless. This is the Northern Cape, the country's far-flung
badlands, flat and unending, reaching up to Botswana, down
into the Drakensberg. In the ground: diamonds. In the sky:

millennia of gods belonging to the !Xam; the Nlu; the Setswana; the Calvinist Boer. The history of the Northern Cape is one of lost deities, and of lost words. It is a place defined by absence, by extinction – a palimpsest, scoured clean (but not so clean) and inscribed upon repeatedly, not by nations with prose, but *with* nations *by* prose: entire peoples erased, at the stroke of a pen. Who, then, does this land belong to? How to define its history? And what language does it speak?

If we are to answer any of these questions, we must meet a man named Solomon Tshekisho Plaatje. All roads in the Northern Cape lead to his intellectual doorstep. He died in the township of Pimville, which would eventually metastasize into Soweto, in 1932, but he is the giant on whose shoulders we stand. The view is, shall we say, confounding.

Take, for instance, the accident scene before me – rich as it is with Plaatje-isms. Minutes earlier, I split the difference and called both the woman's brother and the authorities. The brother arrives first, making his entrance in a pick-up truck with two black workers in the bed. They right the destroyed Toyota, push it off the tarmac, dig through it for valuables. Then the cops and the paramedics arrive. The white brother is massively fat and the black SAPS captain painfully skinny, like characters in a bad *Amos and Andy* knock-off. The brother barks orders at the captain; the captain balks. The sister sits forlornly in the ambulance, while more family arrives. The accident morphs into a sibling reunion.

They speak furiously in Afrikaans, an indigenous South African language based in the main on Dutch. It is hereabouts called, with grave simplicity, *Die Taal.* The Language. Some think of it as a bastard dialect, rough and music-less. This sells *Die Taal* short. It is an entirely South African idiom, rich with compound nouns tumbling over each other, pulling this way and that, exerting the laws of the apposite and the opposite in an attempt to describe this indescribable place. It is a poet's plaything, Afrikaans. But strip it down, and it becomes the cudgel with which some of history's vilest laws were bashed into being.

Which brings us back to Solomon Plaatje, who wrote many millions of words in his decades as a journalist, author, orthographer, politician, linguist, intellectual, teacher, and film exhibitor, almost none of them in Afrikaans. He only ever referred to the whites arriving from the interior to live and farm this land – the trek Boers – as "the Dutch." By linking them so definitively to Europe, he was suggesting that their status was tentative, and the land they used borrowed. But he could not ignore the political force of their language. Encoded in verbs and adverbs and noun and prepositions was the country's future as a divided land. *Die Taal* was a fenced-off universe, and Plaatje would never be invited in.

The argument between the brother and the police captain, despite the broken vehicle between them, is about much more than just a car crash. It's an altercation that Plaatje foresaw, and did as much as anyone in the country to head off. He was born a Setswana (a major southern African tribe) in rural Barolong, in what was, before the union of the four South African colonies, the Orange Free State. (A South African joke: There are no oranges, no one is free, and it's in a terrible state.) His family moved to a Lutheran mission in Pniel, where Plaatje was schooled by a committed missionary educator. The young Solomon – nicknamed Sol in an attempt to humanize the superhumanly gifted boy – was brilliant, serious, devout. Destined for the civil service, he found himself working as a court interpreter during the Boer War siege of the northern city of Mafeking, in 1900. His diary entries and citizen journalism rank with, if not above, the Boer War writings of Winston Churchill and Arthur

Conan Doyle. He was shortly thereafter hired to edit the Setswana paper *Koranta ea Bechuana.*

Plaatje was resolutely a member of the educated native class (a cohort Jan Smuts, two-time South African Prime Minister, described – and he meant this as a compliment – as "pseudo-Europeans"). His political career kicked off with his founding of the South African Native Press Association; this led to his later appointment as the first Secretary General of the South African National Native Council (SANNC), forerunner to the African National Congress (ANC). Last of the great wide-eyed African Anglophiles, first of the great anguished African Anglophiles, Plaatje worshipped Shakespeare, more so, perhaps, than he did Christ, infusing the SANNC with the mélange of Christian fellowship and liberal humanism that he saw as patently Bard-like.

He believed that Union in 1910 would provide franchise to all educated, propertied South African men; he held that the British who (nominally) controlled Parliament would do the right thing by the black majority. He was mistaken. A new breed of soulless late-Victorian – led by the especially soulless Cecil John Rhodes – had come to own Kimberley (and swathes of Africa along with it) shortly after the discovery of diamonds in 1866. By their urging, the British colonial establishment ditched the vestiges of its missionary and civilizing impetus for an unbending social Darwinism. The Boers – Plaatje's Dutch – would never so much as consider universal franchise. Blacks were thus cut out of political life, as surely as if they had been murdered wholesale. It was a betrayal that would define the rest of Plaatje's life.

Those hundred-year-old decisions help explain the scene before me on the strip of road leading from Kimberley to nowhere. They are the forces of history positioning brother against police captain, one fat and white and prosperous, the other thin and black and poor. Language? Skin colour? Tribe? Class? All cast members in the South African pageant, certainly. But what divides our protagonists paradoxically unites them: their existence is defined by laws passed before their grandparents were born. And one law in particular defines them all. "A policy more foredoomed to failure could not be initiated," wrote Plaatje at the time. "It was a policy that would keep South Africa back, perhaps forever. They were going into a thing that would stir South Africa end to end, and which affected hundreds of thousands of both races."

That "thing" – the massively influential Native Land Act of 1913 – would provide legislated racial segregation in South Africa its bedrock foundation. It forbade individual blacks from owning property, and confined communal black ownership to about 17 per cent of the country's poorest land. This was the zygote that, after fifty years of gestation, would finally be whelped in 1962 as apartheid. Plaatje grasped the sweeping implications of the Land Act, sneered at the pre-Orwellian doublespeak describing it as "separate equality," and set out for Britain in 1914 to argue his case before the colonial commission. He was already an experienced writer of polemical texts – the title of his 1910 pamphlet, *The Black Dreyfus,* says it all – and during passage to England wrote one of the foundational tomes of the African struggle movement. *Native Life in South Africa,* the result of a year touring the Free State and Eastern Cape investigating the effect of the Land Act on local blacks, boasts, among other things, the most affecting opening line in South African literature:

Awaking on Friday morning, June 20, 1913, the South African native found himself, not actually a slave, but a pariah in the land of his birth.

It is the fourth comma that lends the sentence its dreadful power – "the South African native *found himself*" – because Plaatje understood that on a winter's day in 1913, black agency ceased to exist.

What's more, *Native Life in South Africa* depicted a country that did not need sweeping racial legislation, a country that wasn't moving backward because of miscegenation, but creeping forward based on the very British notions of class and individual vigour. Plaatje's views would not be especially salutary now, but they were certainly representative of liberalism at the time – the educated of all races would advance, with the "barbarian native" accorded his rightful lower rung in the hierarchy. (Which wasn't, to Plaatje's way of thinking, the same thing as disenfranchisement.) He saw the Land Act, and other draconian measures ushered in with Union, as a disruption to the natural development of a society built along Protestant, meritocratic lines.

He wrote *Native Life* in strident, sparkling English because it was meant for the British intelligentsia. Its rhetorical construction snared colonial hypocrisy in trap after tightly conceived trap, and its notions of the civilizing effects of franchise had an encompassing, wide-angle aperture; the future was not an abstraction, but a field of being in which black South Africans would be forced to live with whites who now held all the power. Plaatje's work cries out at the betrayal of the real South African experience for the narrow expediency of empire. He foresaw, with mantic clarity, the African tragedy to come.

Pictures of Solomon Plaatje show a stiff Victorian gentleman in high collar, unsmiling, eyes creased with laugh lines. A contradiction. In England, he must have conjured up Conrad's vicious image of the educated native as "a parody of a dog in britches." But to dismiss Plaatje was to sacrifice morality, rigour, reason.

He was a cumulus in the otherwise clear sky of a newly segregated South Africa. And so I wonder what Plaatje would have made of this spat between brother and policeman. More accurately, I wonder if he divined this little affair, wrote it somewhere, preached its possibility in a classroom or church hall.

The angry brother is now fixated on chasing down the truck driver who caused his sister's fateful swerve. The argument has entered a new phase; there are other legacies at work here. While Act I took place entirely in *Die Taal,* Act II is peppered with Setswana. If the Northern Cape is a place of lost words – and it is – Plaatje endeavoured to gather the seedlings of language and plant them in the dust, watering them, nurturing them. He wanted to make sure that Setswana words would not disappear with Setswana rights. And so the police captain speaks a language that the brother's ancestors tried to erase.

Plaatje wrote *Native Life* in English. His next major literary achievement, the first novel by a black African, called *Mhudi: A Historical Novel,* was written in the same language. Those were, of course, conscious choices – Plaatje meant to insinuate the South African native into the British intellectual and literary continuum. He was also serious about bringing Setswana into that conversation, offering a bridge between the genius of a predominantly oral culture and a largely literary one. Setswana is particularly rich with the moralistic parables that found easy corollary in Victorian and Edwardian Protestantism; while in England, he compiled *Sechuana Proverbs with Literal Translations and Their European Equivalents,* published by Kegan Paul.

Plaatje never intended this to be a one-way intellectual conversation – he was uninterested in serving vol-au-vents of African primitivism to a European public gorging on Henri Rousseau and freakshow Zulu chieftans. Time and again, he articulated the relationship between printing and culture (he named one son

Johannes Gutenberg), and he knew that Setswana would not survive were it not nailed to the page. Yet he battled the imposition of a Setswana orthography he insisted did not match the rhythm, the African-ness, of the language. (And lost.) He spent years of his life translating Shakespeare into Setswana; first *Julius Caesar,* then *The Comedy of Errors* and *The Merchant of Venice.* He refused the role of the modest translingual courier, would not pantomime invisibility. He saw in Shakespeare's makeshift biography his own: bumpkin who makes good, brings renown on his rural land (Stratford-upon-Avon as Barolong), speaks uncomfortable truth to power, enters the canon. He *became* Shakespeare, took on his mantle.

Plaatje was preternaturally aware of something Walter Benjamin would observe years later: "Translation exposes the kinship between languages, not necessarily their resemblance." In this, translation becomes a moral endeavour, a great civilizing project that forms a web of knowledge linking people, disassembling Babel one beam at a time. And what of Benjamin's further assertion that translation and exile go hand in hand? Did this mean that Plaatje saw himself as an exile – "a pariah in the land of his birth"? Or did he see Shakespeare as exiled from a culture that had forfeited the liberal humanism at the heart of his work for something altogether cruder? The answer lies in the honorific Plaatje afforded the Bard: *Tshinkinya-Chaka.* Man above men. This was no mere sobriquet. It was a means of making Shakespeare indigenous, of weaving him into the eons-old fabric of Setswana culture. And of distancing him from the England of the Native Land Act.

The medium Plaatje used was the International Phonetic Alphabet, or IPA, a result of the late nineteenth century's obsession with taxonomy, classification, the flattening of knowledge. Along with the renowned linguistics master Professor Daniel Jones – the real-life inspiration for Shaw's Henry Higgins – Plaatje compiled *A Sechuana Reader in International Phonetic Orthography (with English Translations),* which was published by London University Press.

The choice of IPA seems essentially Plaatje-esque: elitist, pragmatic – phlegmatic, even – with nary a nod to the gallery. Parsing its intricacies required an educated mind. The phonetic alphabet, the result of a collaboration between French and English linguistics professionals, was formally instituted in 1886 (incidentally the same year that gold was discovered in Johannesburg, consolidating South Africa's status as the richest, most important country in Africa). The IPA employs the Latin alphabet – with some subbing from the Greeks – to create a sort of typesetting gymnastics: letters perform handstands, dangle between bars and betwixt parentheses, do push-ups and sit-ups, all in an effort to render glottal stops and pharyngeal fricatives and affricates and the drenched articulations of the cleft palate: the great sweep of spoken human expression, standardized.

How could Plaatje not want Setswana to join this massive family? How could he not posit it against *Die Taal,* a tongue that refused company like a muttering hermit? The IPA was, however, a final dalliance in his love affair with European culture. He visited Canada as an intellectual sorbet between courses, and then made for the United States in 1921, where he spent time with Booker T. Washington at the Tuskegee Institute. Nineteenth-century liberal humanism had betrayed Plaatje's cause; he saw in Washington's mélange of free-market capitalism and evangelicalism a way forward for the South African native. The break was complete, except that Plaatje never could get Shakespeare out of his soul. He translated *Othello* on passage back home.

South Africa continued on the path Plaatje foretold. Not twenty kilometres from his Kimberley home, the remaining Khoisan people, the Nlu, were forcibly moved from their makeshift housing to the Namibian desert, an act of cruelty repeated endlessly over the course of the twentieth century. Plaatje watched as history was bowdlerized, his people written out of its narrative:

> School books are now being changed and . . . white and black children are being taught that the extinct Bushmen and Hottentots alone were indigenous to South Africa; that the Bantu are interlopers from across the Zambesi and that they only landed here at the same time, if not later than, Van Riebeck [South Africa's "founding father," who arrived at the behest of the Dutch East India Company in 1652].

Everything Plaatje had worked for was being disemboweled. The SANNC, now the ANC, had adopted an unbending Bolshevism. Native education was worse than a joke; there were few Setswana able to read anything, let alone the gloriously named *Diphosho-phoso – The Comedy of Errors –* in IPA.

Plaatje was a leader without a people; he had lost almost every battle he'd fought. He described the black South African status quo as one of "blank gloom," and tried to pray his way out of it. He joined the Christian Brotherhood, he joined the Independent Order of True Templars. He toured rural areas with educational films he shlepped back from America. He wrote for the black press and the white press, decrying new legislation after new legislation that pushed South Africa not so much backward as inward. He died in winter in the mess of Pimville from endemic township diseases – bronchitis, pneumonia. One thousand people came to his funeral. They were celebrating a Renaissance man who would not live to see his renaissance.

Astonishingly, considering the era, Plaatje's voice has survived. In 1923, he was asked to do some recordings for Zonophone Records. At the end of one record, in a powerful, melodious preacher's voice, he sings "N'kosi Sikelel' iAfrika," the first time the song had ever been immortalized in such a way. It is now South Africa's national anthem. It is the song millions sang when Nelson Mandela walked free from prison seventy long, bitter years later.

The brother and his black henchmen are gone, leaving behind a cloud of slow-settling dust. The police captain pisses into the tall grass on the gravel shoulder; it is an act of disgust and of petulance. I have no idea what will become of the Toyota. Perhaps the brother will come back for it after he has indiscriminately shot a truck driver. "Oh, we'll find him," one of the family members assures me.

No doubt.

I look northeast, where Kimberley's township crumbles into shacks and meets the Platteland. The Setswana have settled most of their land claims here, but in the late nineties, the ANC attempted to redress the horrible wrongs visited upon the Nlu during apartheid. They were ceded several hundred hectares of land on the Platteland, given money to build some infrastructure and institutions, and left to make a go of it. Theirs is a culture that was thoroughly destroyed – so much so that Plaatje himself considered them extinct – and now a few thousand eke out an existence for themselves on an atom of the Africa they used to wander before their time ran out.

Their language is a dizzying compendium of clicks and grunts reaching so far back into human existence that it becomes a vital document of what we are and how we became so. But for a few individual efforts, it would have evaporated. There is a young woman at Cornell who is compiling the !Xam and Nlu lexicon using, of course, the IPA. A page of Nlu prose is gloriously indecipherable, an orgy of dexterous typography: southern Africa in code. It is a précis of Northern Cape: land of aphasics, constantly looking for words amidst all the confusion, occasionally finding them.

PASHA MALLA AND MOEZ SURANI

The Ethical Code for Writers, According to
Fifty People Who Are Not Writers

We asked fifty people who do not consider themselves writers, young and old, from across Canada and beyond, the same question: "What is one ethical rule that you think all writers should follow?" We were interested in the relationships, real or imagined, that exist between readers and writers, as well as readers' expectations of writers. Do readers care about a writer's process or methodology? Do writers have responsibilities to their readers, or simply to "the work"? Does "finding the right words" imply something beyond aesthetics, beyond the subjective experience of the artist – perhaps accountability to representing a broader public, and their own moral beliefs? Does writing carry with it ethical considerations at all?

Here, in their own words, are the non-writers' suggestions:

1. Maintain confidentiality: if someone tells you not to reveal an identity, then respect your subject's decision.
2. Don't use the word "nigger" unless you are one of us – and that goes for all cultures.
3. Writers shalt not bang their best friends' wives/husbands.
4. Remember your place in relation to your writing.

5. Remember where you stand in relation to your subject.

6. Remember your responsibility to the work.

7. Don't stop seeing your friends.

8. If you don't feel good about it in your gut, you can't publish it.

9. Writers need not feel bound by any ethical rules in their writing.

10. There are no ethical rules, strictly speaking.

11. Ethics are for doctors, lawyers, and tweed-clad philosophers. Writers ought not concern themselves with such banalities.

12. A great piece of art (in whatever medium) might make everyday ethical standards irrelevant.

13. There's no such thing as a bad word.

14. Don't name fictional axe murderers, pedophiles, or otherwise reprehensible characters after exes out of spite.

15. Use unique experience in a way that is not exploitive of others' kindness.

16. Make sure that you live in the present.

17. Don't copy.

18. Don't plagiarize someone else's work.

19. Attribute. If you're borrowing someone's words, say so.

20. Don't overuse exclamation points or caps because it makes you look like a spaz.

21. Don't lie about your influences.

22. Don't pretend you came up with a style when you didn't.

23. Don't live voyeuristically, seeing every human interaction as a potential source for sport.

24. Don't pretend you aren't part of the machine.
25. Don't waste a reader's time.
26. Don't. Write. Short. Sentences. To. Make. Something. Sound. Important.
27. Don't put your face on the cover of your own book.
28. Innovation without compromise.
29. If you're going to reinforce a stereotype, do it consciously and intentionally, and not because you haven't considered your beliefs and their impact.
30. If you are going to lie to your readers, lie big.
31. Protect your sources.
32. Read widely.
33. Like anyone else, at minimum, know to say no.
34. Like Lyotard said, Incredulity toward metanarratives.
35. "The preoccupation with what should be is estimable only when the respect for what is has been exhausted." – José Ortega y Gasset
36. Do to others what you would have them do to you.
37. Write about your truth. What you believe to be true, not what conventional wisdom tells you or what you think your audience wants to hear. Even if it turns out that you are factually wrong in the end, you still need to write about your truth. If you don't believe something to be true, why bother writing about it?
38. Always speak the truth. Even in fiction.
39. Never let the truth get in the way of a good story.
40. Never let a good story get in the way of the truth.
41. BE TRUE TO YOUR SELF.
42. Therapeutic writing belongs in a diary, not the public sphere; therapy should not be your primary reason for writing.

43. If therapy is your primary reason for writing, hide it well.
44. Integrity of voice. Integrity preserves art from offending.
45. Don't start drinking before noon.
46. Edit thoroughly and make prodigious use of the semicolon.
47. Writers should read more than they write.
48. Own responsibility for what you create.
49. Own your motives for writing.
50. Proofread?

STACEY MAY FOWLES

The First Time

"You can't prepare for it. You can't stop it. You can only
hope that each time it happens, you are near something to
break your fall. Or that you are in a place where no one
cares if you scream."

> – On your unborn child kicking you in the cervix,
> "What pregnant women won't tell you. Ever." Skepchick.org

1

This year, against my better judgment, I read a blog entry called
"What pregnant women won't tell you. Ever." I read this incredibly off-putting list out of equal parts morbid curiosity and deaf-
ening biological clock. Despite the fact that I am a writer interested
in the bedroom-and-booze antics of slutty, wayward twenty-
somethings, I had reached the point in life where you climb off
the bar, put down your tequila shot, and contemplate progeny.

I was at that dangerous age where people no longer told me
that I was "so young" and that I "have so much time." I'd gotten
into the nasty habit of talking about babies at parties, and asking
about babies over dinner, not really sure I wanted to have one, but
more than sure I wanted to talk about it with anyone who would
listen. Because of this interest, a blog post on pregnancy-related

bodily difficulties should have been something educational, if not an all-out breeding deterrent. But ever the self-absorbed writer, I found myself comparing all of the post's sordid details – constantly wetting oneself, pseudo-narcolepsy, projectile vomiting, something called "swollen junk" – to the experience of publishing a first novel.

Don't get me wrong – I don't think the miracle of child-birth should be diminished by some irrational life-decision-challenged author equating typing out a few hundred pages with bringing a child into the world. (That's in the same sad category as people who bring up their dogs when a friend mentions how difficult child-rearing is.) But I do think there's something to be said about the tendency of first-time novelists to conceal the emotional consequences of publication from the naïve scribes that follow in their footsteps. Few writers talk about the meta-phorical kicks to the cervix they experience while writing a first novel, and the result is that many debut novelists believe their debilitating neuroses to be unique. I know that if I'd been able to read a convenient blog post about the horrors of becoming a published author, I probably wouldn't have fallen apart so dra-matically when my first book hit the shelves.

No one wants to hear about what really happens to writers when they finally achieve a bound book with their name on it, just as no one wants hear about a pregnant woman's Poise pads or mangled vagina. Publishing a novel is one of those accom-plishments that most people laud and envy. At parties, people say things like "I've always wanted to write a novel," and you feel obligated to nod and smile and say that yes, you're really lucky/happy/proud/excited. For these occasions, you perfect a healthy combination of pride, modesty, and graciousness. The first novel experience is so littered with misconceptions that the easiest way to deal with such conversations is simply to state, with liberal amounts of humility and self-deprecation, how amazing it has all been and move on.

These misconceptions are understandable. When, after a stream of rejections, I received the acceptance letter for my first novel, I thought I was on the cusp of greatness. I had visions of glamorous book signings, glowing newspaper reviews, Champagne glasses raised in my honour. I was ill-prepared for how insane publication would actually make me – not because it wasn't as enchanting as I had imagined it, but because of how completely naked it made me feel. Equally unprepared were the people who loved me (and who surprisingly still love me). The caricature of the crazy writer can be amusing, but not when you're having a chat with a cognitive behavioural therapist about your very real fear of being consumed by a bear.

Writing a novel *does* have the capacity to make you feel satisfied, exciting, even cool at times. However deluded the belief may be, you feel like you're actually contributing something worthwhile to the world, that you will touch people (*strangers*, even) with your words, and that you will be admired, appreciated, and, for some, worshipped for doing so. Most writers won't admit it, but there is a narcissistic thrill in explaining to someone that you've spent an afternoon writing, in answering the question of what your novel is about, in pounding away at a keyboard in a public place: "Look at me! I am the mythical writer! I am celebrated by society! I am wonderfully misunderstood!" Everything you think about writing a novel is true.

It's the rest of the experience that's deceptive. I don't mean to sound ungrateful, but once it's written, actually *publishing* a first novel sucks. You can read hundreds of those crappy "how to write, sell, and market your novel" books and never be ready for the car-crash reality of becoming so exposed, so suddenly. And as during any positive, life-changing event – marriage, acquiring property, childbirth, career advancement – you are never once allowed to say, "Hey, feel sorry for me. This is really fucking hard."

The first misconception that the pregnancy blog explores is the belief that *you must be happy*: "Except," the blog says, "you're not. Don't try to talk about it with anyone. It's like explaining mustard to a frog." In my experience, people who have not published a novel do not care about the fact that it's hard and you're unravelling because of it. They want you to say it's the best thing that's ever happened to you because, really, it should be. It's true that finishing a novel is fantastic – the sigh of relief and the clinking of glasses that signify the slog is over. And having people actually read it is a dream come true. But all the other stuff – the readings, interviews, reviews, the rocking back and forth in a corner sobbing – is hard for even the most resilient of us. What people don't want to hear is that the experience manages to bring out and magnify the very worst parts of your personality.

If you're prone to mild hypochondria, welcome to an unending world of ailments and the pervasive practice of Googling them. Slightly agoraphobic? Claustrophobic? Good luck ever leaving the house again. Best to buy an unending supply of television on DVD and a durable bathrobe. Your self-deprecation, once a quirky and amusing personality trait that charmed friends and made you fun to be around, has now become crippling insecurity only made worse by the fact that people are writing about you, *in public*. The cliché of the reclusive writer exists for a reason. Putting a first novel out into the world is a terrifying exercise in exposure, and the natural impulse is to want to hide.

Before my novel was published, I had actually been quite brash, even foolish, about exposing my life in print. I had written openly and explicitly about controversial, sexual, personal, and taboo subjects. I had publicly, and carelessly, shared details of my life and the lives of those I loved. If you took the time to look, you could find out about my family, my messy break-ups, my struggles with sexual identity, even what I like in bed. But essays, stories, and blog posts have a short shelf life; the bound book has staying power, immovable in your biography. If it's a disappointment, your career is stained for years, and anticipating that massive anticlimax can be crippling.

As the fictional world populated by people I'd made up came off the press, I was terrified of anyone knowing me by means of what was inside. As a defense mechanism, I had prepared myself for the worst – surely no one would like what I had to expose.

As an older, better, and wiser writer friend of mine said quite succinctly: "Sweetie, get a therapist. Now."

2

About three months before the launch of my first book, something broke inside me. That's the only real way to describe it. My ability to live as a functional human being – a human being who, for the record, had travelled widely, slept in bus stations and on strangers' couches (and, yes, in their beds), who lived fearlessly, sometimes recklessly, and always vibrantly – disappeared. People who know me now (or even knew me then) may find this surprising. While panic disorder manifests itself internally as a tidal wave of pervasive and inexplicable doom, external symptoms are rarely seen. The only thing that people may have noticed was that I was the jerk who left the party early, or who needed to be re-seated at the restaurant because the table was too close to or too far from the door. If things were particularly bad, I was the jerk who never showed up at all.

When a person says they are feeling anxious, we generally tell them to calm down or that they have nothing to worry about. So often, we see mental illness as weakness, not as the mark of a thoughtful person weighed down by their insight into the world. I've tried many times to write about and explain the hold of anxiety to non-sufferers, but it's impossible to accurately describe its vise grip if you haven't felt it yourself. When it comes to anxiety, there is no snapping out of it, no exit from being trapped by your own mind and body, each of them betraying you. In my case, I could only numb it with substances.

My earliest concrete memory of something being terribly wrong: I was on my way to go speak to a group of high school students about becoming a writer. Halfway through the eleven-stop subway ride, an overwhelming feeling of dread came over me, one that had no known source, and one that demanded I get off the subway immediately. Disoriented, suffocated, nauseated, and sweating, I vomited in the street, much to the disgust of nearby pedestrians. I arrived at the high school and got on my knees in a bathroom stall, an act that filled me with a terrifying nostalgia of teenage heartbreak, purging myself of some unknown sickness and angst. I did speak to that group of teens: I told them how wonderful it is to be a writer, that their dreams would come true if only they would work and care hard enough, and that all would be magnificent. With the taste of vomit still in my mouth, I lied to them.

I dismissed my symptoms as the flu and spent a few subsequent days in bed. However, it soon became clear that this was not something bed rest would cure. And things only became worse when the book was released.

The vomiting and dizzy spells came first. Then the sweaty, hyperventilating fits. Numbness in the extremities, increased heartbeat, depersonalization, a fear of losing complete control.

I became obsessed with exit strategies and nearby hospitals. The subway, enclosed and deep underground, without any reliable escape, became completely out of the question. Poison thoughts ate at my brain, irrational and pervasive, involving my imminent demise. Walls collapsing, dogs attacking, my insides riddled with disease. The characters in my novel were reckless, fearless creatures, intent on the most enjoyable road to complete self-destruction. I, on the other hand, became obsessed with intense self-preservation, every minor decision a possible doorway to complete disaster. The only exception to that being my ability to self-medicate. Alcohol and marijuana had the uncanny ability to provide me with an intoxicated window of reprieve where, although still sure of my imminent degradation and demise, I did not give a shit.

Eventually I became housebound, hiding in a false safe zone of my own creation, capable only of sporadic writing, basic personal hygiene, and making sure the dog was fed. After the mysterious development of a permanent "lump" in my throat ("globus pharynges" to those in the know), lasting a full three weeks and requiring visits to three separate doctors to convince me it wasn't cancer, I was finally diagnosed and treated for generalized anxiety disorder.

It took less than twenty minutes for a cognitive behavioural therapist to determine the book was to blame. She claimed what I was facing was common, and then proceeded to gloat over the award-winning, bestselling authors she'd successfully treated. My only thought was that if this was such an epidemic, something that a therapist could base an entire lucrative business on, why hadn't anyone told me that Novel Number One would be instrumental in the loss of my sanity? Why hadn't I stumbled across a blog post titled "What first-time novelists won't tell you. Ever"?

A doctor prescribed me antidepressants, but after noting that one of the side effects was *increased* anxiety, I opted instead for regular exercise and an intense regimen of costly cognitive behavioural therapy, an absurd (yet effective) series of exposures to the innocuous things I was terrified of. By the time I began my treatment, I was so far gone that I had to relearn how to grocery shop, how to buy shoes, how to order take-out, how to make a phone call.

At the exact time that the literary community was deciding who I was as a writer, I was forced to relearn how to be a human being.

3

But why the anxiety at all? Why am I not dancing on a bar some-where shooting tequila and singing the "I'm the queen of the world" song? Shouldn't I be happy? Doesn't all this whining and vomiting in the street make me ungrateful?

Anxiety is a form of narcissism, as is writing. The fear that consumes the panicked comes from believing that people, the universe at large, and even fate itself care enough about us to destroy us. My romanticism had turned against me to the point where the poetry I saw in the world was now responsible for my poetic downfall. In retrospect, the fact that I believed my tiny little short-run book to be vital enough for potential public hu-miliation is comical. Ultimately, my anxiety was assuaged only by my realization that in the grand scheme of things my life, and my book, were pretty much meaningless (a realization that conveniently came via intoxicants before therapy gave me other options). I am only anxious when I am consumed with myself and my imprint on the world. My novel was precisely that: a fifty-thousand-word prayer to force my inner workings on the reading public. The very idea that I would fail after five long years of creating that effort was crippling.

The connection between writing and anxiety disorders? Everyone from Alfred Lord Tennyson to Emily Dickinson to Michael Crichton had a case of it. Yeats, Burns, Brontë, Steinbeck, Asimov – the list is endless. My rather generous therapist claimed that creative minds have the ability to see a situation from all angles, and while this makes them good storytellers, it also leads them to believe that anvils are falling from the sky. Those who are anxiety-prone focus on the possible, not the probable, and what is a good story but finding the most dramatic possibility?

I don't have some scientific explanation for why publishing a first novel makes you a total lunatic, and my evidence that it happens to many writers is purely anecdotal. I only speak from personal experience, but the coping mechanism available to me (besides $175-an-hour therapy and a generous supply of bong hits) was to pretend it never happened. While many a small-press author is forced to be a one-person public relations machine, I rarely brought up the fact that my five-year labour of love was now printed and bound. I perfected a bashful act when the topic was raised and had a stock of subject-changers at my disposal. The only choice was to move on from it, to let it go, to let it be adored or decimated by strangers and friends.

I would be lying if I didn't say I'm not still afraid. The poison thoughts still plague me, I still need to be seated in a restaurant with a decent view of the door, and those who are close to me know I tend to be irrational about ailments and consequences. I still always know where all the exits are. The girl who trusted unconditionally and travelled the world recklessly is probably gone forever. But exposure therapy dictates that the only way to overcome anxiety is to be exposed to the object or context one fears, so naturally the only way to overcome the anxiety of publishing the first novel is to publish a second, and a third, and a fourth. The deeper I go into this thing called "being a writer," the less its consequences eat away at me.

The comments section of that disturbing pregnancy blog post ran into the hundreds, the majority of them simple all-caps missives of the commenter's intention to now NEVER HAVE CHILDREN. The reality is that I doubt the sordid information provided will have any real effect on whether a reader gets knocked up or not, just like warning of a post-publication life shift will have zero effect on whether people write novels. I'm sure I'll write another novel just like I'm sure, despite the horror of the online warnings, that I'll have a baby one day.

Knowing something beautiful and necessary will be awful rarely prevents us from wanting it and making it happen.

LEE HENDERSON

On Tuition Row

"If you want to learn about nature, to appreciate nature, it
is necessary to understand the language that she speaks in."
— Richard Feynman, physicist, lecturer, adventurer

"In general, every country has the language it deserves."
— Jorge Luis Borges

For a couple of desperate years in the middle of the last decade,
I worked for a company that sold post-secondary tuition to way-
laid young adults with low averages and show business dreams.
There were about two dozen staff in our department, split into
two offices. I was included in the group that was seated in a
poorly ventilated space the shape of the cabin in a prop plane.
We all took turns playing passenger, flight attendant, or pilot.
On one side of the aisle, the office windows looked down at
computer classrooms on the first floor, and on the other side,
over what would be the wing of the plane, the windows looked
down at a room set up with a cinematic green screen for making
special effects.

Our unique position between these rooms, and not far
from a latex lab and a fry kitchen, meant that some days a dark
burning smell would permeate our recycled oxygen. A sulfuric

fume or a grease explosion or a nauseating solvent leak would pour from the overhead vents and stall work altogether. I was not the only person in our department who found the stifling atmosphere hard on the throat. Our manager would call expecting project updates. We each had our ways to clear our throats. One resorted to talking louder – as if a lion's roar ever stalled a managerial gas! Others crouched low over their desks below the level of the toxic air, gripping their plastic banana-protecting holsters at their sides in a rainbow of muskets, and spoke only in exfoliating doomsday voices about the workload, all the while nibbling ruefully from their unbruised fruit or from a Ziploc bag of carrot sticks in water – don't get these crouchers going! Their trench jitters slowly pumiced you down to a depressing nut.

"But that's why we're here," I'd always say, "to work. And then to work more."

"One thing at a time, then," they jittered. "Give me one thing. Not five things. Ten things at a time? I need more IT."

Actually, the word my colleagues used was not *thing;* it would most likely have been *deliverables.* As a synonym for whatever thing we were working on, *deliverables* has whipcrack. It's active, it's got looming deadlines. As part of my job in this office, I was faced daily with all sorts of words like *deliverables,* words I was hearing used for the first time outside of business books and sitcom television. So as not to expose myself for harbouring what I sensed were insubordinate feelings, I bit my true tongue and made somewhat of an attempt to sound like a professional by faking a palate for the office vocab. In this department we were all hired to sell tuition to *prospective* customers because in our other lives we were artists and writers and actors and webmasters, and we had some idea of how people, regular people, communicate. Nevertheless, during my three-month probationary period,

I made it my first priority to understand the dialect spoken within the company.

Three days a week I bicycled to the office and worked with a team of other desperate artists, happy to be paid to find ways to convince the youth of today to buy our tuition. We defined our brand and were in the middle of updating our website: our tagline was, "Something-something *dream.*" We sold a fair deal of tuition every year. It was a solid product with lots of options, and it was expensive. Most of my time was spent updating the company's website with new anecdotes about our customers. It was a fun, slow, caterpillaring process.

Over time the company expanded and spread out, leasing floors here and there in the neighbourhood to make room for more customers. At the time I worked there we had three buildings all to ourselves, and floors of towers and low-rise industrial buildings elsewhere in town.

Other companies who sold rival tuition leased offices nearby. A reputable trade school had a whole city block south of us for culinary, legal aid, nursing, and electronics tuitions. A major humanities university was located on the bottom floors of a mushroom-shaped tower to our north. There were two or three single-room schools down towards the pier that specialized in glamour makeup and hair styling. It was kind of the town's educational ghetto.

A dozen or more separate companies sold ESL, a popular tuition package that appealed to young, unfussy foreigners who wanted freedom from home and the opportunity to learn conversational English at their parents' expense. While we toiled to highlight our company's uniqueness, the ESL companies preferred to avoid being identified and focused instead on service-oriented advertising. And ESL was everywhere: ESL signage showed up in our neighbourhood looking like illegible multi-lingual Scrabble boards tacked onto the windows of corner storefronts and three-storey office buildings, although few had actual classrooms (their employees met with customers in coffee shops to talk grammar). Little one-room ESL companies would rather make their interchangeable private services seem like part of one big sprawling corporate entity. I thought their signage was graphically incorrect by any design standard besides ano-nymity, but making it hard to tell one company from the next protected them all. One cold rainy Thursday in the middle of winter, I remember walking past some stunned-looking ESL cus-tomers who had showed up for a verb class that morning to find their school gone. Overnight, the company had imploded in a single bankroll.

Other companies sold tuition packages that did not com-pete with our product at all. Anyone who wanted to pay for lessons in traditional English combat could visit the second floor of the building next to ours, with its full kit of medieval weapons – broadsword, claymore, round shield, plate armour, halberd, flanged mace, ear dagger – and receive instruction in this martial vocabulary for a fee. A peaceful alternative across the street sold fitness and aerobics outfits and one-hour hot yoga sessions.

I observed the many kinds of educations one could receive on these streets. The main offices of the company I worked for were located between these schools, skid row, and a centre for Scientology. Our customers might be outside smoking between classes on aspect ratio and artificial light and get mixed up with a dangerous fanatic from the Dianetics office or a spaced-out zealot on a fresh fix. After class our customers might wait for the next bus with a role-playing knight, and fall in love with an ESL pupil gone astray.

Before I locked up my bike in the morning, someone in front of the Scientology centre would always ask, "Would you like to take a personality test?"

We all offered tests. Working on tuition row, I heard people from around the world struggle to learn the intricacies of the English language. In the office, I was an ESL student of sorts myself as I listened and tried to remember all the nuances of the language I was surrounded by: what is known as Corporate English.

Corporate English (CE), or what the Rutgers linguist William Lutz calls *doublespeak,* conflating two words from Orwell's *1984* (*newspeak* and *doubletalk*), is certainly the dominant slang among the English-speaking world's offices. As a result, it has an influence on the way the rest of us speak, too, even if we lack an office or find our desks cut off from the conversation. As Lutz observes in his comparison of Orwell's novel and his America, doublespeak is an anti-mode of speaking that swaps the rococo of the castle aristocracy with a coarse jargon to suit the age of nano-capitalists. "Doublespeak is language that only pretends to say something; it's language that hides, evades or misleads," Lutz writes. But language can't hide from meaning as Lutz argues this slang does. For slang to inhere, the words must be wonderfully vivid, imposing, and direct – impressed on your cultural perspective from high authority. But I found Corporate English unfamiliar and intimidating, and alienated from the source of its power. Every time I heard it used in the office, I could also hear Lutz's reproach echoing in my head, distracting me from my work even as I tried to decipher the language to stay employed.

I think that calling it doublespeak miscasts the problem, however. Blaming the feudal system of business on the incoherence of the language and not the perspective of the speakers is like bailing out the banks, so to speak. Labelling CE as "language that only pretends to say something" is too quick a dismissal. Such an accusation has been applied to every foreign tongue in the world, and it's never true. Rap slang is likewise dissed, and the same reaction was experienced by the foreigners who encountered the language of the Algonquin Abenaki four hundred years ago, or Australia's reservation Kriol in the 1960s.

Even the ever spacious and sensitive thinker Henry David Thoreau, when describing his first encounter with the First Nation language of Abenakis in *The Maine Woods,* wrote of how it was "a purely wild and primitive American sound, as much as the barking of a chickaree, and I could not understand a syllable of it." But where the linguist Lutz sees only nightmare in Corporate English, the unfettered Thoreau also wrote of how "these Abenakis gossiped, laughed, and jested, in the language in which Eliot's Indian Bible is written, the language which has been spoken in New England who shall say how long? These were the sounds that issued from the wigwams of this country before Columbus was born: they have not yet died away; and, with remarkably few exceptions, the language of their forefathers is still copious enough for them." Is there some such joy and pleasure in CE?

Even before I was hired by the company, I knew how copious a language Corporate English was, but until my first staff meeting I had never heard it so assiduously employed. Before then, my notion of CE came from its reputation, its place in American business, and online spoofs, blogs featuring catchphrases like *drink the Kool-Aid* and fake words like *blamestorm.* But I never knew which words were seriously used in an office and which ones were disgruntled-employee gags. Did anyone really say that you climb the corporate ladder through *assmosis?* Did any boss really expect, even metaphorically, to *boil the ocean?*

In my experience, it was the tuition company's pyramidal hierarchy itself that regulated the flow of speech. My boss was an MBA-by-correspondence and routinely dropped his knowledge in conversation. I learned to differentiate between what was business-certified terminology and what was mere regional coinage by listening to him and my various superiors. *Action item. Deliverables. M.O.U. Team.* The slang was used with a fuzzy grey-partitioned sincerity that was not to be fucked with. Along with the engineering of the highway system, the strict doctrines of the military-industrial complex are another perennial role model and loanword cache for Corporate English – the three languages are all tribally connected. Even tuition companies like ours operated on a loose highway-military model. Our online project organizer was even called Basecamp.

One night, after the boss's sudden layoff of a talented employee had rattled my morale, I lay in bed wondering: *Should I become more than a desktop soldier and learn to speak fluent Corporate English? Implement a few new words and . . . downsize a few others? Just use cliché at the office, that's all, never at home?* I knew that to accept the merits of each new word was part of my job; it was required of me to swallow CE wholeheartedly to keep this sweet part-time gig. But could I get my tongue around the corny patois?

Corporate English is an office creole in which many speakers are so fluent that they might not even notice a change in dialects when they come home in the evening to their dinner and children and a backlog of *Mad Men* episodes to catch up on. It is a jargon full of cog-wheel images of monetary and managerial thought. It doesn't suit home life. The *metrics* of making something from scratch with a small child are impossible to *measure.* Have you ever watched a PowerPoint presentation on upcoming lovemaking? What is the *added value* in cleaning your own spotted trout? Family problems are never *irregardless* of alcohol.

Corporate English is made up of business metaphors; money and power are its inspiration.

Slow learner. Black humour. Kiss ass. Karaoke nights. Overstress. Sexual harrassment. Everyone in the office had an *exit strategy* they might not have realized they were hatching. And the hole I was digging for myself was this empty space where my voice used to be. The academy is derided for its pettiness, the office for its fickleness. At least three of our meetings were about un-expected changes in cubicle seating.

Listening to CE spoken left me stupefied. But to actually *see* Corporate English can give the trench jitters to even the hardiest war generals. "When we understand that slide, we'll have won the war," is the famous remark of U.S. General Stanley McChrystal after seeing a PowerPoint on Afghanistan that looked like a bowl of angel hair pasta. It is believed that some kind of value is added to CE when it's paired with a PowerPoint presentation. "It's dangerous because it can create the illusion of understanding and the illusion of control," the general added. "Some problems in the world are not bullet-izable." (Some prob-lems in the world are not solved by a bullet, either.) In my time with the tuition company I had the opportunity to witness my boss perform three PowerPoint slideshows. They were definitely displays of power, full of bullets, aspirational if there was any point to them at all. In PowerPoint, utopia is stock footage. Stock replaces real. No true documentation will suffice. And graphs and Venn diagrams and other non-representational Miro-esque abstractions are meant to interpret metaphors like *human re-sources* and *risk premium.*

I thought of PowerPoint presentations as office rhapso-dies. I tried to imagine my boss as a rapper and this slideshow as his music video. Rap is a slang also joined by metaphors for money and power, and among the staff *bling, gangsta, hater,* and *pimped* were rap loanwords used when discussing the look of our website.

I was foreign to CE, frustrated by it. I was a CESL student in need of a tutor. All I heard in the company's slang was Lutz's awful doublespeak, and I didn't respect the sincerity of the inflection in my bosses' voices. I chalked it up to cant, another money language – a secret thesaurus of the criminal class. Cant's enticements are its colourful verbiage and vivid metaphors, obscurities which serve to veil in plain sight all the less-savoury aspects of illegal business. Rap and mob movies are the most entertaining outlet for hearing North American cant, but CE is by far the most visible form of cant used in English.

Most slang is teasing and ironic and a nuanced antisocial statement, a reaction to the preconceptions of others; not so for Corporate English. CE's cultural status makes it a self-imposed, deadpan, face-value cant. With its pithiest phrases and acronyms minted by journalists (*future shock, tipping point, prospects,* USP), and its many words lifted from laboratories, road crews, rap, and the military, CE is not ironic; it trusts wholeheartedly in the tested value of its language's debtors.

Outliers. Change agents. Blue sky. Actionable. Integrated. Embed. Diss. Props. Skill set. Narrative. Go live.

Irregardless has been in use in CE longer than *i-fad, the long tail, tipping point,* and *metrics* combined. The stubbornness of *irregardless* in CE usage is found in the dialect's meaning of the word, its close attachment to the central theme of power. *Irregardless:* the prefix hangs a double-negative flaw on the word that is so unnecessary, and suffuses it with pungent ironies that staff cannot mention in front of the boss. Power is never corrected. Power corrects bad behaviour. But I could not tell my boss the correct way of saying *irregardless*. It is a pointless word. But the staff must remain quiet and loyal to the boss even *irregardless* of the nettle word. Maybe practitioners of CE perpetuate this disgrace unconsciously, but that is rarely the case with language, which is communally enforced. To remain employed, staff must accept *irregardless*. To make its power plainspoken, and plainly spoken, so that only a petty snob on staff would correct his boss during a meeting for such a slummy and irrelevant act of stupidity – I offer *irregardless* as the locus for Corporate English and the kryptonite source of its stamina.

The misadjudication of *penultimate* has likely found its correct place in CE usage, coming second after *irregardless* in CE's list of most enduring words.

A similar theme of power can be found in the *green economy*, a concept that makes everyone go digging in their mind-gardens for ways to *grow* their business, *grow* their brand, *grow* their sales. What kind of bitter seed must a boss plant to grow sales? But in CE, sales and debt are all there is to talk about, so you constantly need fresh money synonyms, the way rappers use new aspects of materialism to express their success.

Likewise, while at the company I looked for opportunities to *grow* my vocabulary. But it never sunk in what was being said at meetings, because my fascination with the language was as a fiction writer. I was a part-time dummy, and I used that as my excuse to remain detached and amused and ultimately fail at being employed.

I found Corporate English was not mine to drop into conversation. I held no possession over its glossary. After this realization, I sat through our Monday morning meetings silently smiling. My boss never made me learn how to open PowerPoint. But I did not find any other clear ways to communicate my thoughts either, not without feeling condescended to. But speaking without CE is an obstinate and snobby way to work. I learned the choice was to make life difficult for myself, or assimilate.

In the time I worked there, I watched plenty of others in my department with an ironic handle on CE get laid off without notice and given an hour to clear out. The trench jitters were setting in. I expected my time to come any day. I recalled how in eight years of French immersion at public school I had never learned to speak or write it as well as I could read it. With my tongue tied by my occupation in this company, I figured my chances of survival in it were dim. I lamented my condition and my paycheque hanging in the balance.

So, as my ever patient and sympathetic reader might have gleaned, one spring afternoon on my lunch break I decided to visit the library to find books about the greater destiny of language, in the hopes that what I found might help me learn CE and bolster my sense of duty to my employer. If all languages are fundamentally alike in our brains, as Noam Chomsky has asserted, then what is my hairy problem with Corporate English, besides a fussy academic stubbornness?

My reading related my resistance to this lame English dialect to the seven thousand living languages on the planet that are at risk of going extinct this century. I began to come back to Lutz's side. The more I read, the more I considered Corporate English as possibly the ultimate pine beetle of William Burroughs's imagining, one language as an all-exterminating virus. MBA petri dishes breeding fire ants capable of wiping out the planet.

"I don't mean to downplay the challenge of conserving species and ecosystems," said the linguist and author David Harrison, whose life work is to archive dying languages, "but languages are more critically endangered. They are going extinct faster. And these languages contain some of the secrets to human survival and adaptation."

Already fewer than a hundred languages are spoken copiously around the world. Before the end of this century, half of all languages spoken today will be extinct. Soon we will all speak Corporate English.

At the tuition company, I saw only one way for employees to learn any of the outside world's secrets to survival and adaptation. It came in the form of a request to the boss for a *Pro-D* (professional development) day. A Monday away from your desk will be granted, but only on condition of successful application to attend a three-night conference on CSS and Google analytics in the windowless basement rooms of a remote hotel in Maple Ridge.

I worked at a slang's pace already, what with my full-time salary and twenty-four-hour work week. I never had the added gall to request one; I came to the office with gall enough to think doing so was my *Pro-D*.

"Each language is a way of perceiving the universe," said Borges.

"All people are simply different options," Wade Davis often says. Davis is a Canadian ethnobotanist who gave the 2009 Massey Lecture on his study of the history and language of the Polynesian "Wayfinders," an extinct culture that once spread across the Pacific Ocean: "Ten thousand square kilometres. Tens of thousands of islands flung like jewels across the open sea." The navigators of Polynesia, as Davis learned, could name by memory over two hundred and fifty stars in the night sky, and could make their way through "vast oceans to distant atolls" by interpreting the colour of the clouds and the way the waves broke, "each island with its own distinct refractive pattern as unique as a fingerprint." Davis has said, "If you took all of the genius that put a man to the moon and applied it to the ocean, you'd get Polynesia."

The ethnobotanist Davis and the linguist Harrison agree that one universal language for all mankind spells disaster. A universal tongue does not imply or promise peace and unity but does, at least, mean the extinction of every other way we have for seeing the world. Davis asks us to imagine how we would feel if, instead of English, our universal language was Swahili or Inuktitut. But what I find more distressing and easier to picture is the day when everyone on Earth speaks CE.

"As for English," the French revolutionary Bertrand Barère said in a political speech given in January 1794, "a great and free language on the day when it mastered the words 'The Power of the People,' English is now no more than the dialect of a tyrannous and despicable government, the dialect of banks and letters of credit. Our enemies turned French into a court language, and thus they brought it low. It is for us to make it the language of peoples. . . . It is the destiny of French alone, to become the universal language."

Meanwhile, two thousand species of birds, and their wild songs, have gone extinct along the Pacific Ocean since Polynesians sailed by wind and oar for thousands of kilometres in the open sea.

In his book *Spoken Here: Travels Among Threatened Languages,* the Canadian writer Mark Abley finds remarkable differences in perspective between English and the Australian aboriginal language of Jaru: "Writing in English, I naturally say 'Jaru speakers.' But I should probably say 'Jaru listeners.' Being wise, in Jaru, is 'having ears': *mangir-djaru.* Being unwise or silly is 'having no ears': *mangirgir-mulungu.* What in colloquial English we mean when we say somebody is dumb, the Jaru language conveys by saying a person is deaf." How much more of the Jaru life is spent deliberately listening, and how much more often are we expected to simply talk? To go from Jaru to Corporate English would make an attentive listener look dumb. To go from Corporate English to Jaru would make an assertive speaker look deaf.

On my lunch break I read another example in Abley's book – an Inuktitut word with a double meaning like *dumb,* but to describe someone who is nervous. *Puijilittatuq* means something like *nervous* but is commonly translated in its literal form as, "He does not know which way to face because of how many seals he sees at the ice surface." One word for that. Is there a word like *puijilittatuq,* is there an English moment like it? Might the South's closest equivalent to *puijilittatuq* be when we feel frozen with stage fright? But add to that an empty stomach, feeling truly frozen, and possibly in more danger? It puts the speaker in the eye of a common experience, with a clear point of view, and a high poetry in the compactness of its imagery.

For Canadians to the south, a word like *puijilittatuq* has roots in modern medical observations instead. Our English words for *puijilittatuq* are not images of a landscape or other animals, or our relationship to these external forces. Totems are out of fashion in talk of the Western mind. *Nervous* is a disconnected landscape; its roots are in the tangled threads of a medical cadaver. *Nervous* is a self-centred, biological, and inert word. Nerves: we should prefer them to *puijilittatuq?* I can easily see my prickly nerves and I become preoccupied with the frayed physical condition of my electrified feelings, and in trying to *see* my nerves maybe I fail to notice the seals and fragile ice around me. When seals surface in the office, what am I capable of? The word *puijilittatuq* implies some call to action. The word *nervous* asks that the speaker's consciousness please hold still, irregardless of the seals, and take this or that medicine to calm the *puijilittatuq.*

Depression, something to be paved over.

Leverage knowledge capital, to steal an employee's ideas.

Language directs one's mental picture of life. And when I spoke Corporate English I saw the world as managers do, as a very tiny, manageable place. Through the lens of CE, the Earth was the size of a circle on a PowerPoint slide, and all the new customers were like grains of sand. Even when I spoke the language of CE it made me sound tiny: in its world I was as small as a byte passing through our network bandwidth. CE is from the point of view of the boss. In the poetry of Corporate English, *bandwidth* is a manager's near-synonym for *puijilittatuq*.

I told myself, *I should ungrit my teeth and speak it.*

I learned on my lunch break that in the Hopi language spoken in Arizona and New Mexico for thousands of years, one can talk of things happening without mentioning the thing. The subject and noun can be absent from the sentence and implied by an *i* suffix on the verb – Abley uses the example of *rehpi*, "flash (occurred)." How can the Pueblo of Arizona and New Mexico speak in a tongue without a necessity for nouns when nouns are so crucial to *our* ability to speak at all?

"Your inner voice quiets down. Internal dialogue is stimulated by a preparatory desire to speak, but it is not actually useful if there are no other people around." This was the sense of extreme solitude, as described to a master journalist, felt by the itinerant Julian Assange, master hacker and creator of the whistleblower website Wikileaks, a man absorbed in the most probing forms of decipherment, of computer languages, and of top secret corporate jargon. Solitude, as Assange describes it, is a Hopi experience, without nouns – the opposite of living in Corporate English, which is a deeply social dialect that relies on nouns to make its point. CE is metonymic, a cluttered dashboard of bobbleheaded headhunters and late deliverables. Whereas Hopi speaks easily of a horizonless horizon.

After lunch I put my library loans beside my computer, and before I had time to finish one email my boss came by to chat. A project that I was responsible for had *bottlenecked* on my desk. The idea I had was to buy hundreds of used records and swap all the labels to ones that read, "Something-something *dream*." But months after the first pitch meeting, the new labels still had not been designed yet. Our company now owned hundreds and hundreds of used records that were being stored in my cubicle. And I had completely forgotten about the added cost of glue. My boss wanted to know what I was reading. He told me he was reading David Mitchell's *Cloud Atlas,* on loan from one of the staff he had hired recently to write for our website. "Funny," I said, hearing the off-rhyme in our reading habits, and showed him my library book, David Crystal's *Language Death.*

"That's fictional?" My boss took the book from my hands and began reading at random from the top of a page:

> " . . . this comment by Ezra Pound: 'The sum of human wisdom is not contained in any one language, and no single language is capable of expressing all forms and degrees of human comprehension.'"

My boss continued aloud with Crystal's reply:

> "So, one way of increasing our stock of human wisdom is to learn more languages, and to learn more about languages. And one way of ensuring that this sum of human wisdom is made available – if not for ourselves, then for the benefit of future generations – is to do as much as we can to preserve them now, at a time when they seem to be most

in danger. As each language dies, another precious source of data – for philosophers, scientists, anthropologists, folk-lorists, historians, psychologists, linguist, writers – is lost."

"Interesting stuff. Is it for a class?" he said and shut *Language Death,* passed it back to me.

"Yes," I said.

"Listen," he said to me, "we need to discuss some items. The company can no longer afford you at this salary when you're part-time."

"I'm sorry to hear that," I said, and after listening a little longer to his prorogations about American customers and mortgages and so on, I shook his hand and said goodbye to the other staff – I had an hour to pack my things and get out of there. I went out into the sun. It was the end of May, 2008, and not yet lunchtime, so I bought a sandwich and a San Pellegrino and I went and sat in the park with friends all afternoon.

After I split from the company and no longer felt threatened by the dialect, I regained ninety percent of the movement in my tongue. No one says anything about it, and I don't notice any difference in how I talk.

When I walked out that day with my severance promise, I was reminded by our neighbour on tuition row that the tyranny of a single stupid mindset is what disturbs level-headed people about the popularity of something like Scientology. Scientology is based on a paperback novel. And when I walked by the Scientology centre on my way home from my last day at work at the tuition company, I saw they even had a picture of the paperback novel out in front of the centre. The door greeters asked me if I wanted a free personality test. I thought it was impossible that anyone inside there could be assiduously using the vocabulary of this pulp fiction sci-fi cult. I found it more plausible to hear the language of the bleeding drunks and lost schizoids and crack addicts down the block – that goosebrained babble made more sense to me than Scientology. I unlocked my bike and rode away in the direction of skid row.

Language is an ecology of tongues that rhapsodizes or goes dry on the same principles of diversity as any species in the ocean, forest, or plain. I try to ride along the old roads of language, those left seedy and outgrown by the latest English, because I believe that truth is heard in every writer's other secret duty: to come up with one new joke, and help recirculate into a common tongue at least one word from the stories of the dead.

LISA MOORE

My Character

A man in an airport tips some salted peanuts into his loose fist. He tilts his head back and taps the fist to his mouth. A small circle of frenetic light jiggles on the carpet and up a wall, the sun through the big windows hitting the man's wristwatch. He shakes the small bag of peanuts as he looks down the row of chairs. Waiting for someone.

I want my character to be sitting there, eating those peanuts. The salt. He'll need a swig of something.

My character will be in an airport with a bag of peanuts. I want him to fall in love. I want to fall in love with him. I want him to be ordinary and to overcome extraordinary peril. Is he ordinary? I want him to have a revelation or provoke one. He will be young and brazen.

I want this man to know what to do with a pomegranate.

I imagine him in a graveyard at dawn. There's a backhoe on a tilt of red earth and a grave with a blue tarp. Three identical angels with pocked faces and fingers held near their lips. They are telling him to be quiet.

Because I was in a graveyard like that in Buenos Aires, with crypts the size of garden sheds and ornate grillwork on the doors and glass windows covered in cobwebs. You could look in through the dusty glass at the stacked coffins and narrow marble staircases leading down to the dark.

I turned a corner in this graveyard and there was a little trolley with a bucket of suds, the bubbles breaking soundlessly, and a duster with fluorescent pink feathers. My character has to see that feather duster in the bright sun, the synthetic pinkness, and he'll hear the cleaning woman who is humming, and he will realize she has gone down the narrow marble stairs into the dark; she's down there cleaning the caskets.

I want him to be stealing an identity off a gravestone. I am basing this character on a real person, but I don't want to meet him. I want to make him up.

He has gigantic ambition. He will crawl on his knees and elbows through long grass. He will hitchhike on a highway after a jail break and in the dawn there will be a luminous object on the road. I hit one just like it two days ago. I was upon it before I knew it.

I didn't know and then I knew. A little crack under my tire, the pieces fluttering up like butterflies, the very queasy-making penumbra of knowing and not knowing at the same moment: a phenomenon that accompanies an omen.

It will be a plastic spaghetti strainer of Day-Glo lemon. It will smash to bits and the bits will whirl in the vortex of the transport truck's backdraft. My character will have lots of stuff in his backdraft. A history.

Character flits and builds. It moves accidentally, requires costume, a big cosmos, it crashes up against peril. Is formed and unformed. Hurtles forward; stays still.

When he is a child, my character will go into the fireweed after a soccer ball that lands with a whisper of leaves. There will be spittle in the stalks and muggy summer heat. The flowers will tremble and he will see that each flower has a bee. A bee will dive-bomb a blossom and stagger back and hover as if tethered by an invisible thread. My character will grab the soccer ball and beat it out of there. Because this happened to my son once, just before a game of spotlight.

Sometimes I look into my son's eyes and look and look and look. His character unfolds and unfolds. Then he blinks. He has freckles, a brush cut of pale gold. In certain kinds of light it's gold.

My character will have a son like that. They come out of the mall and the kid will have a fresh new brush cut and he'll say *wha-hoo* when the wind touches his scalp.

Character is plot. Elizabeth Bowen said that. It means the gathering up of force and fate and the surging forward and breaking apart of the who-ness of a person. Who-ness is movement. Who-ness is action. Action is the plot that unfurls inside a character.

I have to decide if fate is the same thing as destiny. What will just happen to my character and what does he make happen all on his own? He will jiggle one knee and tip some peanuts in a loose fist and then there will be an announcement. The flight to Buenos Aires is now boarding.

He will see the tango performed by a woman in a turquoise dress with lots of white ruffles and a man with oiled black ringlets, and my character will be impressed by how humourless the dancers are. They are as serious as serious can be. My character will realize he is capable of that kind of solemnity.

I love the people whom I love for these reasons: freckles, trampolines, barley salad soaked with lemon, black wetsuits in the surf, a ruffle of white foam around their waists. They are overcome and engulfed and lifted up. They get lost in a hurl of bubbles and they're dragged along the bottom. They get drunk and dance to Blondie's "Heart of Glass." They are always sputtering and choking with laughter. They are always hungry. They get sad, sure, but they never get sad. Or their eyes are tearing from the barbeque smoke. Some of them can sing. One can play the mandolin. One jumped out of a plane. One never loses her temper. One got pregnant by accident. Five times. One is my sister.

My character will know these people and love them. Everything he does, he does for them. He does everything to show them. He's going to show them.

The people I love have green eyes and they had dirt bikes growing up. They say things like: "Look at the little cappuccino cup I got at a yard sale in Montreal" and "This parka that had a tampon and forty dollars in the pocket." They say: "The dog has an ear infection." Or: "I'm building a floating dining room." Or: "Where are you from is a different question than where do you live. But it never used to be different."

One of the people I love prefers delicate jewellery, a little silver ring with a knot in it – her name is Holly. Another one had a neighbour with a white horse, who started a bonfire of old tires which the cops couldn't see because the neighbour parked a yellow school bus between the fire and the road. Everybody got drunk at the tire fire and the wind blew the smoke in my character's direction.

My character does time. He can't come home. He hides out. He becomes a man. He becomes.

And the girl he loves. The girl he loves. Man oh man. She eats watermelon and cups her hand under her chin, and the glossy brown seeds get pushed out her pouted lips.

She has the room in the corner with two giant walls of glass looking out on the beach; this is Uruguay we're talking here now.

I stayed in that room. At the head of the stairs, in that hostel, there was the mounted head of a wild boar wearing over-sized sunglasses and, hanging from one tusk, a pair of bikini bottoms. His jaw hung open just slightly, as if he had some comment he was about to make. He looked like he was taking notes.

The girl my character loves is asleep on the bed in the corner room, tangled in a white sheet, pinstripes of red sun coming through the reed blind, curving over her bare back, the sole of her foot. But I think she's with someone else. She's with someone else.

MADELEINE THIEN

Photocopies of Photocopies: On Bao Ninh

Bao Ninh, now living in Hanoi, became a novelist in the second half of his life. Until the age of forty, he served in the North Vietnamese Army, fighting the Americans for a decade along the Ho Chi Minh trail, then passing another decade as part of the NVA's body-gathering team. Demobilized in 1987, he began to write. Three years later, he published his first and only novel, *The Sorrow of War*. It is a slim book, so small that it would fit easily into a coat pocket.

My own copy, an English translation, came from a bookseller in Phnom Penh. The paper is thin and nearly transparent; dog-eared and worn, the book is, in fact, a photocopy of a photocopy. On each page, the sentences slope crookedly across the page and, in some places, the text is smudged and faded from humidity. These counterfeit copies are everywhere in Southeast Asia, available in bookshops, in sidewalk stalls, sold by children roaming the streets. Reading from it in the April heat of Phnom Penh, I feel as if the very air changes. The novel collapses time, collapses worlds.

—

Kien, the novel's central character, joins the North Vietnamese Army in Hanoi when he is eighteen years old. By the time Saigon falls, in 1975, his brigade of five hundred men has been completely obliterated and more than three million Vietnamese have died in the war. His last duty is to travel the length of the country, trying to find and identify the bodies of those who remain missing in action, a mission that takes eleven years. "If you can't identify them by name," the head of his team tells him, "we'll be burdened by their deaths forever."

As Kien works his way across the post-war battlefields – abandoned now, brazenly lush, idyllic – ghosts free themselves from the mud. They play cards, drink, lose themselves in romantic and lustful abandon, they die, decay, sing and tell dirty jokes, while Kien drinks cup after cup of brandy, "the way a barbarian would, as if to insult life." The dead step from every corner, every house, every jungle trail, creating a narrative structure that feels like a tide coming in and washing out – relentless – more like labyrinth upon labyrinth than any solid, Aristotelian form.

Here, the dead remember other dead, they call up their own ghosts, so that we are always remembering, and living, through an infinite corridor of others.

Unable to comprehend the present, Kien begins writing about the past, "mixing his own fate with that of his heroes," embracing a turbulence of memory anchored to neither time nor space, that adheres only to "that circled arena of his soul." The uprush of so many beings, writes Bao Ninh, "penetrated Kien's mind, ate away into his consciousness." Kien takes it upon himself to make a place for as many of the lost, the unnamed, as he can, writing a story in which "any page seemed like the first, any page could have been the last," becoming, in the process, a kind of composite, invoking the dead in order to keep his life afloat, dissolving himself in first-, second-, and even third-hand remembrances. Their stories, of a time when "all of us were young, very pure and very sincere," become his only reality in a world reborn.

Eventually, even Kien himself will disappear, replaced by a different storyteller, perhaps the author himself, perhaps not.

"Who else but you can experience your life?" A simple question, voiced by Kien's stepfather, but one that Bao Ninh turns inside out. Rather, the reader experiences just how many lives Bao Ninh can bequeath to us through the single, solitary mind of Kien, through a character who never quite solidifies, who floats from night to night, from the jungle to the city, from existence to disappearance.

Near the end of the novel, Bao Ninh asks, "As for the author, although he wrote 'I,' who was he in the scout platoon? Was he any of those ghosts, or of those remains dug up in the jungle?"

Was he any of them, all of them, or none at all? Bao Ninh's literary creation is an empty man, a sieve, who is brought alive by other voices. Kien survives the war but his identity, his self, is ruptured. He becomes both a full and an empty vessel, a character who knows that only a greater humanity, a flood of conflicting voices, will hold his self together. "Let our stories become ashes now," a young woman tells Kien, at the war's end, wanting him to forget the past. In the moment, neither recognizes that ash remains, that the residue survives the conflagration. "I know, of course," wrote Bertolt Brecht. "Only through luck did I survive so many friends. But tonight in a dream I heard these friends say to me, 'Those who are stronger survive.' And I hated myself."

——

On its initial publication in 1990, *The Sorrow of War* was briefly banned in Bao Ninh's homeland. Since then, however, it has become Vietnam's most beloved war novel, a book celebrated for its relentless, humane depiction of the generation that fought the war. Here in North America, Bao Ninh's novel has been criticized for being rambling, incoherent, untidy, and uncontrolled, for lacking the poignancy and clarity of Tim O'Brien's *The Things They Carried*. Perhaps the critics are right. Or perhaps fiction, like the human mind itself, is more elastic than we give it credit for. *The Sorrow of War* defies categorization. It takes apart its own structure, it makes a mockery of linearity, in order to voice its truth.

In Cambodia, the artists who might have told the story of their war – the writers, poets, dancers, filmmakers, painters, artisans, and musicians – were killed. Among the two million Cambodians who lost their lives during the Khmer Rouge revolution, an estimated 90 per cent of the country's artists died of starvation and disease, or were murdered in the fields or in the prisons of the Khmer Rouge. Others still were silenced by exile and poverty. Libraries were emptied and Cambodian writers became like Brecht's banished poets: "Not only their bodies but even their works were destroyed."

Images, not words, have come to represent the Cambodian genocide. The most famous of these are the thousands of photographs from Tuol Sleng, a high school in Phnom Penh that was converted into a prison and used primarily to murder "enemies" within the Khmer Rouge itself. The majority of Tuol Sleng's victims were peasants, cadres, cooperative leaders, soldiers, and commandants who fought for Pol Pot and his ministers, as well as students and teachers who returned home from abroad, hoping to serve their country; the remaining victims came from all walks of life, all age groups, and all professions. Of the sixteen thousand prisoners who were brought there, there are eleven known survivors.

Nhem Ein, the Khmer Rouge cadre who photographed each prisoner, was asked how he wanted people to react when they viewed his pictures. "Firstly," he said, "they should thank me. . . . When they see that the pictures are nice and clear, they [should] admire the photographer's skill. None have any technical errors. Secondly, they would feel pity and compassion towards the prisoners." I have been to Tuol Sleng many times. In the hot, stale rooms, air disappears. The tiled floors are dirty and stained. After grief and pity, what I feel is rage and a determination to understand. Movements and ideologies do not spring from the air; we are building them all the time, persuading ourselves of their value, following their bright promises to utopia. Such tidy narratives, in myth or in literature, succeed only in evoking an illusory land, more false than the ghosts of Bao Ninh's landscapes.

—

In the photocopies of photocopies, translations upon translations, Bao Ninh's ghosts have been granted a second, enduring life. *The Sorrow of War* can be found in the placid, northern guesthouses of Laos, and in the endless shelves of the Kinokuniya Bookstore in San Francisco. In June 2010, I took a bus from Bucharest to the Black Sea, where some two thousand years ago, Ovid passed his final decade in lonely exile. I spoke about *The Sorrow of War* to a colloquium of Romanian and international writers, carrying in my pocket the same dog-eared, photocopied book I acquired in Phnom Penh. Reading from the novel's pages on the edge of the Black Sea – the salty air slowly diminished, and Kien's jungle, once again, grew lush. Such is the strange world of fiction, where words allow us to live again an unlived experience, where memory can be preserved on paper. Between ourselves and the most enduring works of art – whether a poem, a painting, a piece of music, a film – every return widens our vision. We hope, each time, to carry ourselves deeper into the encounter. We hope to carry more of the world, and our own experiences, with us.

In 1997, twenty-two of Nhem Ein's Tuol Sleng photos were enlarged and exhibited at New York's Museum of Modern Art. In MoMA's brief exhibition text, there was little context and almost no history. The viewer, gazing into the faces of children about to be executed, would not know, for instance, how Khmer Rouge leaders had educated themselves in the Marxist study groups of Paris, how some Western, leftist intellectuals had shrugged off criticism of the Khmer Rouge revolution – dismissing the stories of Cambodian refugees as American propaganda – or how our governments supported Pol Pot after 1979, how we allowed his foreign ministers to hold Cambodia's seat at the United Nations until 1993. The photographer was credited as "unknown" – a falsehood – and the individuals in the photos as "unidentifiable."

In a country where so many lost their voices, it seems absurd that pictures, taken by executioners, were believed capable of telling the entire story. Perhaps MoMA's curators, like Nhem Ein himself, believed the pictures to be so complete that they could exist independently as artistic objects: images of suffering, relics of tragedy so powerful that they required no words, no prior knowledge when a stranger approached them. Nhem Ein's photographs are distressingly beautiful. Thousands and thousands of times, men, women, and children stared directly into the camera's lens, unsure if they were seeing their brother or their murderer. Unable to hope, yet unwilling to despair, their faces remain fixed in a grievous calm.

But here, in the present, the ghosts should be allowed words and a history, a time and a place of living, a specificity. It seems so little to give or to receive. Instead, they became mute images from a foreign war, distorted by our projections: of suffering, innocence, brutality, madness, and incomprehensible ethnic conflict. As the journalist Nic Dunlop wrote, "The victims are presented as the Khmer Rouge saw them: without a name, without family, without an identity or country."

"The philosophy," wrote Hannah Arendt, "of art for art's sake ends, if it has the courage to pursue its tenets to their logical conclusions, in the idolization of beauty. Should we happen to conceive of the beautiful in terms of burning torches we will be prepared, like Nero, to set living human bodies aflame." Pol Pot was, as Arendt described Hitler, true, until the end, to his own ideology, enacting a revolution he believed would strengthen Cambodia and purify its people. Both men were "prepared to sacrifice everything to this consonance, this 'beautiful consistency.'"

A few years ago, attending a writers' conference in Boston, Bao Ninh was interviewed by an American who had served in Vietnam. The American, Marc Levy, was met with reticence when he asked Bao Ninh to describe the NVA's tactics, jungle strategies, and ideological training. Finally, Levy asked Bao Ninh if there was something more he wished to say, something their interview had overlooked. "We were human beings," Bao Ninh said simply. "That is what you must tell people. We were human beings."

In 2006, rumoured to have finished a second novel, Bao Ninh admitted that, since the publication of *The Sorrow of War*, he had written continuously but he did not know if he would ever publish again. "I keep stopping myself," he said. "I keep holding myself back." Now, at the age of fifty-eight, he edits a weekly literary supplement in Hanoi, and he lives the life of a reclusive author made famous by a book that, in its selflessness, in its lost individuality, managed to speak for a generation. Like Denis Johnson's *Tree of Smoke*, the novel spans not only the unfolding of many lives, but a profound psychological plummet. "There's been a lie told," says a former Vietcong, now double agent, in Johnson's novel. "I've told it. I'm going to let the truth reclaim me."

Soon, I'll return to Cambodia, a country that I love, and one that continues in an uneasy peace. There, another generation, born after the last UN peacekeepers withdrew from the country in 1993, is slowly finding its voice. I have met dancers, journalists, painters, and musicians alive in their art. They do not idolize beauty. They create art not for art's sake, but from necessity, to hold together what is beautiful and what was broken, to seduce, to escape, and to conjure from themselves some small thing that will last, to be encountered again and again, retold, experienced anew, like photocopies scattered across a region, like persistent efforts, as all of us grow older.

MICHAEL WINTER

Thinly Veiled

When I was twenty-one, I bought a pair of dress pants and applied for a summer job with Public Legal Information in St. John's. I lived in a one-room ground-floor apartment where, at night, you could hear people talking as they walked along the street. Their feet were a foot away from my pillow.

I first met Lisa Moore at this job. We were both hired to write radio scripts that dealt with legal issues; the scripts were to be read by the in-house lawyer and a regional CBC radio host, so they had to be written in a conversational tone, as though the speakers were thinking up these legal issues on the spot.

As part of our research, we were encouraged to drop down to the courthouse and watch the proceedings, to get a feel for how justice is conducted. The courthouse was being sandblasted, and each stone removed, cleaned, and reinserted in the wall. It was a process that had been going on ever since I'd moved to St. John's and I sort of thought that's what you did with the stones of justice: spruce them up to keep things spotless. There was a police lock-up in the basement and sometimes you'd see policemen wearing bulletproof vests opening the trunk of a cruiser to deposit their arms and ammunition, and then escorting a handcuffed character in through the lock-up's two heavy doors.

St. John's is small place, and you end up drinking in bars with the best writers and musicians and lawyers and criminals. A man could come into the bar and lift his shirt and there'd be two grocery store steaks on Styrofoam pads shoved in his pants. And he'd walk around until he'd sold them. There was one long night when a friend of mine cautioned me that I was accepting White Russians from a man named Hook the Crook whose specialty was aiming for the soft areas.

Once, on our lunch break, eating sandwiches on the roof of a store just below Public Legal, Lisa noticed two women running between parked cars below our building. They knelt down to tear the price tags off clothes from Woolworth's. They had been shoplifting.

So petty crime was something you saw a lot of. There were massage parlours and prescription drug rings and across the street from my apartment was a man who made counterfeit hundred-dollar bills and sold them for five dollars each. One night late in the summer, my curtains were lit up with the red and blue strobes from several police cars – his house was getting busted, the garbage bags of bills confiscated. Those bags of money ended up in the safe at Public Legal Information, which also shared office space with the Law Society upstairs, and I remember thinking that the ceiling to the safe was a drop ceiling, and that, if you pushed up an acoustic tile, perhaps you'd have access to that safe. That was as illegal as I got, thought crimes.

Lisa Moore was writing short stories and encouraging everyone around her to do the same. She suggested I take notes the way a painter might make a sketch to later reproduce accurately the colours in a landscape. The other thing I started doing was copying down what people said, the words they used, and I remember discovering that how someone says a thing is often more important than the content of what they are saying.

I recall one trial of a man who had allegedly stolen a car. He testified that he had found the car on Horsechops Lane down the Witless Bay Line and he had a car similar to it Your Honour that needed a driver door and so all he took off the stolen car was the door, and the police are tracking the ID plate from that door, but no he didn't steal that car at all, that car was found and it's still there down Horsechops Lane if the police ever got it together to go down there and take a look.

His story sounded plausible to us. The police had made a big mistake, and his explanation of events seemed entirely credible. We were convinced of his innocence, or at least doubted his guilt, until the judge, at sentencing, made some weary remarks. The judge, holding his head as though it took all of his patience not to blow up, tore apart every statement the accused had made, and suddenly, in a matter of five minutes, even I realized that the person in the docket had brazenly stolen the car in question and lied through his teeth about it.

It made me realize how gullible I am, and how professional criminals can sound honest. They are used to lying so proficiently that they in fact must believe what they are saying – they have convinced themselves that they are innocent.

Soon after this job ended, Lisa persuaded me to take a creative writing class taught by Larry Mathews, and since then, I'm sorry to say, I haven't really had a decent job. But I've learned from that courthouse experience, and I use the same format that lawyers and judges use in coming to a decision. I realized, too, that often in our domestic lives, when we're in an argument and feel hard done by, we all, to some degree, lie to ourselves about what we are guilty of. We steal the good nature from others and then pretend we are innocent as babies. I've written stories with this sort of theme in them. And when I started writing fiction, I liked observing life and writing down those details and those emotional crests and troughs. It was sort of selfish, but it can be satisfying to make art of events that happen to you or to the people around you.

And in the twenty years since then, I've written stories and novels that had this hidden sort of jury and testimony, concealing from the reader my agenda in order to convince you that what I was telling was the truth. When someone asks me if my work is autobiographical, I say *thank you, I got you, you believed me, I was convincing.* I fooled the judge!

Five books like that. Perhaps that is enough of that form. But what if I went the other way? What if, instead of making things up and forming them in patterns to convince a reader that the story is a copy of life, what if I took found words, words that exist concerning a true event, and formed them into fiction? In the early 1990s, there was a horrific murder in St. John's that galvanized the city's attention for several years. I found my way to the court transcripts from the murder trial and was stunned by the strength in the witness testimony. I thought at first I could write this up in a dramatized Truman Capote style, and I did that for about six months. But I was waking up at night in a cold sweat. I was upset with myself for turning a family's grief into entertainment. Here was I, writing about a real woman who had been brutally murdered, and if any praise came my way for the novel I wrote about it, it would be as if I were profiting from her death.

Also, when I reread the transcripts, I realized my attempts to dramatize the scenes could not match the raw power of what had been said in the courtroom. I was weakening the text by altering it from its original form.

And so I made the decision not to add a word to the text in the transcripts. Instead, I would choose the best eighty thousand words out of the three million available. I'd curate my way to a book.

I spent three years doing just that. Going through a stack of paper five feet high, looking for the sentences that had power, and stringing them together. Court transcripts are tedious to read, but sifting through them and stripping out the question-and-answer tempo to create more of a narrative helped to make dramatic scenes out of banal information:

PROSECUTOR: Can you tell the court your name?

WITNESS: Sheldon Troke.

PROSECUTOR: Where were you on the night before Donna Whalen was murdered?

WITNESS: Down at Trapper John's.

PROSECUTOR: Were you with anyone?

WITNESS: My brother had some coke on him and Harvey Rowe we met up with him and we were shooting pool and had some coke in the washroom.

PROSECUTOR: What did you do then?

WITNESS: I got a cab and it let me out at Shopper's Drug Mart.

PROSECUTOR: Where is that?

WITNESS: On Empire Avenue.

PROSECUTOR: At what time?

WITNESS: I'd say around midnight.

PROSECUTOR: Proceed.

WITNESS: I went to Tang Man's takeout then and ordered Donna the Number Four.

This sample reads well enough, but imagine reading fifty or a hundred pages of it – or, as I did, ten thousand pages. I turned the above testimony into this:

Sheldon Troke was down at Trapper John's with his brother and they met up with Harvey Rowe. They did some coke in the washroom and then Sheldon got a cab to Shopper's Drug Mart on Empire Avenue. It was around midnight. He

went into Tang Man's takeout and ordered Donna the
Number Four.

You'll notice that I did not add a word, except to convert the first
person account into third person. Yet I created a scene with narrative drive. The length of the sentences and the details I chose
to include make the text read like something I'd written myself.
The structure gives the content the flavour of a specific author
– which tells you that any writer can approach ten thousand
pages of text and find his or her own voice in there.

Instead of writing thinly veiled autobiography, I ended up
with thinly veiled biography: a biography that is trying its best, in
the courtroom of your imagination, to convince you it's a novel.

MARK KINGWELL

As It Were: On the ~~Metaphysics~~ Ethics of Fiction

In the Western tradition of inquiry, the subfield of metaphysics, with its questions about the nature of substance and existence, is considered "first philosophy." Before we can say anything else, we must establish what is real. Everything follows from that. As a philosopher who has been bewitched by fiction since childhood, and whose own books show alarming (to some) elements of narrative, I want to ask: What are the metaphysics of fiction? What is real here, and what follows from it?

"Art is a lie that makes us realize the truth," Picasso said, to the general satisfaction of everyone. A wondrous paradox! The untruth of the invented form, otherwise known as the mystery of art, reveals the truth better than the bare factuality of the documented one. This puts everyone in their proper place. The creators are elevated above the reporters, and higher truths of emotion and wisdom now trump lower ones of mere accuracy. The sentiment even has classical sanction. In Book x of Plato's *Republic*, Socrates lays down as a general principle that myths, or invented stories that communicate general conclusions, have more to teach us than simple history, which can do no more than recount what happened in particular.

Before we accept this claim, though, we should remember that Plato was no friend to poets and that the myth Socrates is about to recount in Book x – the metempsychotic journey of Er, who has to be reincarnated multiple times before he can un-shackle his immortal soul from his desire-ridden body – is part of a larger program of political control. This is a myth to tame a population, an afterlife fable that has inspired everything from Christian eschatology to the dark-future visions of *Nineteen Eighty-Four* and *Logan's Run*. The myth shall set you free!

Except it won't. Socrates and Picasso were both mistaken, and maybe dangerously so, because their lies are justified as noble from a special point of view with only elite access – the transcen-dental Forms, modernist aesthetics. In reality there is no paradox here, wondrous or otherwise. Art is not a lie; it is a fiction, and that is a very different thing. In fact, to call art a lie is itself a lie – when, at least, it is not simply a self-serving confusion. A lie, if it is anything, is a deliberate untruth presented as though it were a truth. Lies may not always be advanced with deliberate inten-tion to deceive, but that intention is certainly captured by the most common use of the word *lie*. Someone lies if and only if they speak or write what they know to be false *even as* they also know, or believe, that the hearer or reader does not know that.

So what is fiction if it is not a lie? Following the clear analysis of philosopher Harry Frankfurt, I think we must con-clude that it is *bullshit*.

Why? Well, no matter how comprehensive or extreme, all falsity or lying remains a function, albeit a negative one, of regard for the truth. That is, something cannot be false unless it is also possible for it to be true, and one cannot lie except as a departure from telling the truth. Bullshit, by contrast, is neither true nor false – in the philosophical jargon, it has no *truth-value*. The bullshitter "does not reject the authority of the truth, as the liar does, and oppose himself to it," Frankfurt notes. "He pays no attention to it at all. By virtue of this, bullshit is the greater enemy of the truth than lies are."

Fiction is likewise composed of a set of sentences that are neither true nor false; a novel has no truth-value, nor does it purport to. This latter fact, especially, makes it clear that fiction is an example of what one philosopher has described as "nonserious illocutionary utterance" – which is to say that it is composed of meaningful sentences which, however, are not meant in the normal sense of meaning. Thus fiction is a matter of *pretending*, or if one prefers the peculiar language of my tribe, a matter of "nondeceptive pseudoperformance." This basic fact about fiction – that it is composed of sentences that only act *as if* they stated that which is the case – has led some people, including a few of my more literal-minded colleagues, to abandon it. For some people, life is too short to read sentences that have no truth-value, that do not even purport to be true.

Such a position may sound crazy, and it probably is a little. I'm happy to say that the closest I have ever come to this pathology was a moment in a university library during graduate school when I was asked by a friend what I was reading. I replied, with great embarrassment as at the admission of a guilty secret, or being caught masturbating, that it was "just a novel." And even though I regard the essay as the highest literary form there is, a locus of intellectual and emotional power, and think Wittgenstein's *Philosophical Investigations* perhaps the most accomplished work of human imagination of the past hundred years, the novel's deep appeal is woven through my everyday life.

Of course, the boundary between fiction and non-fiction is much discussed and disputed, especially in the recent era of "fictionalized memoir" and "creative non-fiction," but actually the distinction is straightforward. Search as we might, we can find nothing in the words themselves, no formal qualities of the prose, that reliably distinguishes fiction from non-fiction. Both may employ any of narrative, discursive argument, dialogue, metaphor, and flights of imagination with impunity. Therefore, it must be the case that the distinction is a matter of intention and presentation. Fiction is as fiction does; placing the words "a novel" underneath a title declares an intention, even if sometimes a sly one. That is, if an author wishes to blur the distinction by setting up ironies between said and meant, well, we can take that under advisement. But if the blurring is sneaky or disguised, we may end up feeling abused, even outraged.

So much is obvious. But what about the background charge that the bullshitter is an enemy of the truth? The Plato-Picasso line is that the artist was a servant of the truth, or at least of some kind of truth, not an enemy at all. How can we untangle this skein of judgmental confusion?

We begin with further analysis of the varieties of bullshit, or more precisely, of bullshitters. In a crisp review of Frankfurt's book, Jonathan Lear – a psychoanalyst as well as a philosopher – made a telling point about the larger ambit of communication: Frankfurt had apparently ignored the special case of the *bullshit artist*. The bullshit artist, in contrast to the bullshitter simpliciter, is not just shooting a line for the hell of it. He or she (but usually he) is attempting to create a kind of complicity between himself and us. Lear writes: "The bullshit artist in effect says, 'This is bullshit, but you will accept it anyway. You may accept it as bullshit, but you will honor it anyway.' In this respect, the bullshit artist is a knight of decadence. Frankfurt ignores this example; indeed, his analysis of bullshit rules it out as impossible. And in this way he fails to confront the most interesting – and influential – style of bullshit in our time."

This, Lear notes, is really a demonstration of power, and so it raises ethical and political problems that are not in play with ordinary bullshit. Lear's example of a paradigmatic bullshit artist is former U.S. president Bill Clinton, a judgment that retains validity even as that statesman enters a distinguished period of less rampant influence.

Despite their differences, both Frankfurt and Lear discuss these questions under a general rubric of suspicion. This is an occupational hazard for philosophers, since we like to imagine we have some sort of duty to the truth, or at least a responsibility for clearing up conceptual confusions. But suppose that a really accomplished bullshit artist is not an enemy, but an edgy kind of friend. Not to the truth, but to something else that we find compelling enough to take up the book: the resonant, the moving, the revelatory. The fiction writer is the bullshit artist extraordinaire, the perfection of the bullshit artist.

No mere knight but a monarch of decadence, the writer of fiction establishes complicity between the author and the reader, and does so in one of the most intimate ways we know: the whispering inner voice of a human consciousness engaged in the act of silent reading. We accept this, may even accept it as bullshit (what else is the willing suspension of disbelief?); but the main difference is that we accept it with great and willing pleasure.

The question then becomes: what sort of pleasure is this, and how can we possibly justify it in light of our basic commitments, often ethical and political, to telling the truth?

It is a commonplace among philosophers that there is nothing meaningful to be said about the future actions of fictional characters, or even about possible actions not taken. Such talk forms a special class of what we like to call nonsense, meaningless utterance, or defective speech. Yes, there are different classes of nonsense. Don't worry: philosophers invoke this charge of nonsense against themselves more than anyone else. A.J. Ayer notoriously said that most metaphysicians were poets *manqués*, spouting fine-sounding gibberish as if it were truth. At least the plain old poet is not, allowing for a few Keatsian exceptions, self-deceived on that score!

So: "The present king of France is bald" is defective because the definite description names an empty set, and no meaningful attributions can be made of it. There is sense to the sentence, but no reference. (The present king of France is not *not-bald* either.) This is different from saying, "Colourless green ideas sleep furiously," another standard example of nonsense. Here, there is both direct contradiction (ideas that are green and colourless) and bizarre attribution (ideas that are either coloured or not; furious sleep). Both classes of nonsense are distinct from this: "Mr. Darcy wrote a great work of political economy soon after his marriage." That, too, is nonsense even though there are no logical contradictions in it and, moreover, "Mr. Darcy" names a character who enjoys a sort of existence and hence can support genuine reference. Such characters may even have their own Wikipedia entries, when lots of "real" people do not, and enjoy a degree of immortality – their existence called into the consciousness of another – denied most mere mortals.

But things get very confusing when we *can* say, meaningfully, that Mr. Darcy married the former Elizabeth Bennett, or that there is no Mrs. Sherlock Holmes but there is a Mrs. John Watson, married to that affable veteran of the second Anglo-Afghan War. These latter claims are contained by the "as if" contract between writer and reader, and so count as notional facts within the fictional frame. There may be real facts in the frame too: Regency habits of dress, historical events like naval battles, actual London streets and Bath establishments. Authors can make mistakes about these. They cannot make mistakes about characters they have invented, though they can of course strain credulity (too-rapid shifts in action, incoherent motivation) or introduce internal errors (hair that is brown in Chapter One turns red in later ones). These gaffes may generate a breach of contract: I throw the book across the room.

All that granted, rare is the reader who confines his or her thoughts about a novel just to the "facts" contained within it. We think and talk about fictional characters all the time as if they had real possibilities. We bemoan Dorothea's bad choices in *Middlemarch* or celebrate Pip's complicated good fortune in *Great Expectations*; we wonder what would have become of Huck Finn or Jay Gatsby if things had gone a bit differently; we allow our impatience to rise at Holden Caulfield or indulge our revulsion at the sociopathology of Anton Chigurh. Indeed, our emotional attachment to these characters constitutes one of the most important ways that fiction matters to us. A given character becomes part of our consciousness, not just for the duration of the reading experience, but often for a lifetime.

The subjunctive mood of many of these sentences about fiction's own conditional sentences ("would have happened") clearly answers an emotional mood in us that lacks a precise name but might as well be labelled the subjunctive imagination. We derive great pleasure not only from the implied comprehensive contingency of all fiction ("If all this were true . . . though of course it isn't"), but also from the micro-contingencies opened up by relating to characters as if they were real people, with both past actions and future choices – which by definition they do not have.

Fine, and nobody is going to take that pleasure – call it the pleasure of costless gossip – away from us pretense-lovers without a fight. But consider two rival versions of what is going on here, both hinging on the argument that fiction, in particular the naturalistic novel, performs an ideological function. We can call the two versions, respectively, the ideology of bourgeois opiate and the ideology of culture-critique. Suspicion and belief. Take the second position first.

On this view, which has been associated with, for example, Roland Barthes and Martha Nussbaum and more recently with James Wood, the importance of the novel is that it enacts imaginative possibilities that are otherwise absent from social discourse. Thus, the fictionality of the novel and its characters are an advantage, not a drawback, precisely because the open-endedness of questions about them – What is married life going to be like for Emma and Mr. Knightley? Would Emma Bovary have been happier if she had married a different man? – prompts investigations, maybe ethical, maybe political, that cannot be pursued by other means. The novel is a lever of normative insight about life and its demands *in virtue of* its being neither true nor false. The novel alone can challenge existing patterns of desire and standards of behaviour in a manner that cultivates emotional engagement and exercises ethical imagination.

On the other side lies the countervailing theory, perhaps most vividly argued by Theodor Adorno and Fredric Jameson, but finding its recent voice with David Shields, that the novel is a drug of conformity, an easily digestible wafer of communion with the current arrangement. On this view, fiction at best palliates its readers and at worst makes them actively complicit with a given social order. By breaking market forces and structural inequalities down into enticing morsels of narrative, even superficially critical fictions play the role of court jester to the dominant culture: they amuse and titillate, but do not challenge power. The naturalistic novel is at one with the mass culture of production and consumption, dominated by sentiment and spectacle. David Foster Wallace defined popular culture as "the symbolic representation of what people already believe." Here, the naturalistic novel becomes just a tony adjunct to the larger institutions of the popular market and, worse, the generalized narcissism of web-based social media. They are all facilitators of the great modern fetish of selfhood, the wonderfulness of me.

Most readers of novels, especially so-called "literary" ones, would be dismayed and annoyed to find themselves lumped together with the audiences flocking to the latest 3-D big-screen cartoon or the dopes who dote on their Facebook profiles, but it is consistent with the tenets of this view that such feelings of distinction are themselves ideological markers. The sense of edification one may indulge in reading "quality" fiction rather than watching television or going to the movies is nothing more than a cultural-capital dividend, something we consume alongside the novel itself, like a cocaine bump taken with your cocktail.

It is perhaps a mark of respect for the sting in this insight that some people label it "nihilistic," as Michiko Kakutani of the *New York Times* did when discussing Shields's 2009 book, *Reality Hunger*. It is not nihilistic, in my view, but it generates its own set of problems. What, after all, is the "reality" we hunger for, in Shields's version, and how is it immune from ideological infection? We know that much of the outrage mentioned earlier, aroused when fiction masquerades as fact, is rooted in twisted Oprahnic desires for "authentic" experiences and "real" suffering. Dashed by the deception of James Frey, say, these ideological bits of cultural detritus emerge in anger, with braying calls for the blood of author and publisher alike. Adorno, the musicologist turned philosopher, placed his faith in innovative classical music, not realizing how smoothly Schoenberg and even John Cage could be assimilated to a highly capitalized and bourgeois version of the concert situation. Neither Adorno nor Shields seems attuned, in fact, to the late-capitalist hybrid known as the bourgeois bohemian, or bobo, which today dominates cultural discourse and practices.

All true. But, on the other side, can anyone be sanguine about the idea of fiction as exerting some special ethical traction? This position seems to demand both too much and too little from the form. Let us put the matter in the terms suggested by Archibald MacLeish's often-quoted line that "a poem should not mean, but be" – itself a paradoxical statement, perhaps an intentional one, since this meaningful message of non-meaning is delivered via a poem.

The fiction-as-morality position calls for *too much* because it asks fiction to mean rather than be, reducing it to a moralistic vehicle; at the same time, it calls for *too little* because, well, it asks fiction to mean rather than be, when being in the relevant sense is a higher task altogether than merely meaning. Worse, and without reeling headlong into Adorno territory, it seems doubtful that one can hold this view without raising some ethical questions of another sort, questions concerning the ethics of doing ethics with fiction. To see what I mean, consider this little story – that is, a narrative with a possible moral.

For some years I taught a small university course called "Ethics and the Creative Imagination." The idea was to use literature, in my case mostly twentieth-century novels and a few films, as the primary texts for what was in reality a seminar on ethics. So I assigned some obvious works, such as *A Clockwork Orange* and *The Fountainhead*, not so much for their literary merit (whatever that might mean, as Adorno would say!) but because they illustrated easily discernible, and debatable, moral issues. Other works, such as *Lucky Jim* and *A Complicated Kindness*, extended a loose theme of individuals struggling, sometimes comically, between sets of moral obligations. I always ended with Louis Begley's *The Man Who Was Late*, his best work and an underappreciated minor masterpiece. There was a good deal of parent-child conflict in the books, which the students could relate to; there was also a good deal of suicide, which I did not consciously plan, but there you go.

I enjoyed this seminar tremendously at first, even though it was an extra commitment and the students, high achievers all, were very demanding. It seemed exactly right to spend three hours a week discussing a book we had all read and wondering about Iris Murdoch's distinction between the nice and the good, or whether Philip Marlowe was a cynic or a knight of virtue. Did Lily Bart, that beautiful fool, take too much sleeping draught deliberately? Was Dr. Sloper, that narcissistic egotist, too harsh in cutting himself off from daughter Catherine? How exactly, apart from being dead, was Ben, the Holocaust survivor so successful at self-creation and living the American dream, "late"?

As time went on, however, doubts began to nag at me. Was this a proper use of literature, to make it a vehicle of value? Was it not, perhaps, to instrumentalize fiction in just the way that Plato used his myths and lies? Well, maybe not *just* the way, since I had no transcendental program of social control on the table, but still, was it not in some important sense unethical to deploy fiction as ethics? A little of this, even in a seminar room, and pretty soon you're veering into that disreputable book-club territory where a book is no longer judged according to whether or not it is any good, but whether you "like" or "can relate to" the characters – indeed, where its being any good or not becomes *a function* of that "liking" or "relating to." The conjunction in the titular phrase "ethics and the creative imagination" started to mock me with its vagueness. What did that "and" signify? More importantly, what justified it? Should it be, could it be, replaced by another word or phrase: "of," or "as," or even (maybe best) "as if"? What would happen then?

Possibly I was losing my mind, but only in the sense that philosophers habitually do. In that madness, it seemed to me, the metaphysical questions of fiction reveal themselves as ethical questions all along. Let us go further and say, with Emmanuel Levinas, that ethics, not metaphysics, is first philosophy. Answering the call of the Other is a philosophically prior task to answering the call of being. Or, more precisely, we can only ever answer the latter call in the form of the former. The Other is who calls us; the Other asks us for recognition and care. Thus philosophy, so often translated as the *love of wisdom*, receives its proper translation as the *wisdom of love*. Love means openness to the call of difference; and wisdom – not happiness, not consolation – is what the openness may eventually bring us. What could this pregnant insight mean when it comes to fiction?

It is pretty obvious why we enjoy the inventions of narrative and imagery, the subjunctive contracts of *as if* and *as it were*. These contracts are undertaken in the gift economy that runs beneath, or maybe above, the transactional economy at large. Fictions are not possible worlds in the technical sense of the term used by modal realism, the philosophical position which holds that all possible worlds are real. Fictions exist in this actual world, after all, and we must account for their ontology here, not elsewhere. If there are other possible worlds, certainly some if not most of them also contain fictions. But the fictions of any world depict *aspects of possibility*, and no matter how naturalistic or otherwise – the differences negotiated by sub-contracts against time travel, in favour of levitation, and so on – they allow us to lose ourselves in something that is not actual. I think that getting lost is in fact the chief druggy pleasure of fiction, the immediate contact high of suspension from reality. We experience the frisson of tension between our rational beliefs (the fictional world is not real, the roller coaster is safe) and what psychologists have come to call our "aliefs," those primitive cognitions typically provoked by threat or risk: Emma Bovary is going to die! I am going to fly off the summit of this speeding metal contraption!

On this view, we do not in fact suspend disbelief when we experience the pleasures of fictional narrative; instead, we simultaneously set belief off to one side, indulge alief, and cover over the whole process by performing it without hesitation or forethought. Add the larger cognate pleasures of big themes, eye for detail or image, narrative coherence, and perhaps the meta-pleasures of narrative twists or reversals, postmodern tricks of line-blurring, authors-as-characters, and so on – it's a heady tonic of complicated imaginative excitement, all conducted with appropriate safety mechanisms.

Meanwhile, the organic structure of most narrative tames the contingencies of life into linear coherence. The end of a narrative retroactively confers meaning on what came before, making sense of events in a way that is painfully absent from lived experience. Counter-narratives – inversions, multiple perspectives, fractures in the timeline – only call attention to the dominance of linearity in the act of deviating from it. Sometimes unwilling prisoners of contingency in life, we are willing prisoners of meaning in narrative fictions. Roland Barthes's celebrated five codes of narrative are just different aspects of this happy self-imprisonment, where the text gives pleasure by offering resistance. Barthes distinguishes the codes this way: (1) the hermeneutic code, where the fiction's meaning is withheld, subject to interpretation; (2) the prohairetic code, where what happens later is structured by what happens first; (3) the semantic code, where elements in the story signify certain ideas; (4) the symbolic code, where larger meanings are structured in the story as a whole; and (5) the cultural code, which enfolds and sometimes critiques elements of shared knowledge or taken-for-granted belief. Perhaps most important, from the reader's perspective, is the prohairetic code. This code dictates – as Chekhov famously put it – that if a gun appears onstage in Act One, it must be used by Act Three.

That *must*, the implied aesthetic-ethical force of Chekhov's gun, can stand for the whole issue. Such a necessary combination of the contingent and the necessary – fiction's basic premise cluster, its presupposition payload – is absent when it comes to created personae, such as the avatars of *Second Life* or the game-characters we play in video games such as *Halo* or *Grand Theft Auto*. Here we may identify with a character, but we can never empathize with one; we can experience excitement, but not compassion. Whether or not these forms of leisure are art is not to my present purpose, but one thing is clear: there is no possibility of tragedy in such pastimes, because there is no structure of inevitability. Only narrative can deliver the peculiar emotional engagement Aristotle described as catharsis, the experience of fear and pity aroused when Oedipus drives events to his own doom. There is no doom in *Doom*.

The attractions of fiction are thus centrally aesthetic, in the root sense: arousing a set of *feelings*, by which I mean to include emotional, psychological, intellectual, and moral reactions. Contrary to the ideology of suspicion, the presumption of the contract is that none of these feelings are possible, or anyway *as* possible, outside the contractual space of as-if. The temporary loss, or bracketing, of reality is essential to the phenomenological task of revealing consciousness. In this sense, every great work of fiction is also an *ars poetica*, a fictional manifesto about the possibility of fiction. (Note for completists: the MacLeish poem referenced earlier is called "Ars Poetica.")

But, contrary to the ideology of belief, fiction is not the servant of some cognitive payload, or "message." A novel is like the Scandinavian legend about life, recalled by the central character in Turgenev's *Rudin*. Our mortal span is likened to the flight of a bird entering a feast hall at one end and exiting at the other. The flight represents the experience of living, our fleeting span of consciousness with voids before and after. No life has a simple moral – or, if it does, it likely falls into the category of the unlived life not worth examining. Likewise, no great fiction has a simple moral, though it may have many serious things to communicate using its nonserious discourse. Taking seriously the ethics of doing ethics with fiction shows us that using fiction as ethical tutelage is dubious – not because literature has no ethical heft, but rather because reading that heft as argument by other means instrumentalizes, and hence violates, fiction itself. If fiction were reducible to propositions, that would obviate fiction. Fiction speaks something, but it is not something as simple as the truth, ethical or otherwise.

At this point, we could have recourse to other notions of "truth": psychological acuity, emotional subtlety, cultural deftness. But why not use those notions instead? After all, they're more precise and do not confuse the issue in the Platonic/Picassan manner. Nor are fancier theories of truth much more helpful. I might favour Heidegger's claim that the work of art opens a clearing of Being, the truth of *aletheia*; but saying so doesn't much help in understanding why *Underworld* is a great novel and *Cosmopolis* is not.

We do better to adopt a different approach. It has the benefit of resolving some of the apparent paradoxes of fiction, such as the fact that meaningful words are used in a meaningless manner, even as it takes seriously the provocation that beauty, in all forms, offers a promise of happiness, but never happiness itself. What if we were to distinguish the normative in general from the ethical in particular, noting that fiction can prompt direction-altering reactions or expansions of compassion without ever having to issue, or embody, any particular directive? Then I believe we would be able to say – subjunctively, but in keeping with our peculiar pretended contracts – after the manner of Rilke's meditation on the archaic torso of Apollo, that the moral of all great art is simply this: *You must change your life.*

DIANA ATHILL AND ALICE MUNRO

A Conversation

Diana Athill and Alice Munro appeared in conversation together on October 21, 2009, as part of the opening night gala for the International Festival of Authors in Toronto. This is an abridged transcript of their conversation, which was moderated by Bill Richardson.

BILL RICHARDSON: How was this invitation extended to you both?

DIANA ATHILL: As far as I'm concerned, it was the most amazing surprise. I was invited to come and talk to Alice. I thought, no, no, I can't go; I can't make that long journey. But I don't know – talk to Alice! I've loved this woman's writing for years and years and years. And now that I've got a chance to meet her, I've damned well got to do it. So here I am, and it's a tremendous honour to be here.

BR: You've written about Alice Munro a couple of times in your books. You mentioned her in *Stet* and *Somewhere Towards the End*. What about Alice Munro's writing drew you in so much?

DA: It meant so much to me because I've always rather resented the fact that one has just one life to live. I remember years and years ago, the first time I read George Eliot's *Middlemarch*, as the last pages were coming, I thought, "Oh, I'm coming to the end, I'm going to have to leave this world that I've just learned about." Well, Alice has given me that same thing. She's given me, over the years – and not just in one book – she's given me a world that I now feel that I know in ways that I couldn't possibly know. If I were put down in the world of Alice's early stories, particularly, I could walk down those streets, I could go from the silver fox farm and up the road to the town, and I would recognize it. I would know the people; I love the people. And this has built up in me. I suddenly realize that I've added to my life a whole world that I've not experienced myself. And that's what books do.

ALICE MUNRO: Yes, yes it is. I think you've given me somehow the same thing. Because in writing about your life, I feel I know lots of things that are wonderful to me to know because they've been described so well. And the emotion – the emotional ease somehow of the things you tell us about yourself. This is wonderful, I don't know anybody else who does it as well. So I wanted very much to meet you, though I felt I already had met you, and knew a great deal about you.

DA: I envy you, as a publisher. I envy you very much because as a writer of fiction, which is, alas, something I am not and never will be, but I've dealt with many writers of fiction. You in Canada and the people who live in Australia have marvellous subjects – my goodness, you have subjects! In England, I feel that novels have explored one way or the other pretty well every inch of life. We're all becoming now very navel-gazing writers in England because we've done so much. Whereas people who live in a country that is developing in the extraordinary fashion Canada is, changing and growing all the time . . . I was talking to a wonderful Australian writer called Kate Grenville, and she has said the same thing. I said to her, "You're so lucky. You've got this vast amount of subjects around you." And she said, "Yes, you're right, there's no end to it. We're only just starting to explore it."

AM: But you know, when I started to write, there was a feeling that you couldn't write about Canada because nobody would be interested. There was an extraordinary shyness, or a feeling that somehow you had to go to Europe in order to bring out your creativity.

DA: That was very strong in the days when people like Mordecai Richler and Margaret Atwood –

AM: Yes, that's my generation –

DA: They came to London. They felt that somehow that's where writing happened.

AM: And I couldn't do that because I had children. And I wasn't going to take them off to London so that I could discover my creative roots. I mean, I was dealing with them!

DA: Alice, did you always, always know that you were going to write the kind of thing you are writing?

AM: Oh, I didn't know I was going to write the kind of thing I've written, but I knew that I was going to write – I just had to. The first thing I remember reading was Hans Christian Andersen's "The Little Mermaid." And you know about how sadly it ends. When I came to that sad ending, I was appalled. I got up and I went out and I walked round and round outside the house, making up a happy ending for the Little Mermaid. She got the prince! And she didn't have to be changed into foam on the sea. And so I think that was the beginning of my writing career. I knew I had to do something about what I found in life around me. I can't remember a time when I didn't make up stories. I don't think I called it writing.

DA: It's quite extraordinary how some people make up stories, and some people can't. And what is the difference? Why does it work like that? I was thinking about this the other day, and I thought, well, really in every society, in every clan and every tribe, there is honour given to the storyteller. I believe that a group of Neolithic men would come home to the cave and the women would say, "What happened today?" And one of them would say, "Oh, it was awful today! We didn't get a touch of a rabbit until we were across the creek . . ." And he would tell a little story, and he was the one they valued. I think some people are natural storytellers. And it is necessary that they should be, because they perform a function for human beings.

BR: In your childhoods, what do you first remember reading?

DA: What was your first memory?

AM: Well, there was "The Little Mermaid," which I already told you about. But Charles Dickens wrote a history of England for children. Somehow this was lying around our house – I think it had been given to my father when he was a little boy – and I started to read it. And I was at the stage where I didn't know about Ireland. I didn't know how you pronounced it, so I came to this place where the headline read, "Troubles in Eerieland." I didn't know anything about Eerieland! But I read it anyway. It's a wonderful history – I don't know how accurate it is *as* history, but it has lots of beheadings in it. And it describes them in detail – how many strokes it took to separate the head. And here was I, this seven-year-old or eight-year-old girl, just devouring this stuff. And so that was the great book of my earliest childhood. Not *Peter Rabbit* or anything like this. *A Child's History of England*.

DA: I was very lucky – mine was a very bookish family. There were books, books, books everywhere. I think the first thing I can remember reading is *Peter Rabbit*, which still remains a very good story. And we read all the time. It was a country house, and we used to say, if we're out of doors, we're riding, and if we're indoors, we're reading. And that's what we were doing. And I can't imagine life without books. And when I think of the persecution of writers, it's unbelievably awful.

BR: May I ask about your experience of reading Marie Stopes? You talk about finding her when you were just the right age – the birth control advocate. Have I got the name right?

DA: Oh yes, that's how I learned about sex. I was eleven years old, and there was a little tiny black book with nothing written on the outside. It was in a corner. My mother didn't believe in hiding away books, but she had put it in a corner, hoping that I wouldn't find it. I pulled the book out, and I opened it, and on the title page, it said, *Wise Parenthood*. And I thought, in a sort of cynical way, oh, Mum must have been trying to learn how to bring us up – ha ha. And I thought I'd have a look at it. And there it all was – the whole facts of how sex works. My word! I went rushing up the garden through a fence to our neighbour, my best friend, to pass this great news on. That was a very important part of what I learned from books.

AM: You know, I read a book that was supposed to open my eyes to life. But it was quite different. The title was *Beautiful Girlhood*, and my mother gave it to me in hopes that I would give up Charles Dickens. But I hated that book. I think children detect anything that is trying to shape them –

DA: Anything that is going to do you good.

AM: Yes! But my mother didn't say, "This is going to do you good, and you can stand some doing good." It was her idea – though I can't remember if sex was in it or not. It would be very guarded if it was. It was mostly about being unselfish. There was quite a lot about doing chores around the house. I did my share of chores, but I didn't want to be told this. I wonder if all children aren't like that. Or if some children really do enjoy being told.

DA: I don't think they do.

AM: I wouldn't think so.

DA: I used to be given many, many books for Christmas and birthdays, the sort of book that a well-meaning aunt who didn't know one very well, of a sort of improving nature – one could smell it at once!

BR: Do you think that part of the gift that makes a writer is the gift of memory? I mean, it's astonishing to me that you hold so vividly these books in your heads.

DA: I think I remember what I've learned from books and felt in books almost more than from life. And when you think of what you've experienced through books, it's extraordinary. When one thinks of the whole of the Second World War, one knows things, about the Holocaust, one knows about what terrible things happened – one can see it, one can feel it. Of course, one read about it. It feels, in our generation, anyway, that reading has built most of our lives.

AM: Yes, it has – I don't know if it still does. I think there are various rivals for reading right now. But the vividness of the stories we read when we're young – that does diminish somewhat as we get older. I know the last book that I read over and over again obsessively – and can still quote – was a book I read as a teenager, starting when I was about thirteen. *Wuthering Heights*. *Wuthering Heights* was the great book of my growing up. Now, I never did meet Heathcliff, fortunately. But there was a lot of sex in that book.

DA: Terrific passion in it.

AM: Yes, I can remember lines from it now. I can remember: "Love for my life urged a compliance." This is, I think, poor little Isabella, who managed to marry Heathcliff. She was in love with him and she married him, and I think he was chasing her upstairs. He was a very crude sort of man. He wasn't chasing her upstairs so they could make love. He was just getting her out of the room so she couldn't talk to somebody or something like that. But great big passages stay in my head. I won't bore you by repeating them all or we'll be here until midnight. But that book I think was sexually so exciting to a young girl without ever –

DA: Without ever mentioning the word.

AM: But what kind of lesson! To fall in love with a horrible man like Heathcliff? Why was he so much more interesting than Edgar, who was nice all the way through? One was dark and one was fair. You can tell that way.

BR: Let's talk about sex. You write about sex in a very candid, vivid way in your books. What sort of reaction do you get from people? Are they amazed?

DA: People are, in England, incredibly polite. They very rarely mention it. I have had to argue with people about it. I'm rather ashamed about writing so much about my own life and my own self, having been brought up with this as a shocking thing to do, to talk about yourself. "You're not the only pebble on the beach," they used to say to me. So people say, "Why do you write that sort of book? What's the point of telling everything?" A sort of shudder of guilt still goes through me about being so – not *indiscreet* – but about myself. I shouldn't be doing it. But if you're trying to write about something because you're trying to get to the bottom of it, whether it's your own life or something else, there is no point in doing it unless you try as hard as you can to do it honestly, and to say how it really was. And that is the only lesson I learned from other writers. Jean Rhys the novelist used to say, "I must try to get it as it really was. I must get it right." And of course that is what good writers do – they get it right.

Vidiadhar Naipaul, who was another one of my authors when I was a publisher, he wrote when he was young about life in Trinidad, and he often used the Trinidad dialect in his work. We were talking about the problem of trying to sell his books in England, where people didn't know this place and weren't very interested in it. And I remember Vidiadhar saying that the proof is that if you get something right, people will understand, even if they don't know it. And he's perfectly right – I mean, it's what good writing does. And it's what you do, all the time.

AM: Well, I got things right, but it didn't always please the people I got it right about. I can remember really hurting people. I wrote a story in my first year at university, and it was published in the university magazine. It was rather a silly story about a dried-up spinster of thirty-four. This spinster had hallucinations about one of her students – she thought he was in love with her. But at the end, she's walking alone and two girls are following her, trying to hear what she's saying to herself. And she is talking to this boy, this imaginary lover, and one of the girls says to the other, "Jesus Christ." And that was the end of the story.

Now, that magazine went to my hometown. And not only to my hometown. I had become engaged to a young man who took a copy home – can you imagine this? – for his mother to read! The whole shock was in the "Jesus Christ," and yet, it had to be there. I hadn't thought about shocking people, I really hadn't. And this sort of thing was happening all the time. And about sex, too. So I was always hurting people a little bit. I always hoped they wouldn't read what I'd written.

DA: Yes, one does hope that.

AM: Do you feel that, too?

DA: But I find that, on the whole, people are much more accepting now than they used to – much more!

AM: I don't think you could shock people now the way you used to.

DIANA ATHILL AND ALICE MUNRO

DA: It's a problem if you're writing about other people. You can be, after all, as indiscreet about yourself as you like. I found that when I was writing my first autobiographical book. My friends had been very important in my life, and I would have liked them to have come into that book much more. But I found that if I had to bring other people in, I had to use a different tone of voice completely. So I had to leave them out.

AM: Because you couldn't get it right.

DA: I couldn't write quite as unsparingly about them as I could write about myself.

BR: Was that *Instead of a Letter*?

DA: Yes.

BR: And in that book you write, for instance, about having an abortion. Very frank, full of disclosure. What was the reaction to it?

DA: One of the nicest reactions was I had a darling aunt who I loved, and who loved me. She wrote to me, and said, "Darling Di, I've been reading your book. I've read it up to page so and so, and I want to tell you that you write wonderfully and I liked it so much, but I'm not going read any further because I don't think perhaps that I would be able to like the rest." That was a very generous and wonderful reaction. My mother's reaction was that it was never, never mentioned – ever. And she'd read the book, and I knew she'd read the book. And for a long time, I thought that was hypocrisy, really. And in the end I came to the conclusion that it's a technique of getting through life. You've got a daughter. You love your daughter. You want to go on loving your daughter. She does something that you rather wish very much she wouldn't do. Let's pretend she hasn't done it.

AM: Yes, I think that's what people have to do. *She's a nice person! You'd be surprised how nice she is, really!* Though there is all this to be ignored. I live in a small town, and everyone rushes out to buy the latest book, because we have a writer living in town. I feel for them. I'm not saying that some of them aren't very good, sophisticated readers. But some are not used to reading this sort of book, and I want to protect them.

DA: You had a bigger problem than I did, because I came from a bookish background, and you didn't.

AM: No.

DA: Therefore you were really breaking all the rules.

AM: Yes, but also what you said about not drawing attention to yourself, that was the way I was brought up, too. I think it was our generation. I always broke the rules when I was writing. But I didn't think about it while I was writing – you probably didn't, either – that somebody was going to read this.

DA: While you're actually writing, you don't think about it. You don't say to yourself, "Oh goodness me, can I say that?" Of course, while you're actually writing, what you're interested in is what you're doing. Then when you've written it, you look at it and wonder what they're going to make of *that*.

DAVID CHARIANDY

The Words for a Place

In December of 2009, I was fortunate enough to be invited to give an onstage interview at the Literary Colloquium Berlin, one of the oldest and grandest of the literature houses of Berlin. I happened to visit at a time when no other writers were staying in the guest quarters, and so I was assigned an alarmingly fine suite with an office overlooking a lake. I spent every spare moment of my three-day stay in that office, working intensely on a draft of my latest book, and understanding all the while how precious this time would be away from the chaos of work and family. When I needed to rest my eyes, I looked out upon the lake, which was grey and olive beneath the overcast sky and like a painting in its stillness. When I needed a walk, I visited a nearby forest, its walkways carpeted with leaves, its trees bare and black and wet. It rained throughout my visit, but it was one of those soft rains that I know well from winters spent in Vancouver. During my walks through the German forest, or along the roads by the lake, the rain offered me a very welcome solitude and anonymity. It seemed to discourage others from strolling about, and it acted as a sort of canopy over me, absorbing sound, limiting my view of the surroundings, and encouraging me to focus inward upon the challenges of voice and form that my new book was presenting me. I should explain that I am not the sort of writer who can ever hope to rely upon times spent away in retreat in order to be productive, or one who generally draws inspiration from nature. I am also of a working-class background, and not by upbringing a traveller of cosmopolitan confidence and ease; I do not automatically expect to enjoy moments of peaceful anonymity in Europe, where I imagine, rightly or not, that my dark skin will mark me quickly as a foreigner, and, for some at least, a person of special concern. But I did feel comfortable during my stay in that house by the lake in Berlin. At least as comfortable as I ever do. Whether or not I had any right to feel that way.

My interview at the Literary Colloquium Berlin was part of a year-long series of talks on the new global literatures, and it was conducted by Sigrid Löffler, an accomplished critic who asked me thoughtful questions about my first novel, entitled, in English, *Soucouyant*. I remember explaining to her that my novel, which tells the story of a woman afflicted with dementia, is also about the vulnerability of cultural memory, about the sometimes quite precarious belonging of migrant peoples and ethnic minorities, and about the hope that individual words, no matter how obscure, might teach us something about the unacknowledged past when they are recalled and rearticulated. I remember my explanation not because it was in any way original or compellingly put, but because of what I discovered on the day of the interview, and what I am now, in this bit of writing, still struggling to understand. Shortly before taking the stage, I had dinner with the staff of the Colloquium and other generous people from Berlin's writing and publishing scene, including a representative from my publisher, Surhkamp Verlag, a press that, among its many extraordinary distinctions, was started in Frankfurt in 1949 by a Jewish survivor of a concentration camp. The representative from Surhkamp was himself from the American South, and not only surpassingly knowledgeable about world literature in English, but also warm and welcoming. We talked about many things, but, at one moment, he asked how it felt to be staying "here." I confess that I didn't entirely know what he meant by this question, but I ended up responding, quite truthfully, that I had found the accommodation almost embarrassingly luxurious and that everyone had treated me very nicely. I sensed instantly that my response was inadequate, that I was somehow missing the point. After the interview was over, I had the chance to talk with my friends Chloe and Sam, who happened to be living in Berlin, and they gave me some information about the district where I was staying. Later that night, sitting alone in my suite, I used my laptop to go online and find out more. I remember at one point looking up from my computer screen and towards the window of the office, and this time seeing only my face lit up and reflected in the darkened glass, and not the lake outside, which I had only just learned was named Wannsee.

On January 20, 1942, in a villa very close to the Colloquium, and which likely shared the same view of the lake whose serenity and beauty I had enjoyed while writing, the Wannsee Conference took place. The meeting was presided over by Reinhard Heydrich, and it was attended by various senior officials of the Nazi regime (including Adolf Eichmann), who gathered to address what they officially described as "The Final Solution to the Jewish Question." We know of this because of the surfacing, in 1947, of carefully censored minutes from the conference, and from the direct testimony of Eichmann himself. During his interrogation in 1962, Eichmann admitted that the minutes did not include the very blunt discussions that had taken place about the participants' ambitions for the "liquidation" and "extermination" of the Jews of Europe. The Holocaust, in fact, had begun before the Wannsee Conference. But the Conference could still be considered a turning point, one in which active practice and ingrained ideology became invested with newfound political authority and official language. I already knew some things about this. I felt compelled to learn about the Holocaust not only because it is a paradigmatic evil of the twentieth century, but also because I believe I have a personal investment in understanding how catastrophic suffering can be inflicted upon those we elaborately imagine to be our ethnic or racial enemies. I know that it is naïve to think that historic programs of persecution are over, or that they cannot return, in old forms or new, to afflict either the same peoples or the new dark "others" of the twenty-first century. I wanted to believe that I was vigilant and broadly principled about all of this. But the fact remained that in that hauntingly beautiful setting in Berlin, where I managed, against certain odds, to feel comfortable, and where I imagined myself withdrawing from worldly vagaries in order to enter some personal and ever elusive state of creativity, I had failed to read the history. I had not drawn the link between a landscape and its story. Caught up in the hectic pace of my personal life before leaving for Berlin, and in my preoccupation with work immediately upon my arrival, I had not noticed the name Wannsee on any map; and the fact is that I might not automatically have recalled its significance even had I done so. And, worst of all, I had failed to do all of the aforementioned in my specific capacity as a writer.

Marianne Hirsch asks these difficult questions about "the ethics and the aesthetics of remembrance in the aftermath of catastrophe": "How, in our present, do we regard and recall what Susan Sontag . . . has so powerfully described as the 'pain of others'? What do we owe the victims? How can we best carry their stories forward without appropriating them, without unduly calling attention to ourselves, and without, in turn, having our own stories displaced by them? How are we implicated in the crimes? Can the memory of genocide be transformed into action and resistance?" As a writer, I know that these questions are also precisely ones about style and narrative form, about the ethics inherent in the words we choose and the voices we adopt and the ways we story together individual circumstances and events. I know that in writing something like a personal essay about my experience in Berlin, I risk reducing unspeakable suffering to a matter of my own individual awareness, as if whatever I might feel or realize about the Holocaust could in any way be adequate, as if my belated awakening could actually matter in the slightest respect. Yet I see no alternative but to adopt this personal voice, and to risk what may be inappropriate in attempting to articulate this catastrophe against the terms of my own life. For those of us living after the unique horror of the Holocaust, and also, I believe, for those of us dwelling in the long shadows of transatlantic slavery or the decimation of aboriginal societies during the colonization of the Americas, it is impossible to remain at some impersonal distance. As readers and writers, we are implicated into these events in deep and discomforting ways. For me in Germany, on the shore of Lake Wannsee, I became implicated when I failed to know where I stood and what had happened there, regardless of whether or not I was explicitly briefed in this regard. But I continue to hope that this specific failure might awaken me to other challenges, and help me think more clearly about that essential but perennially fraught relationship between the occupation of writing and the historical spaces that writers often come to occupy.

Theodor Adorno is a Surhkamp author who is known for his frequently cited, philosophically complicated, and perhaps ultimately recanted line about the impossibility of poetry after

Auschwitz. Yet Adorno is also the author of many other striking maxims or aphorisms, including the one, found in *Minima Moralia,* that suggests that "it is part of morality not to be at home in one's home." Unlike his friend Walter Benjamin – another (posthumous) Surhkamp author, who, in 1940, apparently chose suicide over being captured by the Gestapo – Adorno, whose father was Jewish, managed to flee Nazi Germany for America before eventually returning to Frankfurt in 1949. Likely, the "home" to which Adorno alludes is in part his birthplace, Germany, where absolutist ideologies of homeland and ethnic belonging had wrought so much evil, and where, upon his return, Adorno could never be expected to feel comfortable. But "home" for him might also have alluded to the high mansions of traditional European philosophy and art, which, he seemed to suggest, had offered little real shelter from the Nazis, and, at times, had appeared to play their own role in lending an aura of authority and decorum to genocidal hatred. I am not someone who could begin to outline Adorno's often daunting analyses of art and of the different pathologies of contemporary societies, which did not limit themselves to Nazi Germany, but also critically addressed, for instance, the rapidly expanding "culture industry" of post–Second World War America. However, I have been struck by the fact that the philosopher who came to express grave doubts about both traditional art and contemporary mass culture could nevertheless express faith in particular forms of art to help us both critique and demur from the dangerously unexamined ideologies and social structures that we might find ourselves within. For Adorno, these forms of art were almost exclusively of the high modernist sort: self-consciously difficult art that appeared particularly resistant to being cynically harnessed by the powerful or else reduced to mere commodities; art that seemed to arise from and re-affirm an exilic relationship to modern society and its automatic patterns of thought, representation, and feeling; art, above all, that was itself "not at home in one's home" in that it was restless with stylistic convention, and promised to act upon its viewers, listeners, or readers in ways that were productively unsettling.

Adorno's thoughts about art, society, and morality arose under specific and extreme circumstances, and, as compelling as they remain, they may not necessarily provide the best answers (or even questions) for the complex terrains that writers and readers have to navigate today. In the twenty-first century, people around the world continue to suffer enormously as a result of the violent promotion of homeland and ethnic belonging that Adorno both experienced and struggled to assess. And the persistence today of both old and new forms of racism and xenophobia articulated as matters of national "pride," and practised at the bitter expense of those who are not "us" (or not *really* us), may indeed suggest that being "not at home in one's home" is now, more than ever, a crucial aspect or indicator of contemporary morality. But the companion reality of the twenty-first century is that millions upon millions of people are involuntarily denied anything like the security we might associate with home, having been expulsed from their lands and physical homes by war and ethnic conflict, environmental catastrophe, and preventable resource shortages. These people are stranded within states that are either impoverished or violently unstable, or wealthy and powerful but unwilling, until pressured, to accord genuine security and dignity of life to both citizens and to those noncitizens within the shadow of their control. Oftentimes, we imagine these people to be living elsewhere or in entirely different times, the victims of the cruelty or irresponsibility of others; but I am thinking here of circumstances when these people are not so remote or disconnected from our lives, people who are our neighbours or else those whose lives are directly affected by the goods and services we consume or profit from, the governments we elect, and the wars we support.

Writing is not, in my mind, wholly reducible to these difficult politics of home, but I do believe that writers need to think seriously about these matters, not only because lives are at stake (and we are, ultimately, never neutral in the affairs of the world), but also because the practice and occasion of writing are inextricably tied to these politics. However much one might insist that writers and writing ought to be "free," meaning at a remove from the dictates of political parties, pressure groups, religious authorities, ethnic chauvinists, or corporations, the plain fact is that writers and writing both need homes. Writers of all backgrounds need space to work without the threat of death or imprisonment, and also the existence and support of schools and libraries, progressive presses and sponsors of writing, open networks of information and the broader terrain of genuine democracy, without which the freedom of writing is either impossible or meaningless. Institutions such as the Literary Colloquium Berlin play their own specific and valuable role in providing homes for writers and literature, and they are often established and run with fully admirable vision and dedication. A writer must be grateful for the precious gift of shelter and support that they provide. But this does not change the fact that these homes, whatever one might initially imagine, are inevitably haunted – by the dead and by the barely living.

I am writing this in Vancouver, in March of 2010, in the wake of the Winter Olympics, which were held here in February only a month ago. My six-year-old daughter was absolutely enthralled by the Games, which we often watched on television together since tickets were very difficult to come by. Between events, and especially when bedtime threatened, she would urgently invent new sports for our living room, such as straight-armed and blind-folded pillow-toss, and flying couch-propelled bum-bounce. Each time she won an event, she would proudly declare herself "the Canadian," and, standing on the podium of the couch, sing the national anthem, before springing towards me for a congrat-ulatory hug. I thought a lot about her during our quieter mo-ments, when she was just watching the television, her eyelashes touched with blue, her skin that shade midway between the brown of my own and the "pink" (as she once called it) of her mother's. I wondered, of course, about the wireless technology of nationalism, and how it envelops all of us, young and old, with a field of power and unconscious feeling that we do not always think clearly about. I wondered about how my daughter might be being manipulated by those primarily interested in sell-ing furry mascots and official memorabilia and, perhaps, uncon-scious acquiescence to questionable civic and national priorities, rather than celebrating human perseverance and peaceful col-lectivity and the raw energy of our bodies. I was wary about what my daughter was being subjected to, but I also wondered what kind of genuine possibility a six-year-old girl might be find-ing for herself in the often very cynical world of television.

A few months earlier, when my daughter and I were finish-ing lunch together in a cafeteria and quietly giggly with our chocolate cake, a very well-dressed woman, who had perhaps had a rough day at the office, turned to us and angrily stated that she genuinely had a right to be sitting there, since she was born here. She was "*really*" Canadian. My daughter and I were both born in Canada, a fact that contributes nothing, of course, toward our right to be sitting at a cafeteria table in a public space. But the truth is that I have not always felt an uncomplicated sense of belonging to the land of my birth. I offer this statement without apology, but also without complaint. For of the processes, violent or subtle, through which certain people are made to feel alien in their homeland, one can never complain; one can only attempt to change them through the help of others. I am very aware of the privileges that I now possess, mostly because of the principled labours and sacrifices of my own parents (who were not born here), but also because I have had the fortune of encountering other Canadians, of many different racial and ethnic backgrounds, who would never literally or symbolically begrudge people like me or my daughter a seat at the table. I have tried to make my occasional feelings of being not at home in my own home not a bitterness, nor an excuse for despair and withdrawal, but, as Adorno suggests, a morality – an effort to learn and connect with others, to safeguard and contribute to what is good about this country, and also an opportunity to learn from those around me who have their own good reasons for feeling not at home, and who aspire not simply to personal belonging, but to the wider space of justice. Yet I am painfully aware of my own limitations in what I have learned and accomplished, and also of the contradictions in what I appreciate consciously, and what I bear in my heart. For it is one thing to take inspiration from the work of an Adorno, who through the extremes of personal experience, and in the contexts of high philosophy and scrupulously elite art, finds a morality in being not at home in his own home. It is quite another thing to watch your daughter, whom you have always hoped would someday belong here, struggling to find her footing in a land that has not always accepted people like her.

When the men's hockey team won gold, and Canada had broken the world record of gold medals for a winter Olympics, we went outside, my daughter and me, and also my wife and toddler son, a gloriously mongrel family trailing cracker crumbs and potato chips from plastic snack bags as we joined the crowds celebrating the victory. It was not at all a day of rain like the one that I had experienced three short months before in Berlin, but one of brilliant sunlight, when from the slopes of Fairview the city of Vancouver stands like pale glass before the metallic blues of the northern mountains. And when we walked down to False Creek and Granville Island, we saw a massive screen set up on which were projected more images of the city and of the province, images which in turn had appeared on our television sets and computer monitors throughout the Olympics: the electric colours of the lakes and oceans, the deepest greens of the forests, and there again, these images, on postcards and official merchandise for sale in shops and special vending facilities set up for the crowds, and here right now in front of us in the manicured surroundings of the seawall, this eternal live feed, this perfect circuit of place as it was so carefully engineered to be viewed and experienced. It was beautiful and unreal, palpable and digitally modified, the way Vancouver often is. And on Granville Island that day, with my daughter's hand in mine, and with the throng of faces around us, I felt so many things. Gratitude, of course, for this moment of safety and security that I could have with my family and our neighbours, for this moment of free sociability in what is sometimes, for many people, a somewhat chilly city. I wanted to relax and enjoy this moment, to participate in what many of us seemed to intuit was bigger and deeper than a sporting event. But I could not do this, not really. Maybe I am just not very good in these sorts of circumstances, and will inevitably, by nature, prefer the quiet of books to the thrall of crowds. Or maybe it was just too soon after my experience in Germany for me to relax and enjoy, the wind punched out of me by the experience of another beautiful landscape, and what I did not see. Or maybe, quite simply, it was that this time, unlike in Berlin, I knew things. About the poverty that would not be projected on those screens. About the crisis of homelessness and affordable housing in the most obscenely expensive place to live in Canada, grotesquely dubbed "the liveable city." About the profound cuts to local culture and arts that the provincial government had arranged immediately before the build-up to the Olympics, and which might result in an all-the-more sanitized and monolithic representation of British Columbia. And so while I stood there in the crowd at False Creek, with my daughter's hand in my own, and feeling slightly remote, as I often do, but also knowing that I too have a stake in this land, and a stake in how it is represented, I thought of words. How the phrase "skid row," known throughout the world, was maybe coined in Vancouver, and remains a bitter reality today for thousands of my neighbours. How the *Komagata Maru* was a ship once sent away from this port, just like the *SS St. Louis* was a ship sent away from another. And how, for the Coast Salish peoples who have endured injustices that still have not been recognized, but who live and write and seek their own way today, this place of False Creek where I live with my family is still sometimes called "Snauq."

STEVEN HEIGHTON

Given to Inspiration

I am not bored at the moment, though it might be better if I were. Boredom might mean I was lagging and loafing my way slowly toward a fresh jag of creative work, creative excitement – a poem, a story, the opening lines of a novel, lines that might lead anywhere, into the expectant offing, off the edge of the storyboard into a sandbox as vast as the Sahara. (I chose writing because I saw no reason that adults should ever cease to play.) Instead I'm expending another day as a compliant, efficient functionary – earnest secretary to my own little career. (If you'll excuse me, another email just blipped into view. I'm going to have to click and skim over, so I can glean that small, fleeting fix of satisfaction that comes from purging the inbox. A sense of accomplishment! – the ensuing narcotic calm! – that deeply licit, Lutheran drug our time-ridden culture starts pushing on us in kindergarten or even sooner.)

I'm afraid that boredom, at least of a certain kind, may be disappearing from the world. And this potential truancy has me worried, partly for the sake of my daughter and her generation, but also (how unsurprising) for myself. Myself and other writers. I mean, the minute I get bored now I check my email. There's often something new there – maybe something rewarding, a note from a friend, some news from my publisher. And if there's nothing there, there's the Internet. For almost all of my writer friends it's the same: like me, they constantly, casually lateralize into the digital realm. Some of them also have cable TV (I don't), so if email and YouTube and other web excursions fail to gratify, they can surf a tsunami of channels. Or else play video games. Whatever. The issue here is screen media. The issue is that staring into space – in that musing, semi-bored state that can precede or help produce creative activity – is impossible when you keep interposing a screen between your seeing mind and the space beyond. The idea is to stare at *nothing* – to let nothingness permeate your field of vision, so the externally unstimulated mind revs down, begins to brood and muse and dream.

What a live screen presents is the opposite of nothing. The info and interactivity it proffers can be vital, instructive, entertaining, usefully subversive, and other good things, sure, but they also keep the mind in a state of hyperstimulation. (All the neurological and anecdotal evidence backs up this claim.)

The twenty-first century brain may be verging on the neural equivalent of adrenal collapse.

———

Just as an hour of boredom – of being at loose ends and staring into space – can serve as precursor to a child's next spate of creative work/play ("work," I write, because a young child's profession is to play), so an adult's month of brooding can open into a year of purposeful creativity.

———

Boredom is the laboratory where new enthusiasms prepare themselves, beakers and test tubes bubbling quietly over Bunsen flames no larger than pilot lights, spectral figures in lab coats moving among them, speaking in hushed voices. (Not one of these figures has the bored dreamer's own face – the face the dreamer wears during the day.)

—

Sign on the wall of a corporate poobah in a Heinrich Böll story – a man who has a treadmill installed under his desk so he can both exercise and generate power for his office while he signs forms and dictates and answers the phone: IT'S A CRIME TO SLEEP.

What he really means is that it's a crime to dream.

—

Boredom is a hibernation, or aestivation, a remission from conscious thought and mental din, a vacancy that starts to fill with micro-dreams that the dreamer never actually *sees* as she gazes into space and the dreams elapse on a deeper level, the way small, unseen fish (not those splashy gold koi on the surface, auditioning, greedy and garish) move in the depths of a pool on which small, suggestive ripples now and then flex – ripples rising to the waking mind in the form of ideas, structural patterns, suggestive phrases or single, germinal words.

—

I suspect Emily Dickinson was often bored. Bored and staring. And out of her boredom, lines erupted, openings like "My life had stood – a loaded gun" and "Safe in their alabaster chambers"

and "Exaltation is the going / Of an inland soul to sea . . ."
Lines that poke holes in the tenuous facade between our public
being and the world's true, ecstatic reality. Or say instead that
after boredom had done its work, her dreaming mind – the nightmind – could reach through the wall into that richer place and
grasp new thoughts in the form of those lines. The daymind, the
wakeful will, always on the make, as conscious and calculating
as a grifter, is too busy and *practical* to receive weird, metamor-
phic couplets like the one uttered by Dickinson's dead speaker
who "died for Beauty": "Until the Moss had reached our lips – /
And covered up – our names –"

—

When you're musing with the nightmind you *have* no name, no
needy ego. You're an anonymous stenographer transcribing
words from some higher or deeper self.

—

Boredom, yes, as in those moments when the eyes stare without
itinerary – when the brain's hard drive revolves at low RPM, un-
coupled from regimen, responsibility, the whole Logistical Life
that *becomes* one's life in the middle years, what Hinduism calls
the Householder Phase, to do to do to do to do to do . . . But now
alpha waves are lapping at the shore of the mind as you depart
the secretarial for the sacramental realm.

—

Flannery O'Connor, ill with the lupus that would kill her, worked
at her typewriter for two hours each morning – when her energy

was at its least feeble – then spent the rest of the day on the front porch of her house, in a rocking chair, doing nothing, she said, but staring.

———

Don't just do something, sit there.

———

Boredom, even of this potentially creative sort, can be experienced as distressing and oppressive partly because the ego, that notorious control freak, feels itself losing control and wants it back. Keep purging that inbox! Keep scratching items off the domestic roster! Advance your agenda! Improve yourself! Perfect and provide, provide, provide. At the end of the day you'll feel you've accomplished, achieved, earned the reward of rest, television, alcohol, sex, sleep, though of course it's a crime to sleep, to sleep too much, to dream and pay attention to dreams. And so the ego, which hates being forgotten, barges back into consciousness, urging you to do something *useful*.

———

(It's the Buddhist teacher and writer Thich Nhat Hahn who says instead, "Don't just do something, sit there." A small act of subversion in a society that has no use for stillness, silence, inward vision – that extols speed, productivity, the manic pursuit of things that by their nature can never be caught and retained.)

———

The ego is as out of place in the sacramental zone as a commercial PR rep would be in the workshop of a woman I know – a woman who hand-sews the bindings of the poetry books she prints on a linotype machine, simply out of a desire to make something beautiful, enduring, and good.

—

Finding the words – or receiving the words, let's say – is a matter of jumpstarting the quiet machinery of dreams while in a fully waking state. A feat more easily described than done.

—

Here's one thing I notice about the ideas that come out of daydream or nightdream: they work, they always work. They might not lead to *Hamlet*, but they work. As for the lines of poetry that come, they're *right*, sufficient unto themselves, in no need of editing. In fact, they seem pre-edited and polished – as if the relaxed mind has done the necessary work and, when the moment is ripe, has issued the lines to the dreamer like a *fait accompli*. "I know I am in a dark place because I / cannot swallow, & the wasps / are weaving hives / into the dead eyes / of the streetlamps." These lines of my own are not great, but they are poetry, possessing poetry's surprise and bizarre aptness and rhythmic/acoustical unity. I'll wager that most people who read them will see that they're nightwork, not daywork, and that editing them would risk introducing foreign material – the material of the daytime will – to lines that have a nocturnal, oneiric integrity. I have a number of lines and poems like this, but not nearly enough. I wish they'd arrive more often, such things – delivered by overnight courier, calling for no editorial surgery, no weeks or months of revision. I can't speak for all writers, but I speak for some of us when I say that we might do more if we could learn to try less, to relax the mind so as to render it vulnerable to inspiration.

—

The corollary: that the daymind is always running interference, censoring, editing, talking over the whisperings and vesperings of something deeper; that if we could sedate the surface chatter, the nightmind could issue its pre-edited offerings more often. (Some of those offerings might not only be poetry, but also key insights into how to change our lives.)

—

Who was the Person from Porlock, anyway? You remember that obtrusive, anonymous figure who rapped, Coleridge tells us, on the door of the poet's residence while he was writing down lines that had come to him in a dream (probably laudanum-induced) from which he'd just awakened. "Kubla Khan." Some have suggested that that Person was simply Coleridge's invented excuse for not being able to bring the poem – which starts so famously, "In Xanadu did Kubla Khan / A stately pleasure-dome decree" – to an equally sublime conclusion.

I think the Person from Porlock is nothing but the daymind, the willful, meddling, obstructively conscious brain, returning to full wakefulness and seizing back control. It raps its officious fist on the door of the imagination and scatters the dusts of a dream that until then had been using the poet as a sort of Dictaphone.

In a wireless world, where the daymind is never allowed to doze off, digital stimulation and busyness amount to a rapping so chronic it grows inaudible, unnoticed.

—

Don't get me wrong. No one finishes a novel or even a book of poems without a hefty contribution from the daymind – specifically the will, overseen by the hungry ego. (Who could finish a four-hundred-page novel without some ego hunger?) Inspiration and good lines can only take a book or writer so far. Still, in the end, writing that's all sweat and disciplined desire for achievement, a story lacking inner vision, a poem untouched by the nudgings of the nightmind – these have no deep resonance or aesthetic staying power. We have to remember how to invite and receive the words and insights we can't force to mind. We have to relearn how to muse and drowse and stare into blankness, adrift, dormant, even bored, especially now when our various screens are always present – firewalls raised between us and the reality of dreams.

MARTHA KUWEE KUMSA

Feeling for Akkoo

Akkoo (Grandma) just died and I'm going to work . . .

I scribble this note as I melt into the hustle and bustle of Toronto. A stranger among strangers, I wonder if anyone in the subway heard my screams. Did anyone see red tears drip from my heart?

Oh my beloved Akkoo! That must be how you felt back then. Screaming and screeching but no one hearing you. Bleeding inside but no one feeling your pain. A stranger among your own. I see traces of your strangeness in my own strangeness. Your anguish is my anguish now.

Write! Write! It's a good way of grieving your loss. People say I'm a born writer. *Am I, really?* Writing is a compulsion from within. *Is it, really?* A writer can't help but write. *Somebody must be joking!*

Write! Write! Give voice to the voiceless! The world around me bombards me with words. What about the silences between the words? What about those gaping gaps of consciousness?

Writing comes to me with bouts of anguish and pain. Each word is brutally torn from my heart, leaving the silences swimming in a bloody stream. My words express the bad things others do and leave out my own inhuman cruelties lurking in their shadows. How can I express the unknown and unknowable stories dancing behind my words? Few are more voiceless than Akkoo, but how can I voice her silences, my silences?

Coming Home

That's my childhood home. See that big odaa tree? It stands at the gate of the homestead. That's my father's house. Thank you Waaqa! At last! I'll rest my throbbing bones and bathe my weary feet. I'm home . . .

My heart ached when I was told these were the last words Akkoo spoke to anyone. She was standing on my mother's veranda when she had the revelation. She called my mother out and joyously uttered these words, pointing to the big tree at the gate of the compound. My mother thought Akkoo was losing her mind and tried to explain that it was not Akkoo's childhood home.

Akkoo refused to hear. She shut out the world that shut her out. She knew that she had come home after a lifetime of yearning. *Never again,* she seemed to say, *will anyone snatch me away from home.* She refused to let go and died there – at home.

Akkoo may well have been standing on her father's land when she uttered those words. The people passing by just outside the gate may well have been her people, the relatives she had always yearned for. Who knows? You see, Akkoo was just a child when she was taken away and she did not know where she was from.

That's my childhood home!

Oh my dearest Akkoo! Your last words ring in my ears as if I heard you say them myself. People didn't understand your language, Akkoo, but everyone else knew that was your childhood home. The night bird knew; it hummed along to your mother's lullaby as she put you to sleep. The moon knew; you sang and danced with her in the misty night. The droplets of dew knew; they bathed your feet as you ran the coffee errands. Tiny siddisa buds knew; they opened up into purple blooms with your gentlest touch. Haadha Dachii (Mother Earth) knew; she embraced you when you lighted on her. The gentle breeze knew; it whispered your childhood dreams into my ears. And now I too know, Akkoo.

You were right! That was where you were born and where you will rest forever, away from yearning and all the suffering.

Oh my dearest Akkoo! Only in my own exile could I begin to feel your exile. Only in my own rupture from home could I begin to feel your pain. Back in the days when I was younger, I thought you were strange. I laughed and jeered at you along with your children and grandchildren. We all thought you were strange but none of us stopped to ask what was underneath all the strangeness.

Now I know a little bit of your alienation and displacement. I feel for you, Akkoo, I ache for you deep in my bones and deep in my soul. And I cry with you until your tears and my tears blend and flow together. I swim with you in that ocean of tears, soul to soul and heart to heart. I cry with you, Akkoo, until my eyes give out their last droplets of tears and melt into a puddle of blood. Your pain is now my pain.

But why does realization come so late, Akkoo? Why are we so numb to each other's feelings? Why are we so hard on each other when we are together? Why was it so hard to sense your pain, Akkoo? Everyone said you were strange. But blessed are those who question what everyone said. I am sorry, Akkoo, that I was not among them.

Is it ever too late to mend, Akkoo? Can I make it up to you by telling your truth? I'm a storyteller too, Akkoo, just like you. But I need words to tell your story. I know you said I'm not a good learner if I waited until the stories found words. I know words leave out too much. Yet, I don't know the world beyond words. I know you want me to tell the story of your life without words. I don't know how, Akkoo.

I am in a strange land, Akkoo. My world is woven from words, thread by thread. I relate to others through words. I can talk with you in the whole of my being, Akkoo – body and soul, heart and mind, gut and viscera. I need words to tell the story of your life to others.

But why is my story so fragmented? Why can I not tell it in a single whole? Why do others spiral in and out? Akkoo, I want to tell your story – and only your story – wholly and fully. But others overwhelm me and weave themselves into the tapestry of your life. I guess you were never you all by yourself; you were you because of and in spite of all those in your life.

Abaabee

Akkoo's family fled her homeland when she was only a child. Akkoo didn't know why. Her father became a goat herder in the new land. Little Akkoo helped by looking after the goats, fetching water, and collecting firewood.

Soon Akkoo fell under the prying eyes of a strange woman who claimed Akkoo as hers. Akkoo's father protested bitterly but the strange woman was too strong for him to challenge. Month after month she came and asked for Akkoo. She embraced and kissed her and took her up on her lap. She touched her, patted her, caressed and massaged her. She grabbed her limbs and kneaded her thighs, her calves, and her arms. Strange! She pressed and rubbed her pelvic bones, her ribs, her breasts, and her back. She pressed and rubbed and kneaded and squeezed again. Very strange!

Akkoo's father resented all this. He had fled his homeland, determined to give Akkoo a good life, but the strange woman was not letting him. What she was doing to his child was against the custom of the people. Secretly, he was planning to flee again and save his child from the predator. But the strange woman saw through his secret schemes. Soon, she too was scheming to keep Akkoo no matter what.

Oblivious to what was happening around her, little Akkoo ran after the goats, revelling in her childhood frivolity, playfully singing her herder's songs and appeasing the goats with her lovely childish voice.

One day the strange woman visited, as usual, but nothing was usual about that day. Akkoo was herding goats in the field, as usual, but nothing was usual about that field. The surrounding bush was swarming with strange men but Akkoo could not see them. They were crouching and crawling and hiding.

Akkoo's father was visiting a neighbour just beyond the ravine when the strange woman came. Akkoo's mother brought Akkoo in to be kneaded, as usual. Akkoo's mother was standing at the door with her back to the outside when she sensed somebody approach from behind her. The men swarming the bush were now at the door. Akkoo's mother turned around but alas! Before she knew it, the huge muscular men picked her up and ran away with her.

Uuuuu'uuu uuuuu'uuu! Akkoo's mother screamed, her shrill voice piercing the still air and rocking the quiet village. The strange woman ran after the men with Akkoo in her arms. She was yelling. *That's the mother! Let her go at once! Mine is this one! Take this one!* She hollered after the men. Akkoo's mother was so young and beautiful that the kidnappers thought she was their girl. They had no idea they were about to kidnap a child. Soon they let Akkoo's mother go, snatched little Akkoo from the strange woman's arms, and ran away with her.

When he heard the terrible screams, Akkoo's father interrupted his visit and ran home. Like a cheetah, he skipped the winding path and came, cutting straight through the ravine. But the men had already run away with his child. He heard Akkoo scream: *Abbaa! Abbaa! Rescue me, Abbaa!* Now the cheetah man blew like a wind. He caught up with the men instantly and clutched his daughter.

Akkoo and her father wrapped their arms around each other's necks, but they were overwhelmed and the men ran with little Akkoo as she screamed: *Abbaa! Abbaa! Save me, Abbaa!* And her father ran after them screaming: *My child! My child! I'm coming, my child!*

The men brought Akkoo to a strange place and shoved her into a dark room in the back of a house. In the darkness, Akkoo waited for the signs of her father. She put her ears to the ground and listened for the hooves of his horse. He had said he was coming and he would be there to rescue her.

When darkness fell across the land, a man came into the room but he was not Akkoo's awaited father. He pinned her down and forced himself into her little body. Akkoo screamed in terror: *Abbaa! Abbaa! Rescue me, Abbaa!*

He muffled her voice and did what he had to do. When he was finished, Akkoo was soaked with blood. As she hugged the ground feeling dizzy, she heard gunshots outside. And she screamed like no time before: *Abbaa! Abbaa! They're shooting me! Save me, Abbaa! They're killing me!*

The revelling outside drowned out her voice. Everyone but Akkoo knew what was going on. And they all laughed at her naïveté. Her entire body burned and throbbed and ached. Soon the strange woman came in with some strange broth and made her drink it. She washed away the blood and kneaded her body. Akkoo felt almost grateful, even as she resented the bestiality she had just experienced.

Outside, people sang and danced and ate and drank. They enjoyed themselves at Akkoo's expense. Her terror dipped a bit when the people fell asleep and the noise died down and the night fell quiet. The moon came out late in the tranquil night and reached out to Akkoo. Akkoo was in no shape to dance with her old misty friend. She collapsed on Mother Earth and slept like a baby.

What a cruel world, Akkoo! What scar did all this leave on you? How did it feel, to be snatched from the embrace of the strongest man you'd ever known? And to realize there were stronger and more merciless others? To cry out for help only to hear their roaring laughter? Even generations later we all laughed at you, Akkoo. Everyone thought life was happening to you when you thought it was death. Only in my own torture could I feel your anguish deeply. And now I know they were violating your personhood, Akkoo. Yes, they were killing you.

Only in my own strangeness could I make sense of your strangeness, Akkoo. Only now could I realize the play of power and how the powerful become normal and others become strangers. And how they turn their own strangeness into the strangeness of others and how ordinary life is turned into the extraordinary. The kneading, the pressing, and the squeezing; it all embodied strangeness in you, Akkoo. It was all a way of turning the strangeness of the strange woman into your strangeness. And everyone around you rubbed it in. Yet that was only the beginning.

Akaakaa

That's how Akkoo married Akaakaa (Grandpa) when she was only twelve. It was entirely crafted by the strange woman. Even Akaakaa was not privy to her schemes. He was hauled from where he was working to come home and take little Akkoo, only after she was kidnapped. He was twenty-two.

This strange woman is my own Abaabee (Great-Grandma), Akaakaa's mother. Abaabee loved Akkoo the moment she set her eyes on her and was determined to get her for her son no matter what. *My God, what a tyranny of love!*

Akaakaa took Akkoo and moved to another far away land to stake out his own life. As he built his career and became a big shot, Akkoo disappeared into his thick shadow. Her stories became mere footnotes in the great stories of a great man. She moved with him from place to place and bore his children, twelve of them.

With every child coming, however, she yearned for her people. She wanted to go home to her mother to give birth. That's what normal women did. But Akkoo could never fill the shoes of a normal woman and, in her profound strangeness, she ached for her kith and kin. With every pang of labour pain, Akkoo cried out for her mother; she howled out for home.

One day, with tears streaming down her cheeks, she asked Akaakaa: *Where are my people? Find them for me at once! Find me my clan! I want to go home, if only for this one birth.* She was pregnant with her fifth child. Akaakaa gently sat her down and lovingly pressed her to let go of the impossible. He rounded up the four children and said: *From now on your children are your kith and kin. For God's sake, don't ask again.* Akkoo was shocked, as she had never seen Akaakaa so stern. She swallowed back her yearning and clung on to her children.

But then some of her children were given to others. Akkoo fought to keep them but every effort she made to cling to her children made her look stranger. *How could she be so selfish? How could she be so mean?* Even some of her own children thought she was cruel and the tighter she clung to them, the harder they fought to get away from her. Alas! Akkoo became the outcast of the family.

I am Akkoo's first grandchild, the first daughter of her first daughter. But she was not the first person I loved and called by the loving name of *Akkoo*, as was the custom. Instead, I was given to Akaakaa's elder sister when I was six months old. And Akkoo's estrangement spilled over to my generation.

Stranger Power

Akkoo rebelled by refusing to speak the language of power through which Akaakaa and the children were rising in their world. As she played dumb for our dumb world, we all sat around and roared with laughter at what she said and what she did. We mocked and ridiculed her, rubbing in her estrangement and lodging it deeper into her soul. How cruel!

We had no idea that by embracing her strangeness and rejecting the language of power, Akkoo was exuding the power of a language we did not understand. We had no clue that by laughing at her we were laughing at ourselves, by mocking and ridiculing her we were mocking and ridiculing ourselves.

Oh dearest Akkoo. Now I know how we made you homeless at home and a stranger among your very own. I'm beginning to realize the depth of the suffering we caused you, and how hard you had to hit the bottle. I want to tell your truth, Akkoo, but the language of power fails me. I need the power of your language.

Stories hidden from me in my youth are surfacing in bits and fragments, but I'm so scared of your truth, Akkoo. I know what happens to those who betray family secrets and I tremble in fear. I get a glimpse of who the real devils in our family might have been and I'm scared stiff. It's much easier to demonize you, Akkoo.

I'd be dishonest to my own sense of justice if I did not tell your truth wholly and fully. But I fall on my knees, wobbling and trembling. I collude with power, Akkoo. My life hinges on it. My world is woven from the words that robbed you of your knowledge and left you out in silence. I thought I was courageous. I thought I spoke truth to power all my life. That's a lie, Akkoo. I'm a coward.

I pray for the power of your language, Akkoo. Then I don't fear the language of power. Then I'm not doomed to understand your strangeness only through my own exile, and I don't have to feel your torture only through the violation of my own personhood.

Now I know, Akkoo. We don't have to go through another's suffering to understand the pain we are causing them. Now I know the power hidden in strangeness and vulnerability too, Akkoo. It gives us back the power of the language part of humanity has lost in its self-centeredness. It contests the language of power that disconnects us from the rest of the universe.

Now I know how much we are all woven together from the cosmic fibre you used to tell me about. And I don't have to wilt with the leaves to know what thirst means. I don't have to suck with the roots to understand what drinking is. I don't have to burn with the sun to know what heat is. I don't have to sing with the birds to know what music is.

Now I know the home you uttered in your last breath. I know the kith and kin you felt you had joined with. Home was the much larger home of the cosmos and your kith and kin were everyone in it.

In that bend of space where the path of light curls into a bow, in that nick of time where there is no beginning nor end, in that blend of life where no one is estranged, I see you clearly, Akkoo, among all creation, animate and inanimate, infinite and infinitesimal. And I can sense the stories before the words.

GUY GAVRIEL KAY

TMI: Authors in Cyberspace

Act 1

Not that long ago I found myself in a bar (no idea how *that* happened) with a literary agent from the United Kingdom. I want to
stress, by way of background, that he wasn't an especially young
man (that matters), and he was an intelligent, well-read person
(that matters, too).

As we watched a World Series game on the big-screen television in the bar (that doesn't *really* matter, but it was an outstanding game), amid a crowd of literary types at a conference,
the agent told me about his current work methods.

He said that when he was dealing with a new submission
by a writer looking to be taken on as a client, he read a chapter
or two. If it didn't work for him, he stopped and moved on. If it
seemed to show promise, he put the manuscript aside and went
to his computer – and undertook a detailed search for the prospective author-client in cyberspace.

He checked Facebook, Twitter, the blogosphere, looked for
a web page. He chased down some online venues that, to me, were
merely a smattering of initials. He did a Google search, looked for
the writer's presence in comments on *other* writers' blogs.

"Why?" I protested.

"Because if I don't see him strongly present online, I am far less likely to take him on as a client," he said. And sipped his Scotch with impeccable timing (he was a former actor, actually).

I made the medieval sign against evil, and looked, in vain, for an oak tree around which to run counterclockwise. (The bar was marble, no help.) "You can't be serious!" cried I.

"Of course I am," he said patiently. "I need to know how much he'll help me sell his books."

I drank from my own Scotch, less smoothly.

What are we to make of this, aside from the absurdity of an author looking for oak trees in a bar in California? My core point here (to make it easy) is that while the book trade has always had an element of writers performing jigs (as Bernard Shaw once put it), the culture today has writers dancing as fast as they can, and on a daily or even hourly basis.

The collision of many trends has created, like a mash-up of elements, a new book-world reality. Take a "cult of personality" society, note a severe cutback in marketing budgets, mix in the seductive ease of "broadcasting" oneself online, be aware of reality shows with their vicious erosion of the very idea of privacy, and you have a literary world where the author is now his or her own marketing machine, however well or badly that machine is tuned.

This has manifold implications, but one of them has to do with a radical revision of what might be called the author-reader relationship. The principal consequence is the disappearance of the space between author and consumer and between author and work.

You sell your books on the strength of your personality online, as the agent suggested to me that night, or, as he put it more carefully a bit later, on the strength of the personality you *construct* for yourself online.

A young writer I know wrote me a little while ago that she was heading for a lunchtime meeting with her publisher to discuss exactly that: the persona she ought to adopt or create in blogging and tweeting and whatever-elsing. She felt – and most young writers offer variants of this – that she had little choice but to get herself "out there."

Not long ago, a bitingly satirical piece in *The New Yorker* underscored this ("Subject: Our Marketing Plan"). It purported to be an email from "the intern hired to replace your publisher's marketing department" to a writer about the marketing plans for his new book. Said plans were that the author would sell *himself* via every online channel known or to come. (I thought a few of these channels and their acronyms were invented, that they had to be; others, more sapient, have told me it isn't so. Reddit bites?) The concept of an intern *replacing* a department is so painfully accurate in light of publishing today, it took the piece to that edge of reality where the best satire lives.

There are consequences of all sorts to this blurring, or erasing, of borders between author and audience, and to the emergence of an author as an online friend to his or her readers, and I'm not just talking about time lost from work or what the word *friend* really means in this context. There's a *value* to keeping how one looks at a work of art separate from one's sense (manufactured or otherwise) of the artist who made it. And there's importance to the space between artist and consumer.

The online world has seen several ugly flare-ups where readers have viciously lambasted authors for (as an example) being late with a promised manuscript. As if the delivery was something *owed* to the readership, part of some unwritten contract, the breach of which could legitimize cyber-rage. One well-known author, struggling with complex challenges (apparently) in a multi-volume project, had readers attack him on his own blog for watching too much football, taking a holiday with his wife, working on an editing project, not *exercising* enough.

One shakes one's head (for starters). But there's an aspect to this that needs to be noted. The only reason the readers knew of the football-watching and the holiday was because the author had *told* them, on that same blog, and he had regularly broadcast other details of his life. One bestselling writer is reported to be tweeting up to a dozen times a day to a massive army of follow- ers on Twitter. This is undeniably effective marketing and fan manipulation. Readers feel a sense of connection – and empow- erment, even personal affection – but anyone who is in any kind of relationship knows that there are expectations that can kick in, and may lead to vitriol, or orders to get on an exercise bike and lose weight so the promised book won't be forestalled by something *really* annoying, like the author dying.

Writers, hastening to forge these new bonds and personal links with readers, to fill the space left by the absence of pub- lisher marketing, are willingly engaged in eroding both their own privacy and the space that can be necessary to produce not only good art but a good life. It feels, at times, lemming-like. Tweet where the cliff is.

Act 2

Two mornings later, I was being driven to the airport from that same literary conference. The driver was a young magazine editor and novelist, my fellow passenger a seriously smart, widely re- spected fiction writer. Making conversation, I asked the established one how her work was going. (I had failed to spark interest in discussing the World Series.) She told me she was having trouble beginning a new book. She was seriously distracted, and finding it hard to focus, especially as she had to spend so much time online.

"You have to spend?" I asked, preemptively looking beside the highway for oak trees.

"Well, yes," she sighed. "It starts to be expected of you. You know that."

She proceeded to tell a story of how she lost a morning to the online world. I'll give the short version. She was ego-surfing for web tidbits (no, not Reddit bites, those are . . . something else) about herself when she stumbled upon an active discussion about one of her own books. (It is alarmingly easy to find one-self online, in all possible senses of the phrase.) She read the discussion posts, which were appearing quickly, almost in real-time – and then she jumped into the conversation.

"They were shocked, of course," she said, grinning. "But they loved it! The downside is I ended up chatting there for so long. And I went back a couple of times."

"Of course they loved it," I said, though I also made the (too easy) joke about no one expecting the arrival of the Spanish Inquisition *or* the author. "But tell me – this is a real question – why did you pop in there?"

As I said, this is a thoughtful woman. She gave it time as we sped along the highway.

"Because I'm human," she finally answered.

Back home, I relayed this story over coffee to an older writer friend. He, too, gave it time. Then he said, "In my day, the idea was that if you overheard people talking about you, you ducked behind a potted plant to avoid embarrassment, *and* to maybe hear a bit more. That's what I'd say 'being human' used to mean, in that situation."

His "day" may well be over. Human nature is, after all, both an individual work in progress *and* contingent upon culture, which is also evolving. It is necessary to remember that "privacy" as a value, as something even substantially *possible,* hasn't been universal or universally accessible. If changing norms in our society now seem to work against it, that doesn't mean a shocking loss of something definitively important in the world.

Feels that way sometimes, however.

There was a website created recently called PleaseRobMe .com that was designed to make people aware of just how much information about their lives could be discovered by complete strangers, based on, among other things, Facebook posts or Twitter feeds. (I do not know if Reddit bites were complicit, and I have made an executive decision not to find out.) If you tweet, "Leaving for Jamaica in an hour!" that is information of use to individuals who might not have your best interests at heart.

It has been reported that British insurance companies were looking to raise premiums by 10 per cent to cover the cost of break-ins occasioned by Facebook alerts that home owners would be away.

The PleaseRobMe.com site has since been discontinued – the creator felt his point had been made and discussed, and he didn't *really* want to be a channel through which thieves gained access to empty homes. But the emerging fact is that most people today, even after noting this truth and chatting about the website's clever warning, offer the cyber-equivalent of a shrug. They treat this self-exposure as a cost of business (and pleasure) in the modern world. 10 per cent premium boosts? A small price for telling the immediate universe you are going south for piña coladas on a white sand beach. How can you star in your own reality show if people don't know where you are?

The implication, or the consequence, is that privacy as a value becomes eroded, or superseded by exposure as a value. Years ago, long before this dramatic acceleration in self-revelation and before the technology existed to facilitate it, I wrote that "nobody knows you if the blinds are down and you're not out," riffing on an old song. Sometimes you can be more right than you want to be.

Is this just grumbling? Antediluvian resistance to getting with the current program? Is it even hypocritical? I *have* an online presence, after all: there are two websites dedicated to my work, developed by others (one publisher-created, one reader-based). When I have a new book coming out, I post a "Tour Journal" to one of these, offering what I hope will be interesting information about the run-up to a book's publication: background details of editing, marketing, jacket design, cover copy, and public events, with a view to lifting the curtain for those interested in how books end up on bookstore shelves (electronic or traditional). I stop the journal when the touring ends, and start another a few years later when a new novel's coming. These two websites even offer a Twitter feed of core information – reviews, articles, interviews, appearances – judged to be of interest to my readers.

The agent in the bar made that point during the seventh-inning stretch. He said I was simply lucky enough to have "arrived" to a degree where I could retain some privacy and time for myself and have others willing to step up as I withdrew, to maintain a "voice" for me in the evolving media world.

There's truth to this; I'd be wrong to deny it. But surely there's another truth to be found: all of us need to work at finding our balance in this process. This isn't an either/or exercise (unless you're a Salinger or a Pynchon, perhaps). We don't need to be, as public figures or simply citizens considering the social networking of the world, violently rejecting of it *or* unconditionally immersed.

But the process of finding this balance, for those of us in the book world, requires an awareness that there is a balance to be found. And that, in turn, requires some resistance to the hype and the need-to-hype, the drum roll of Reddit bites, the pressure to flog *yourself* and your life in order to flog your book.

The jury is still out as to how much this self-exposure helps a book right now, and how much it will continue to do so, as more and more writers try it, altering the signal-to-noise ratio even more.

A celebrated bestselling writer may have tens or hundreds of thousands of fans following her on Twitter, or checking her blog, but – to be banal and obvious – that is a celebrated best-selling writer. A handful of authors may create a persona for themselves through online marketing that *makes* their books bestsellers. One writer was reported to have blogged a million words in a year. That's five or six or seven novels' worth of writing, and time. What is the actual return on investment there, even if a degree of recognition (and even bemused stupefaction) comes to him? What's the opportunity cost? The works lost, or the *quality* of work lost? Maybe there's none. It is possible. Maybe he'd be online that much, or nearly so, even if he wasn't trying to make a living as a writer. This is a factor, too. Every one of us will have his or her own calculations to make along these lines.

But we need to do that calculation, as best we can, and we need to think about implications and consequences, about "being human" and how that idea shifts. This isn't just a matter of some unstable (or just seriously pissed off) people anony-mously screaming at a writer on his own website to get off his ass and starting writing, dammit. It is about who we are, indi-vidually and collectively, and who we are choosing to become. If we boldly go where no man has gone before, in this particular way, it makes some sense to at least have our eyes open.

Maybe bury the house key at the root of an oak tree, rather than leaving it under the mat.

RAWI HAGE

*On the Weight of Separation and the
Lightness of the Non-Belonging*

In the early 1900s, my grandmother, like many Lebanese of the time who witnessed the exodus from the mountains of Lebanon, watched her father leave for the Americas. My great-grandfather never returned. His whereabouts remained unknown, subject to speculation and resulting in a sadness that stayed with my grandmother for the rest of her life. Eventually, a credible but unlikely story surfaced within the family. The story goes like this: my great-grandfather was told, by undefined sources, that all his family and relatives had died during the 1914 famine in the mountains of Lebanon and that it was futile to go back. Upon hearing this news, my great-grandfather experienced an agony of longing and despair.

We were told that he went into a deep depression and eventually took his life. The irony is that my grandmother and the rest of her large family survived the famine, due to a few sacks of grain that my great-grandmother had managed to hide, and to a modest amount of eggs that were luckily available because of the promiscuous nature of a rooster and a sexually liberated group of hens.

As a child, I used to think the story of my great-grandfather was both tragic and suspicious. I often played the scenario in my head, imagining him weeping in a lonely room in the Americas,

227

having lost all hope of being reunited with his family. But what is more fascinating, and at times even shameful to me, is the fact that he didn't immediately take a boat home. He never attempted to save his family from starvation, or to bury his dead.

During my own exile, the story took on different meanings and presented further possibilities. I started to add my own interpretations, my own endless beginnings and endings. One possibility I contemplated was that my great-grandfather became rich, that he remarried and, due to his significant distance from the motherland and his obligations to his new family, he forgot all about his kin in Lebanon and started a new life. In other, less dramatic scenarios, it could well be that he ended up injured, dead, or imprisoned, or that he simply wandered for the rest of his life in a foreign land, hopping from one train to another, an impoverished vagabond, a failed peddler, or simply a drunk.

Leaving one's homeland is an endeavour that is freighted with responsibility. The emigrant carries not only certain obligations from the collective, but also the weight of that collective's expectations. If there is one truism to be found in the old saga of migration and immigration, it is that the act of leaving is loaded with anticipation. Mostly, it is a man who leaves, and who will one day come back to rescue those left behind. This scenario has become one of our most common, almost folkloric, stories: the emigrant will work hard in a foreign country and send money back to the family. And, if he is lucky, he will one day return to his village or place of origin and parade his wealth. The idea of a triumphant return has long sustained and motivated those who leave under precarious conditions, as well as provided a source of hope to those who remain behind.

Indeed, to leave and come back victorious is an idea as old as human history. To sack Troy and return to Penelope, to return to a promised land (regardless of whether that claim is legitimate or absurd), the biblical story of the prodigal son, etcetera. The idea of the return is always an epic of hardship, humility, and grand endeavour. Departures are more permissible and, in some situations, expected, but a homecoming must be earned.

There is always the possibility of oblivion. To leave without a sense of regret, nostalgia, concern, without any promise to return home: this is a legitimate choice for those whose lives have been affected by misery, war, and poverty. And I assure you that during my long exile, I have often met those who left without any desire to go back. There is relief and a sense of efficiency and clearness when such a decision is taken. Those who are capable of so grand a detachment often provoke a sense of admiration and envy in me and other exiles. I have seen stunning, and certainly genuine, metamorphoses in men and women who have overcome the past to rewrite their names and redefine their lives, adapting like chameleons blending into a new tree.

But then again, transformation is bound to affect every immigrant and exile. The transformation can encompass a range of emotional states, from happiness and well-being to depression, culture shock, longing, anger, resistance, acceptance, and, in extreme cases, madness. The existence of an immigrant is volatile, and this volatility can lead to aimlessness and a perpetual sense of loss and non-belonging; it could well be an experience on par with the loss of that first, ever elusive, paradise.

When I am asked in the West about my experiences during the Lebanese war – a legitimate question, and one that I am bound to answer since my first novel was based on that war – my reply is that I found my early years of displacement more brutal and devastating than the war itself. If anything, what one detects in the protagonist of my first novel, *De Niro's Game*, is the sense of non-belonging, of living an existential dilemma, of introversion.

In short, the solemn, brutal existence of the narrator is based on my early experience of immigration. When I tell my audiences that my family's closeness, the support of our community, and a sense of belonging prevented the war and its hardships – though brutal – from being an alienating experience, I am met with a fair degree of skepticism.

In leaving one's country, one becomes a witness to a change in one's own consciousness, a change within the self. To leave is often a product of a sense of stagnation, a refusal to initiate a change, a refusal that comes from a feeling of helplessness. War, famine, oppression, and economic hardship are the main instigators of exile. Once the act of leaving has taken place, there is a duality, a confusing binary, between what was left behind and what one is currently experiencing. I am interested in this duality. In the initial days of adjustment to a new culture and an adopted place, the old country surfaces as a constant reference point. In other words, an immigrant's perception of a new culture is always interposed with another, older one; hence, both experiences become new and to a certain extent, foreign, and even contested.

"The elsewhere" is and will always be a volatile current of change that one, with time, learns not to fight and not to fully accept. One is left with the limiting realities of memories, refutations, and observations. Which brings me to the act of writing.

There are many expectations and taboos that haunt writers who work in a foreign language and in an alien space that is not their own. Writers from the diaspora, like myself, are in a very precarious position. Your primary readership is no longer solely your immediate race, ethnicity, or language group. Further, the writing itself takes place in a self-imposed and self-contested zone: To write about your past is to evoke a place that is no longer fully your own. However, to write in a language that is not your mother tongue is to declare, to speak, and to take ownership of what has been newly acquired as yours.

But why write in a language that is not your own? The public's reaction to such writers ranges from accusations of abandonment of one's culture, and betrayal of one's motherland, to praise and wonder. The number of times I have been asked if I really wrote my novel in English is substantial. And then: Why not in Arabic, my mother tongue, or in French, my second language?

I am certainly not an oddity in these cross-language endeavours. I could mention the Syriac monks who excelled in Arabic and translated Aristotle, among many other Greek philosophers, or remind people of the Greek sections in the New Testament, or list a long tradition of Russian writers who have chosen to write in French, including those who lived during the reign of Catherine II, Empress of Russia, as well as more recent Russian writers like Andreï Makine. In Makine's novel *Le Testament Français*, Charlotte, on the edge of the Siberian steppes, tells her grandchild stories of Paris from before the Great War. The child marvels at Charlotte's recollections of her youth in France and is incited, when grown, to leave for France. Makine's exploration of the links between the histories of France and Russia, and between the French and Russian languages, is woven throughout with a mixture of Proustian and Chekhovian styles. His mastery of and admiration for the French language exists at the centre of his work.

Languages, like unstoppable armies, like siren songs to ships and lonely sailors, embrace us, subdue us, and infiltrate us, only to change us and even cause some of us to leave our mothers in search of those mythical places and stories we heard of as children.

Languages are vital organisms that grow, mutate, and multiply with the speed of reaching branches and the treachery of pests on migrating boats. Language is opportunistic, destructive, embracing, indoctrinating, seductive, and certainly enriching. Language's only loyalty is to its own mutation and message. Those of us, like Aliocha, the narrator of *Le Testament Français*, who are exposed to a multiplicity of languages and images of other places at an early age, unconsciously become the bearers and seekers of "the elsewhere" and its histories. These quests are not quests for promised lands, but for mythical childhood places with which we wish to be reconciled.

As a Lebanese (later Canadian), whose exposure to the French language at an early age was formative and wondrous, my first choice for a place of exile was France. But then, circumstances and the complications of bureaucracies led me to North America, where the English language dictated itself upon me, covered me, and embraced me with the exigency of a fur coat in a cold Siberian landscape.

It is within such a linguistic binary that writers of the diaspora tend to exist. A return, as I previously mentioned, is weighted with certain expectations and responsibilities. In criticizing one's tribe to expose the motherland, one runs the risk of solidifying stereotypes that may already be well-established in the outside world. On the other hand, as Edward Said writes in *Representations of the Intellectual*, to refuse to condemn one's community is to fall into the narrowness of a nationalistic and counterproductive parochialism. Hence, in order to earn our own "return," we must also give voice to our political and intellectual concerns. I am a firm believer that there is no progress, no salvation or advancement, without an acknowledgement of failures and regrets, without a refusal of injustices, and without critical engagement. In the same vein, I believe there is no progress without a good dosage of outside influences, without exchanges of ideas that can be tailored to a culture motivated to change.

Having said that, I should note that outside ideas have also led to failures and disaster. I need only cite the Khmer Rouge leaders who studied in France and were well-rehearsed in the matters of the French Enlightenment, French existentialism, and, to an extent, Maoism and Buddhism. Here, allow me to evoke a recent novel on the Cambodian genocide by the Canadian writer Madeleine Thien, *Dogs at the Perimeter*, which brilliantly and subtly portrays the transnational character and the devastating effect of history on people's lives.

Writers of the diaspora have much to offer because of their contested identities, hybrid existences of here and there, and perpetually divided loyalties and belongings – what the Egyptian-Canadian poet Iman Mersal refers to as the refusal of identity amidst a surplus of identity. Within the telling of a story, ideologies have the potential to be contaminated, imported, discussed, read, dissected, and, most importantly, diffused and disarmed.

In *De Niro's Game*, I have told a story of the Lebanese people. The story of a country at war. Certainly, our unfortunate war had its own intricacies, reasons, and characteristics, be they religious or geopolitical. I have often heard that the most puzzling thing for the world to understand is just how complicated the war was. Who was fighting whom and why. After writing *De Niro's Game*, I had the chance to meet people who had experienced civil war all over the planet. A lady from the former Yugoslavia said to me that while reading my book, she felt as if she were reading a story about the war she herself lived through.

But what obligations does the exile carry towards the many lands that he or she has lived in and even benefited from? All these loyalties, these burdens of nationalism, ethnicity, and origins, become, after a time, an overbearing baggage that opens and fills with self-reflections, doubts, and demands. How to link one's contemporary experience with one's past and beginnings? How to deal with the new self in the context of redefined borders, how to come to terms with uprootedness, with the weight of physical separation, with the lightness of non-belonging?

After publishing my second novel, *Cockroach*, the questions that I had to face most often and which I loathed the most were: Are you Canadian? Do you feel Canadian or Lebanese? In short, where do you belong, and who has a claim on you now? The novel was often perceived as an immigrant story, and furthermore an ungrateful immigrant story, but this reading disregards the multilayered and complex issues that the novel portrays, including questions of displacement, secularity, religion, class, and madness. I have presented a creature that cuts across geographical, cultural, fantastical, and stylistic boundaries.

Cockroach is a personal account of the strata of culture, religion, and language I have been exposed to since the age of three. My homeland of Lebanon, contrary to the nationalistic, narrow, confessional beliefs that are ever present in the daily lives of its citizens, is the product of many stones, tongues, gods, and certainly many revivals after its destruction by consecutive armies. It is a place where the crossing of the ancient and the new is perpetual. I wanted to join in one codex Lebanon's many histories in a new land, in my adopted country, Canada.

What is, at times, dismissively disregarded as an immigrant story is, in fact, one of the most current, most modern stories that exists. Beyond the apparent lamenting of loss and displacement, beyond the newcomer's expected gratefulness or the explanatory missions, immigrant stories emphasize the parallels and the distinctions between here and there. Essentially, these stories are simultaneously as old as human history and continuously new in their modern relevance.

In *Cockroach*, I used a despicable insect as a metaphor for the ever resilient mover for whom the architecture of human boundaries is nothing more than a stroll through the pipes and the underground, whose closeness to the ground mocks the idea of an afterlife, a being who defies upward mobility and its clouds of rewards. The cockroach is a conqueror who can never be eliminated, a carrier of filth and wisdom, an existentialist who never questions his own existence, a reminder that evolution never favours anyone, that the gods are ever absent, and that nature and its elements are ever effacing those feeble, ephemeral demarcations we might call nations.

To be on the margin, to live outside the boundaries, is to be in a permanent state of duality, a condition that is harsh in its losses but rewarding in its gifts of freedom and openness.

But then one wonders why these perpetual carriers of news from elsewhere, these watchers of both shores, are trapped in the turmoil of their own selves? Those who left in tears, who carry a persistent longing for home, and who exist in a new place that will never fully be their own, are both the burdened and the blessed. They gravitate between the roles of public defenders and secret attackers. They live a convoluted but necessary intellectual existence, swinging between the pessimism of the skeptic and the optimism of the absurdist. Theirs is a mixed blessing. Having lost their blind loyalties to the grand constructs of nation-states and the petty chauvinism of their tribes, they are cursed to never see things as they are, but to instead see everything through their own past, layered with images of their own birthplaces, their toddler's steps, and their perpetual flights. We are unable to carry on in exile without seeing in everything a beginning and a cause, and certainly an origin, including our own.

JOSEPH BOYDEN

The Hurting

A Cree woman I've known for a long time up in Moosonee has been in such anguish for the last year that I fear for her life. Although *anguish* – this word – can't begin to describe her tortured suffering. She lives every day in what most of us would consider our worst nightmare. A year ago, her seventeen-year-old son, while at a house party full of friends, walked from the kitchen, where he'd found a short indoor extension cord, through the crowded living room, to a bedroom, and eventually into a closet. There, he wrapped the end of the cord around his neck, and, leaving a foot or two slack, he tied the other end around the clothes rod. This thin young man with pimples on his chin and black hair he wore short and spiky, knelt so that his full weight pulled the cord taut. In this way, he slowly strangled himself to death.

If you have the fortitude, think about that for a minute. He could have stopped at any time; he could have simply stood up to take the pressure off. Possibly he did once or twice or three times when the fear of what awaited overcame him, when the happy noise of his friends in the rooms next door drifted in, muffled. But eventually, with unbelievable will, with a drive he'd never exhibited in his young life before, he managed this gruesome act of self-destruction.

—

In June of 2010, I attended the Truth and Reconciliation Commission's first annual gathering at The Forks in Winnipeg. Residential school survivors and their families came together from all across Canada. The first day alone an estimated twenty thousand people gathered to speak about their experiences or to see old friends or to soak up the evening concert that featured Buffy Sainte-Marie and Blue Rodeo. Despite the rather festive feel of the first day, the pain – the same anguish that my Cree friend feels – was palpable just below the surface. The sunny skies turned to rain for the next couple of days, as if mimicking the mood.

An Anishnabe medicine man I know, when he speaks of the creation of residential schools, says that a door was opened that should never have been unlocked. For Westerners, his rather poetic view might be comparable to letting a sinister genie out of a bottle. One of the many evils that escaped out that door, the medicine man says, is the tremendously high aboriginal youth suicide rate in our country. He believes, as do many, that this suicide epidemic is a direct effect of a residential schools system that tore generation after generation of families apart. What's certainly true is that suicide among aboriginal groups was almost unheard of before the establishment of the residential schools.

As I've mentioned, this Cree woman in Moosonee, my friend, has lived in anguish since the suicide of her son. As did her fifteen-year-old daughter. She was close to her brother and went through most of the stages of grief: disbelief, anger, a stabbing sadness. But she wasn't able to make it to the last stage: acceptance.

Five months after her son was found hanged at a party, my Cree friend found her daughter hanged, this time in her own closet at home, and this time her child was actually kneeling, leaning slightly forward as if in deep prayer.

How does a mother go on after that? This Cree woman, my friend, she's from a tiny, isolated James Bay reserve named

Kashechewan, one hundred and sixty kilometres as the bush plane flies north of Moosonee. Kashechewan is like a hundred other northern Canadian reserves. But unlike most, Kashechewan made the papers a handful of years ago when more than twenty youth attempted suicide in a single month. I remember reading about it on page five of the *Globe and Mail* and not being surprised. I'd lived and taught up there – the reserve's reputation preceded it.

People in Moosonee warned me each time I was to travel to Kash and spend a few days, a week, teaching adult community members reading and writing skills. These people said, "Be careful. It's a dangerous place. It's a rough reserve. A lot of people up there are crazy." None of the warnings – strangely, I might add – were ever more specific than that. What I found were a lot of amazing people who became dear friends.

And I found a sadness difficult to define, lingering just below the surface of day-to-day living. My Cree friend, now the mother of two dead children, had left Kashechewan to live in Moosonee years ago, which to her mind was moving to a big town, in part to escape that insidious sadness of her reserve.

It's the same sadness I can feel seeping from residential school survivors as I wander through this first annual gathering at The Forks in Winnipeg. Groups huddle in large tents, rain popping on the roofs. They sit in circles and take turns speaking about their experiences. Some are resigned and speak matter-of-factly, others in hiccups and sobs. There are very few dry eyes and my initial feeling that I'm eavesdropping on something I shouldn't be dissipates when someone invariably cracks a joke and smiles light up the circle.

My Cree friend didn't know then what she knows now, that this sadness I speak of, this hurting, isn't isolated only to Kash. This hurting has spread across the northern reserves and heavily

Indian communities of Canada. It spreads more easily than HINI, and it's been infecting northern communities for many years. It's deadlier than any epidemic since the smallpox and tuberculosis eras.

The oldest son of one of my dearest friends in the world, he's made something of himself. He's a young Moose Cree man with a brand-new wife and a brand-new career as an OPP officer. On my last visit to Moosonee, he told me something that continues to devastate me, that is so brutal as to sound unbelievable: Over a recent six-month period, there were at least a hundred suicide attempts by teens in Moosonee, and many others in the neighbouring reserve of Moose Factory. At last count, eight youths in Moosonee have been "successful." They've hanged themselves in closets, sometimes in trees behind the high school. It appears a death cult is taking root. More than one hundred attempts. Eight suicides. In a community of 2,500. Yes, it appears to be a death cult.

If this statistic darkened non-Indian towns across, say, British Columbia or Manitoba or Prince Edward Island, if this epidemic struck one of our communities, it would be national news, the media frenzy so saturated that Canadians would suffer empathy burnout within months. My quick Google search – "suicide rates on Canadian reserves" – pulls 36,000 results in 0.28 seconds. Within minutes, I can learn that since at least the year 2000, many experts have declared that the northern reserves of our country are the suicide capitals of the world. The statistics on these pages, I think, quickly stun, then numb us. And the reasons why our aboriginal youth are strangling themselves in closets, are shooting themselves in the head, are drowning themselves in icy rivers? A few more minutes of keyboard tapping on Google and it becomes so obvious: miserable socioeconomic conditions, psychobiological tendencies, the post-traumatic stress of a culture's destruction.

And what can even begin to stem the tide of brutal loss? The one and only family services centre in Moosonee, Payukotayno, which serves all of the 14,000 Cree of the Ontario side of James Bay, almost had to close its doors in December 2009, not long after the deaths of my good friend's children. That was due to a severe lack of government funding. It's expensive to try and furnish these services in such remote areas. The experts agree, though, that it's vital. I've been told of fourteen youth suicides on the west coast of James Bay in 2009. One in a thousand Indian youth committed suicide last year. The Canadian average, I'm told, is one in one hundred thousand. Suicide rates on the west coast of James Bay are one hundred times higher than the Canadian average in 2009. And the only family services facility for the west coast of James Bay came within inches of closing its doors last year due to a lack of funding.

But let me be clear that for each story of loss there is a story of accomplishment, of perseverance. Here's one: While wandering around The Forks last June, I ran into a young man, Patrick Etherington Jr. from Moosonee, a young man I've known since he was a boy. In fact, for much of one year, I homeschooled him. After a brief catching-up, he told me something startling. Over a month before, he and his father, Patrick Sr., along with a few friends, had taken a train from Moosonee to Cochrane and then begun walking. They had walked over sixteen hundred kilometres in just over thirty days in order to get here for this first annual gathering.

Along the way, they had talked to strangers, explaining that they were walking for the people, that this was their own little way of helping to close the door first opened with the founding of the residential schools in Canada 150 years ago.

Patrick Sr. is a man I've held in great regard for fifteen years. When I lived in Moosonee so long ago and became close with the Etherington family, Patrick Sr. shared with me some very tough, shocking stories of his years at St. Anne's in Fort Albany, one of Ontario's most infamous residential schools. And now, here he was walking with four young people across a substantial part of Canada because he understands that the epidemic I speak of is contagious, and one way to protect your children is to engage with them in as direct a way as you can. What better way than to spend more than a month walking and talking and laughing and telling stories and sharing the joys and pain of such an adventure?

Six more Truth and Reconciliation events are planned across Canada over the next five years, six more chances for people to come together and share stories and discuss remedies and keep straining to push that door shut.

What I'm convinced of is this: the simple act of taking that first step on the highway with your father and best friends beside you, the words you exchange as you share of yourself and learn of others, the tension of the fast-moving river through your paddle, the radiant heat in the moose's ribcage as you reach your arm to cut out its heart, the sound of Canada geese honking as they stretch their necks for the south, the tug of the pickerel as it takes your hook, the sickening grind of the outboard's prop as it touches submerged river rock, it's these simple experiences that contain medicine strong enough to start some healing, to start closing that door.

Sometimes I catch myself dreaming about my Cree friend's two children. In my dream they're still alive, and they're out in the bush, paddling the Moose River together, sun on their shoulders and good power in their stroke. They're paddling north, I think, home to Moosonee. And although I can't see her, I know that their mother stands on the shore by town, waiting patiently for them to come into sight.

KAREN CONNELLY

How to Swim in a Sea of Shit

A famous writer wrote the last bit of the title you've just read and I've always wanted to quote him. When I first discovered the correspondence between Gustave Flaubert and Ivan Turgenev fifteen years ago, I laughed aloud at several lines. Every year or two, as the age-gap closes between myself and the writers when they wrote these letters, I flip through the book and laugh some more.

In Paris, on November 8, 1872, Turgenev laments sympathetically: "[It's] the boredom and disgust with all human activity; it's nothing to do with politics, which after all is no more than a game; it's the sadness of one's fiftieth year. And that's why I admire Mme Sand: such serenity, such simplicity, such an interest in everything, such goodness! If for that one has to be a bit over idealistic, democratic or even evangelising – by God! – let's put up with such excesses. . . ."

From Croisset, on November 13, Flaubert responds:

> Thank you for your encouragement! But alas, I fear that my sickness is incurable. Apart from personal sources of grief, . . . *the state of society is crushing me.* It may be stupid. But there you are. I am overwhelmed by public Stupidity. Since 1870, I've been a patriot. Seeing my country die has made me realize that I love it. Prussia may dismantle her guns. We don't need her to bring about our demise.

The bourgeoisie is so stunned that it no longer even has the instinct of self-preservation; and what will follow will be worse! . . . I feel a wave of relentless Barbarism, rising up from below the ground. I hope to be dead before all is swept away. But in the meantime, it is no joke. Never have affairs of the mind counted for less. Never have hatred of everything that is great, contempt for all that is beautiful, abhorrence for literature been so manifest.

I have always tried to live in an ivory tower; but a sea of shit is beating up against its walls, it's enough to bring it down. It's not a question of politics, but of the *mentality* prevalent in France. . . . I can no longer talk with anyone without getting angry; and all the contemporary writing I read makes me wild. A fine state of affairs! – all of which doesn't stop me planning a book in which I shall try to spit out my rancour. I am not admitting defeat as you see. If I didn't work there would be nothing for it but to throw myself in to the river with a stone round my neck. . . .

. . . [In December] I hope to pay you a visit. In the meantime, try to bear your gout, poor dear friend; and believe that I love you.

Must I say more? Isn't it enough, really, to quote these two?

Alas, no. One hundred and thirty-five years later, the metaphorical sea of shit (accompanied by a literal ocean full of oil, thanks to BP) is more expansive and oppressive than ever. To make matters worse, today's humble writer has no ivory tower. We are plugged in, connected, blasted with the same tidal wave of crap that everyone else has to deal with. The last straw was the bloody iPad. I just figured out how to use my cellphone. The BlackBerry? The iPhone? Do I want to write and read emails *all the time?* No, I do not. I am inundated with them, suffocating in apps, entangled in online petitions and Facebook, not waving but drowning in a mass of language from which there is no escape. *There is no escape.* If I go for three days without checking email, people consider calling 911 or think I despise them. Or choose someone else to do the job. The world has become fast and full of appointments, while the writer remains slow, best suited to ambling, fermentation, and unscheduled adventures into unexpected territory.

How nice it would have been to be Turgenev, even with the gout, and receive wonderful letters from Flaubert. I remember letters. I used to write them, five-, ten-, twenty-page letters, hundreds of them over a twenty-year period. Another age, obviously. I wish people would stop calling me a young writer. I wrote *letters*. On paper. With a pen. Daily. Ergo, I cannot be a young writer. I am a relic! Ah, Turgenev, despite your unhappiness in love – something you shared with your French friend – how pleasant to settle down daily to work on your latest book, with a few servants around to bring in your lunch and your afternoon coffee.

What would it be like to know that I was working in a fresh, elastic, powerful form of literature, *le grand roman*, the Novel? Instead of being where I presently am, harried by a hundred emails at the end of an era, wondering what literature will look like when I enter my fifties, with publishers severely diminished and book reviews a thing of the distant past. I will be too old to do acrobatics or walk a tightrope for any book launch I might have in my fifties. Perhaps book launches won't exist in a decade – or books. There will be (and already are) booksellers who print out certain texts on demand, or source out-of-print editions from enormous underground warehouses full of rodent poison to protect the aging and bizarrely ephemeral stock. We will be able to order any book we want on the iPad for a dollar, or probably less, seeing as Apple is already giving away several thousand of them for free.

Hmm. With thoughts like these, why the fuck do I want to write another novel?

I grew up under the impression that books mattered deeply. I grew up *believing* that the Novel was a powerful act of creation; that books could change people's lives; that a brilliant novel, especially if it was brave enough to wade into politics, could constitute a kind of action, be a form of intervention, like the writings of Voltaire, Zola, Rizal, Camus. Or, for that matter, Mary Wollstonecraft, Margaret Fuller, Betty Friedan, Audre Lorde, Susan Griffin. Both distant and recent past are rich with the brave works and the brave acts of writers whose words influenced not only the reading public but also the political forces of their times. I believed in all of them, growing up.

I admit there was some transference going on. I was raised as a fundamentalist Christian, so my original sense of words was, well, you know, The Word. The Most Important Book came directly from Him. When I broke up with Him in puberty, I had to put all that devotion somewhere. I poured it into books and writers.

But in our post-industrial, language-saturated, compassion-fatigued world, am I out of my mind to still believe that the creation and artifact of the novel still matter? And am I a traitor to the cause when I sometimes doubt the relevance of both novel and novelist? What loaded questions! And what a load to place on the venerable Novel's old back, not to mention the writer's, who already has enough chiropractic and massage therapy bills after sitting at a computer five, six, eight, ten hours a day.

Despite all that onerous sitting (and emailing), the novelist of today rarely possesses the kind of transformative power I'm talking about, either in the act of creating or in the resonance his or her work has in the wider world. Sometimes this is not the novelist's fault. The writer spends two years, or four, or ten, walking back and forth on live coals in the service of the Important Novel, the big truth-telling novel. Finally the Novel is published – given over to the world, a gift, even an act of witness, or a call to arms. Not that many writers bother trying to write this kind of book; irony or poetics usually get in the way.

Anyway, the newborn book rises up on the media wave. There is a squall of interviews, a flurry of reviews, opinions. Then the wave is cresting, now it curls over, the beloved novel carried with it – *mais non!* – the wave topples into a deep dark trough, and the novel sinks into . . . the sea of shit.

Not even Flaubert could have imagined it. This is a new sea, never before experienced in the history of human culture. The beloved book – repository of wisdom, experience, craft – is sucked down into a competitive whirlpool of mass media: the iPad, movies, DVDs for sale and rent, advertising (images with their demands and their promises), video game obsessions, cellphone addictions, 24-hour news channels, lifestyle shows, reality TV, and that great lethal octopus the Internet, that sucks in human minds and human hours, wraps powerful tentacles around the imagination, and squeezes it dry, paradoxically, by pumping it full of too much information.

If you disbelieve the power of these new media, then you are either a technophobe or more out of touch than I am. Or you are without teenage sons and daughters. And if you think I describe only a sad North American mania, think again. The last time I was in Paris, a couple of years ago, I read an article that made me feel *je ne sais quoi*: Sick to my stomach? Depressed? As furious as Flaubert? A major poll of *lycées* across the country asked students to suggest the most desirable and important professions. How did the young citizens of the republic answer? *Rock star, movie star, TV personality*. Doctors and writers didn't even make it into the top five. *Tant pis*.

In one hundred years, we will all be dead. Will our children's children, or their children, read books in the next century? If they are *already* not reading them, if they are *already* losing or have lost the habit of mind that makes ample space and time for the Novel, how can the form be a force that influences the world of the real and touches people's minds?

I do not know.

This lack of knowing, this growing hesitation to judge, is partly what makes me a writer. I write *in order* to know, to learn, to not only experience my own life more deeply, but to enter imaginatively into the lives of others. To be uncertain about my power as a writer is perhaps a willed state. If I knew in advance that my work was going to create a certain effect, I would be a rock star. Or a TV personality. Not an artist.

To *not* know is also a way to hold on to the possibility that, against all the evidence to the contrary, it is important that I write another novel. Any other book, for that matter, in any genre. And this essay. Important not just to myself but to this plant-animal-human world. I say plant-animal-human world because, as we continue to desecrate the planet, to destroy land and poison water, and perhaps to drive our own and definitely other species to extinction, it will become a writerly responsibility to bear witness to that violence. Not enough of us are doing this yet, but I believe we will. I believe we will have no choice. Paradoxically, the novel will be reinvigorated by destruction. And it will cease to be a territory reserved for human life.

See? This archaic fundamentalism is hard to get rid of. In a way, as already mentioned, I can trace it all back to God. I can't give up the faith. I cannot help believing in the Novel, poor old thing. The humble bound book, a technology so slow that it doesn't even move. Nor possess a single megabyte. But it is the longest memory we have. I cannot help imagining that the Novel will continue to grow and respond to the contortions of the future, and that people will respond to it, in ways we cannot know. It is a force for truth – the subjective, vital, complex truth of the individual, the truth that changes clothes, the truth with two eyes, one brown, one blue, the embodied truth of narrative. It is not just *this happened, then this, then this happened after that*, but narrative as the essence of human experience. This distillation produces an alchemic liquid similar to blood: that which is invisible but flows everywhere under and even through the surface, enlivening the body of human history, by revealing it to be more than a chronicle of wars and great men and their empires. The Novel is the ultimate alternative history of the world.

That is why I have ignored email and the Internet long enough to write and, as importantly – perhaps more importantly – to read. To read and read books, more books, beautiful books that smell of old paper and sometimes mildew and ink. Crisp new strangely confident books. I *know* that a good novel can change a life. Books changed *my* life. But as importantly, they have given me so much *pleasure*. Something happens when the right pages are opened at the right time; that invisible liquid lifts, flows up off the page and enters the reader's mind and heart.

Let's face it, reading is the wisest form of fundamentalism. It is late. The house is quiet. You are lying in bed in a pool of light with a delicious book. (It is, I can assure you, better than lying in bed with the novelist.) To be alone with a good book! To stem the tide of shit and take back your time and hide yourself away to read! To feel what you would not feel at all, if you were not reading. To travel so far. Late night passes into early morning as written people and ideas and emotions soak into you. Not just your mind. Forget that. This is a bodily experience. Such reading is deeply *lustful*. It is private, between ourselves and the universe of the novel, which is the universe of physics: random possibility, chances, hunches, mystery. You are reading this now because you, too, have had such affairs with books. We cannot do without them.

So, over and over again, despite being repeatedly overwhelmed by public Stupidity, I seduce myself through reading. And the reading convinces me that, by extension, what I write and publish does matter, must be wielded as a tool for truthtelling, celebrating, challenging.

Ten years ago, I was struggling to write a novel about a Burmese man in a Burmese prison, sentenced to solitary confinement. I was writing outside of my culture, my sex, my own formative experiences. I wept every day for a few years. During that time, I had the chance to ask the great Indonesian writer Pramoedya Ananta Toer – a quiet, brave man who spent years in prison for having written his novels – if he had any advice for me. He sat thinking for a while. Then he took a drag on his clove-scented cigarette, exhaled, and announced: "Be daring."

Pramoedya was right. His advice worked. *Be daring* is still my slogan.

I've taken my most profound lessons from writers in countries where writing words is an essential act of courage. There are so many places where telling the unofficial truth – by critiquing governments who abuse their citizenry, by recording the narratives of the silenced and oppressed – is galvanizing, and dangerous, a physical act of bravery, such an assertion of power that the dictators and the tyrants continue to arrest, torture, imprison, and kill writers.

Those writers are creating – when they can, when they survive – a literature of action, even if it is written on toilet paper or scratched onto plastic bags. Or, tapped into a computer to appear instantaneously on other computer screens thousands of miles away. Despite all my bitching about the Internet, it is a marvel, a miracle for writers in places where paper publication is too dangerous or impossible. Even if these writers' words are read only by a few, by those who smuggle texts out of a prison or out of a country, even if no one reads them because the manuscript is confiscated, destroyed, it is still a triumph. A writer wrote her words, his words. The human hand and mind created, acted, summoned up the ghosts not only of famous humanist writers but the spirits of many others, not famous, some without names, the writers in the mass graves, the men and women who died in Argentina's Dirty War and Pinochet's Chile and Soviet Russia and South Africa and Cambodia and the death camps of the Second World War. The list of imprisoned and murdered voices is long, and grows longer each day, and cries out for one act: that we read it.

That we still that churning sea and hear the other voices: from Mexico. Ethiopia. The Congo. Kazahkstan. Iran. Turkey. China. Algeria. The "new" Russia.

If we want to know or to remember what a literature of action is, we must turn our heads and our hearts to those countries and their writers. They make my doubts and worries about the sea of media-shit seem small, another kind of luxury. Those writers remind us all of our real power, especially when the state of society is crushing us. Or when we feel fearful of the latest wave of barbarism. Or convinced that affairs of the mind have never counted for less.

They remind me of lines I read by Camus when I was in my teens and believed so hard in the power of words. Why not believe in it still, without bitter irony or my usual griping? Half a century ago, he exhorted writers to refuse to lie about what we know and to resist oppression, whatever form it takes.

In other words, be courageous. As Pramoedya said, be daring.

DENISE CHONG

Across the Divide and Back

Fifteen-year-old Lu Decheng clashed with his father yet again. It was their worst disagreement yet, this time over his refusal to enroll in high school. His father considered Decheng's disregard for schooling short-sighted, but the boy was adamant that he would not continue beyond junior high; he had lacklustre marks and, with the exception of the time in middle school when he and his classmates spent their days making bricks to build teachers' dormitories – as was common during the Cultural Revolution, when physical labour replaced learning in the classroom – he found no joy in his schoolwork. Besides, he had no ambition to go to university, where you had to study not what you enjoyed or were good at, but what the state decided you would study. While his father considered his decision to quit school shortsighted, for Lu Decheng being branded uneducated would turn out, years later, to be a helping hand of fate. Not in the wider world, but rather, in a most cruel environment – the Chinese prison system.

In imagining his future, the young Decheng considered he had two qualities beyond a record of education working in his favour. One was his curiosity about mechanical things (for example, the first thing he did when he got his hands on a coveted transistor radio was take a screwdriver to the back of it so that he could look inside). The other was his athleticism. Several times, he'd been Sports Commissar at school. Down at the river's edge, where more quotidian contests made one's reputation, no challenger – grown men included – could yet throw a stone, aimed at the opposite bank, farther than him.

In the backwater town of Liuyang, in Hunan province in southern China, other than at the firecracker factories where few wanted to work because of accidents that routinely killed or maimed workers, employment prospects were grim. Even so, to come by a job at any other state enterprise took connections. Decheng passed idle days with friends on the riverbank or playing mahjong. Worried sick that his son would go the way of other jobless and malcontent youth and turn into a *liumang* – a hooligan who courts the antagonism of local police – Decheng's father, a driver at the long-distance bus company in town, pulled rank. He got Decheng a position in the garage as an apprentice mechanic, and considered his worries to be over, now that the promise of the "iron rice bowl," the Communist Party's pledge to workers in socialist China of wages and dormitory housing for life, belonged to his son as well. When, a few short years later, his son had to support a wife and child himself, Decheng's father might have once again thought his progeny had reason to be grateful to the state and content about his future.

But a decade after their showdown over Decheng's education, and amid growing uncertainty in the country about how Beijing's economic reforms would play out, the elder Lu's worst nightmare about his rebellious son seemed to have come true.

—

On May 23, 1989, in the sixth week of the student-led, pro-democracy protests in Tiananmen Square in Beijing and on the fourth day of martial law in the capital, police detained three men from Liuyang: Lu Decheng, now a mechanic, and Yu

Zhijian, a primary school teacher, both aged twenty-five; and Yu
Dongyue (unrelated), an arts editor for the *Liuyang Daily*, aged
nineteen. That afternoon, the three had positioned themselves in
front of the portrait of Chairman Mao that hangs above the central archway into the Forbidden City. On either side of the archway, they hurriedly hung two handwritten scrolls:

> Five thousand years of dictatorship will cease at this point!
> The cult of personality worship will vanish from this point onward!

They retreated a few steps, then lobbed some thirty paint-
filled eggs at the iconic image of Mao. What happened next was
something they had never imagined when they conceived of
their protest: the student leaders turned them over to police.

That evening, people all over China gathered in front of
televisions for the daily update on the students' occupation of
the square. An entire nation gasped at the stained visage of the
Chairman. When Decheng's father saw that one of the three
culprits was none other than his own son, he nearly fainted dead.
Bewildered at why his son would do such a thing, the bus driver
simpered plaintively to his wife, Decheng's stepmother: "Things
are fine in China. Life is okay. What does Decheng have to complain about?"

Facing interrogators from the national security ministry,
Decheng hoped that the government might take a benign atti-
tude to what he and his two friends had done. His contention
that they had come to Beijing to support the students would have
been verified by what interrogators would surely have found in
Dongyue's backpack: photographs taken using a camera he'd
borrowed from his newspaper to record their trip and, in his and
Zhijian's handwriting, texts of pro-democracy slogans and
speeches and a proclamation, signed by all three men, calling on

Beijingers to reject martial law. After their failure to get the students to broadcast the proclamation in the square, their purpose in marring the portrait, Decheng explained, was to reinvigorate the student movement.

Decheng's interrogators dashed his hopes early on that leniency was in the cards. "You've been a reactionary right from the beginning!" Decheng knew that the file held on him by the state was not unblemished. In his early days as an apprentice mechanic, he'd played a foolish prank. Irked by the braggardly ways of a fellow apprentice, he'd taken the man's thermos stored by his bunk, emptied it of hot water, and put in an agricultural pesticide that smelled of manure. Though no harm came to the man, the management of the bus station called in a Party official who declared he would find the "class enemy" responsible. Decheng confessed and police punished him with two months in the town's detention centre.

But to Decheng's surprise, his interrogators had something else in mind, reaching back to when he was but a boy of thirteen. "You didn't cry at the memorial for Chairman Mao!"

Decheng had entirely forgotten that incident.

Before his sixth-grade class had attended the memorial in town, one of thousands held all over China to conclude nine days of official mourning for Mao, his teacher had lectured the students on the depth of the grief he expected them to display: "It's as if your own parent has died." During the three-hour service, the teacher repeatedly glared at Decheng as if to say, "Cry!" He'd glared right back, thinking the behaviour of his classmates, who loudly sniffled and blew their noses on cue, to be downright silly. At the time, Decheng had dismissed the run-in with his teacher as trivial; obviously his teacher had not.

The prison where Decheng was being held soon grew crowded with protestors detained in the wake of the brutal crackdown on June 4, when the regime sent in troops and tanks to clear students from Tiananmen Square. One morning, guards removed a cellmate who'd thrown a Molotov cocktail at a tank. A short while later, they returned with a cardboard box to collect the executed prisoner's belongings. Decheng grew rattled, convinced that at any time, even the dead of night, soldiers would drag him away to be shot. Worse than the bullet to the back of the head, he feared becoming one of the disappeared, whose fate is unknown – there would be no formal record of him in the judicial process, and no body returned to his family to confirm his death.

Mindful that the stained image of Mao had been seen not only in China but televised around the world, the Beijing government decided to make a public lesson of the three from Liuyang. In mid-June, the security ministry announced the formal arrest of the trio on charges of counterrevolutionary propaganda and incitement, counterrevolutionary sabotage, writing reactionary slogans, and counterrevolutionary destruction of state property. One month later, the high court tried the three together, in a closed proceeding. The trial lasted three hours. The crimes carried the death penalty, but the court would spare all three: Decheng was sentenced to sixteen years; the journalist, Yu Dongyue, to twenty years; and the teacher, Yu Zhijian, to life in prison.

———

As winter approached, Beijing emptied its crowded jails of socalled 1989 inmates and transferred them to "reform through labour" prisons in their home provinces. The trio from Liuyang, now reunited, learned that the interrogation and incarceration of the two Yus had been particularly harsh, and Decheng's had been, by comparison, lenient.

In their new prison, where inmates toiled making automotive parts, this pattern continued. The two Yus decided to exploit this. So that Decheng could remain the voice of the three should they come to a dire end, Zhijian and Dongyue kept him on the sidelines while they led a revolt against a group of bullying prisoners. Their efforts succeeded and the fame of the two spread in the prison. Inmates looked to the leadership of the charismatic Yu Zhijian, who impressed with his love of literature, from Chinese classics like Tang dynasty poems and *Dream of the Red Chamber* to the works of Western literary figures like Percy Shelley and Ernest Hemingway. The prisoners lined up to have their portraits sketched by the brilliant Yu Dongyue, who had been a child protégé of a painter of national renown, and who had graduated from university at seventeen. The authorities responded to this new popularity by arranging a transfer of the two Yus to different prisons.

Zhijian and Dongyue's parting gifts for Decheng reminded him of happier days in Liuyang, when he would sit listening to the wide-ranging conversations of the two, awed by their intellects. *They're so far ahead of me*, he'd tell himself, *I can't even see the back of them.* Zhijian wrote out a reading list for him of one hundred titles, mostly works of Western literature and philosophy. Dongyue composed a poem – his choice of words limited lest authorities deem his poem subversive:

> The globe is very small
> but mankind is great
> the wind of humanity blows across the sweet-scented grasslands
> allowing all dreams to thrive.

Decheng had hardly been separated from his friends when he heard through the prison grapevine that they had suffered severe beatings and been placed in solitary confinement. In that dank dog cave of solitary, one either went mad or wasted away on reduced rations for "non-labouring" prisoners. Decheng did not want to believe what else he'd heard, that guards had tortured Dongyue, that they had dented his skull in the front and back, that he'd gone "crazy in the head." Sympathetic guards warned Decheng that even minor provocations would offend authorities – "Yours is the same political case!"

Increasingly, Decheng realized that the regime regarded him, the backward and uneducated one who had gone only as far as junior high school, as a lesser threat. Undeniably, his reading and writing skills were poor, his Mandarin heavily accented, and his vocabulary limited.

In hindsight, Decheng saw that his limited formal schooling, as compared to the two Yus, may have very nearly severed his case from theirs and exposed him to a summary display of justice, as happened with the cellmate who'd thrown the Molotov cocktail. In the early days of his incarceration in Beijing, other cellmates, petty criminals all, had taken it upon themselves to coach him on how to outwit investigators. They had urged him to chat them up, to portray his act as that of a hooligan: "Tell them what you did had nothing to do with politics." The normally taciturn Decheng had been seized with fear: Was this a set-up? A plan of the government to depict him as a repeat offender, a common criminal whose acts of hooliganism, this time, had gone too far?

Decheng saw that in rejecting his cellmates' advice and remaining steadfast before his interrogators and the court about the desire for democratic change in China that had led him and his friends to Beijing in the first place, he'd preserved his own right to a political life. He decided to use his time in prison to do as the two Yus had always encouraged him – to educate himself. In addition, he was motivated to become a more worthy husband for his wife, who was waiting for him on the outside.

Decheng began at the most basic level, methodically working his way through a dictionary. He improved his vocabulary one word at a time, and he built Chinese characters stroke by stroke. He worked on his penmanship, turning his printing into a more cursive style. He improved his literacy by reading newspapers.

Ironically, Decheng's jailers remained blind to his self-education. They persisted in targeting him as uneducated, unformed intellectually, and therefore pliable. Their tactics to make him recant his political beliefs included granting him privileges rarely accorded common criminals, much less a political prisoner. To up the pressure, using the familiar tactic of "attacking from all sides," authorities granted Decheng one week's leave to return home to be with his wife and young daughter. Back in Liuyang, Decheng found out that what he'd heard in prison was true, that guards had beaten his friend Dongyue into a precarious mental state. When the week was over, authorities offered Decheng a sentence reduction from sixteen to fourteen years. Well aware that a prisoner's sentence could just as easily be extended – and he was only three years into his – he rejected the offer. Angered, officials revoked his privileges.

If, to his wife, Decheng's decision appeared to be a choice of prison over her and freedom, Decheng remained certain that he and his friends had a better chance of surviving their time in prison if they continued to stand in solidarity with one another. As for his wife, he was certain that her resolve was as strong as his, that his imprisonment was but another inhumanity they could endure. They'd already been through so much, having prevailed in their love affair – first as teenage lovers, then marrying and starting a family – despite the state's opposition. The encouragement Decheng needed to stay strong came in the form of a note from Zhijian. Concealed in the pages of a book on the Communist perspective on the collapse of the Soviet bloc after the fall of the Berlin Wall, the note, written in Zhijian's familiar handwriting, read: *As old as I am, I am old.*

Decheng interpreted his friend's words to mean, *I too know about our friend, Dongyue, but I'm still the same old me.* Knowing it was risky for the note to be found in his possession, he folded it as small as possible, and the next time his wife visited, when the guards were looking the other way, he tossed it across the divide to her.

—

In an accomplishment that would be extraordinary even for an academic, much less an uneducated prisoner, Decheng dedicated himself to studying in its entirety a tenth-century work written by a Confucian scholar. Entitled *Comprehensive Mirror to Aid in Government,* the four-volume set totalled more than four thousand pages. For the past thousand years, China's governing elite, Mao included, would have consulted its record of events and figures spanning fifteen centuries of dynastic history, using it as a guide to methods and strategies of governing. When Decheng went to pay for his purchase at the remaindered books sale held at the prison, the clerk snorted her contempt at his choice. Other prisoners snapped up books on marketing, economics, and business. Back in his cell, Decheng studied the volumes, intent on probing the failings and worst excesses of Chinese leadership throughout history. His fellow prisoners, who preferred to spend their free time playing cards or making deals for contraband, took one look at the classical text that he was poring over and shook their heads. "You're from another planet," said one.

Six years into his prison term, Decheng's wife divorced him and remarried. Devastated, Decheng fell into a deep depression. He contemplated making a dash for the gate so that guards would shoot him dead, or throwing himself into the path of an oncoming delivery truck. He pulled himself out of despair through introspection. He applied what he had learned from his texts to re-examining his own conduct. Determined to keep his own humanity intact, he resolved that when he was again a free man, he would ask his ex-wife to divorce her husband and re-marry him. Remarriage, he believed, would undo all the misfortunes that the state had brought on the two of them.

In his ninth year in prison, authorities gave Lu Decheng one day's notice that he was to be released. He gave away most of his clothing and his bed quilt and filled the two plastic zipper bags that his father had brought for his belongings with only the books that he'd collected in prison. Decheng's father reproached him. "I can't believe it. You had things that could still be put to good use and you bring out completely useless stuff!"

Decheng arrived back in Liuyang and proposed remarriage to his ex-wife. Wavering, she admitted to still having strong feelings for him. Finally, she said no, choosing to stay in what she confessed was an unhappy marriage. She admonished her ex-husband: "You should not care so much about politics because you can never win." Decheng took solace in the fact that he had never thrown his lot in with his oppressors, inside or outside prison. As one of the conditions of the divorce settlement with his wife, Decheng retrieved the letters and papers that she had held in safekeeping for him while he was in prison.

In the Chinese system of prisoner reform, the state's purpose is to remake a criminal into "a new socialist man." The early release of Lu Decheng had little, if anything, to do with authorities having "corrected" his "wrong thinking." In paroling some high-profile Tiananmen Square prisoners, Beijing sought to garner support from the West for its bid to host the 2000 Summer Olympic Games. The city of Beijing would lose by one vote to Sydney, but it remained in the running for the 2008 Games. In the year 2000, Beijing released Yu Zhijian early, after he'd served eleven years of his life sentence. Yu Dongyue's release came in 2006, after he'd served seventeen years. By the time Beijing hosted the world for the Olympic Games of 2008, the three men from Liuyang had all since fled to the West: the two Yus to the United States, and Decheng to Canada. Still in Decheng's possession is the cryptic note of encouragement that he received from Zhijian: *As old as I am, I am old.*

ALAIN DE BOTTON

On Writing

A young student once wrote to the French novelist André Gide to ask him whether he should try to become a writer. "Only if you have to," answered Gide, neatly summing up the best advice any writer can give a prospective recruit. The job clearly makes no sense from any practical point of view. It only intermittently satisfies ordinary longings for security and status. Trying to tie writing talent to a mortgage is akin to connecting a bicycle to the national power grid. So if one's to become a writer, it clearly has to be from a motive other than the search for money or status. It has to be because of the deep fulfilment that some people feel in arranging thoughts and experiences on the page.

I wrote my first book at the age of eight. It was the diary of my summer holiday, spent in the Normandy seaside resort of Houlgate with my parents, dog, and sister. "Yestday nothing much happend. Today the wether is lovely. We went swiming for the hole day. We had salad for lunch. We had a trout for diner. After diner we saw a film about a man that found gold in Peru," reads a typical entry headed "Wendsay 23 of August, 1978" (not dyslexia, just learning English). If the book is unreadable, it's because, despite the best intentions and neat handwriting, the author is unable to capture much of what is actually happening. There is a list of facts, an account of the trout, and a weather report, but life has slipped out of the picture. It's like watching a home video in which you're shown only the feet or the clouds, and wonder, bemused, what might be going on at head level.

The desire to record experience never left me, but as I matured, my technical skills slowly improved. I learnt that wanting to say something very badly doesn't always mean that one has managed to do so. Writing is about capturing experience. Behind the desire to write is a wish to gain mastery over beautiful as well as painful feelings. Inspiration comes in many forms: a fine weathered brick wall, a humiliation, a painting, a face glimpsed in the street. For me, the finest books are those in which an author has put his or her finger on emotions which we recognize as our own, but which we could not have formulated on our own. We have a feeling that the author knows us – perhaps better than we know ourselves. I aspire to write books that offer a feeling of recognition, and ultimately, of friendship.

The task isn't easy. The writer's life is suffused with anxiety. In a highly productive, entrepreneurial age, it seems odd, even insane, to be locked away in a room, trying to hammer words into their correct places. I often have intense longings to go to an office – in order to share the burdens of my work with other people, as workers in offices can. Currently, I am overwhelmed by a desire to become an architect. I have always been marked by how much the buildings we inhabit shape us and I would love the chance to improve (in my eyes) the environment around me. I have a running dialogue with myself about what is right and wrong with the buildings I pass daily. I admire the ability of architects to be artists and at the same time, practical people of the world, whose visions translate into a solid mass. I don't want to only interpret the world, I also want to change it, and there are days when I am painfully struck by what a modest object a book is as an instrument with which to make a difference, compared, that is, to the power of a government, a university, or a business.

I worry constantly about my future. Few writers are able to turn out a decent book a year – three or four years is more typically necessary, and even this rate is unlikely to go on over an entire working life. The idea of a Muse may be fanciful and politically incorrect, but the lady evokes well enough the insecurity of the hold most writers have on their creative faculties. An element of chance lurks behind the birth of masterpieces, which aggravates financial anxieties: it is one thing to be poor and convinced of the worth of one's work, far harder to combine poverty with an awareness that a book isn't going well.

As for where I write, it seems that my work is always best done in places where it isn't supposed to happen. At a desk, in front of a computer, my mind goes blank, but as soon as I take off (to the supermarket, to Australia), inspiration strikes. Journeys are the midwives of books. Few places are more conducive to the internal conversation that is writing than a moving plane, ship, or train. There is an almost quaint correlation between what is in front of my eyes and the thoughts I am able to have in my head: large thoughts at times requiring large views, new thoughts, new places. Introspective reflections which are liable to stall are helped along by the flow of the landscape. The mind may be reluctant to think properly when thinking is all it is supposed to do. The task can be as paralyzing as having to tell a joke or mimic an accent on demand. Thinking improves when parts of the mind are given other tasks, are charged with listening to music or following a line of trees.

Of all modes of transport, the train is perhaps the best aid to writing: the views have none of the potential monotony of those on a ship or plane, and they move fast enough for me not to get exasperated but slowly enough to allow me to identify objects. They offer me brief, inspiring glimpses into private domains, letting me see a woman at the moment when she takes a cup from a shelf in her kitchen, before carrying me on to a patio where a man is sleeping, and then to a park where a child is catching a ball thrown by a figure I can't see. Out of such fine filaments, books are born.

Hotel rooms offer a similar opportunity to escape my habits of mind. Lying in bed in a hotel, the room quiet except for the occasional swooshing of an elevator in the innards of the building, I can reflect on, and write about, things from a height I could not have reached in the midst of everyday business, subtly assisted in this by the unfamiliar world around me: by the small wrapped soaps on the edge of the basin, by the gallery of minia-ture bottles in the mini-bar, by the room-service menu with its promises of all-night dining, and by the view onto an unknown city stirring silently twenty-five floors below us.

Hotel notepads can be the recipients of unexpectedly in-tense, revelatory thoughts, taken down in the early hours while the breakfast menu ("to be hung outside before 3 a.m.") lies un-attended on the floor. I began my last book in a Sydney hotel room on a jetlagged night in 2004. I'm hoping that the Muse might knock at the door on this visit, too.

GORD DOWNIE

Let It Ride

We were to talk and sing, in front of a crowd, with the CBC's
Laurie Brown along in case it went nowhere. The whole thing
was to be taped for broadcast later on the radio. I didn't know why
I got picked. They told me it was Gordon Lightfoot who picked
me and that was like winning an Olympic gold medal. Then
Gordon told me it wasn't him, it was Sylvia Tyson. That was like
having the medal taken away. Such is the life of the performer.

And yet I was there. Thank you, Sylvia Tyson.

―

I had questions for Gordon Lightfoot, a lot of questions, questions I had prepared on behalf of all the songwriters out there,
lots of things to be off-the-cuff about. I wrote and wrote. I listened and listened. I made lists with headings like:

Gordon Lightfoot. Songwriting. Why?
Songwriting: How?
Whither Songwriting?
Songwriting. Who cares?
Why?
To mourn, Gord? To honour? To provoke?

―

Laurie Brown pulled me aside before the show and said, "I will consider this evening a failure if I do too much of the talking." I reacted as if I'd never heard the word "failure" before. I reacted as if I was being sworn at in another language. "Failure?"

I didn't know how it was going to go, what kind of night it would be. I only knew that for an evening to be great, something has to happen. And I knew that I would never – ever – fuck with Gordon Lightfoot. My biggest question – and I didn't know if I'd get a chance to ask it was simply, *Why?* A song. Why?

Sure, there are other obvious questions, ones that song-writers probably feel more comfortable answering. But *What is songwriting?* can get technical or sentimental or boring. *How do you write a song?* can be Googled. No, the question I wanted to ask is, *Why?* Why write a song? There is no *demand* for it, for what you do. No one *requires* a song. Or do they?

—

I had all these questions to ask. I was going to talk to Gordon Lightfoot. I had Whitman and Carver and Bellow at the ready. I would make Gordon Lightfoot feel comfortable and that would take my mind off how uncomfortable I was. We would talk easily and amiably. We would entertain. We would have chemistry. I would express my best feelings, perfectly. This was my plan.

I would ask him why he had decided to stop writing songs. I would try to convince him why he couldn't.

—

So the show began. Sylvia Tyson walked out and gave the George Weston Recital Hall its requisite churchy thanks. "And now our host, Laurie Brown." Laurie put everyone at ease. She introduced us as "Misters." Gord Lightfoot and I walked out together. The place was amped.

We sat down and I don't remember much of the small talk. Laurie started in: "Songwriter first?"

Lightfoot said, "Entertainer. Performer . . . I just do shows now."

I answered something and watched myself answering it. Something like, "Now, as when we started, as when we're finished, entirely . . . an entertainer." Guh! I kicked myself under the table. There was no table.

Laurie asked Lightfoot to start us off with a song. He walked over, picked up his guitar and stood in front of his long-time bandmates, who have been part of his band since the late sixties, Terry Clements on guitar, Rick Haynes on bass. Within microphone range, sounding a little unsure, he said, "All right."

And then, softly to himself, he said, "First on the list."

—

Lightfoot started into "Rainy Day People," from his 1975 record *Cold on the Shoulder:* "Rainy day people always seem to know when it's time to call."

As Gord played, I was a kid again. It was summer and it was raining outside. It was a Sunday. I was on my bed and I could hear this song coming from the clock radio in my sister's room. I think I knew that the DJ was trying to be "thematic," that the singer was describing a feeling, that memories are like occasions, that occasions are fleeting, temporary, like a dance to a song that is disappearing as it's happening. I think I knew all that.

—

Is that what songwriters are doing, Gord Lightfoot? I was phrasing a question in my mind as he played. *Are we merely serving our memories with a song, trying to grab into the swirl of private memory for a public remembering?*

Is it to be as Tess Gallagher said of Raymond Carver's poetry, "ample and grateful, to make room for those events and people closest to our hearts"? *Is this why you do it, Gordon?* I hoped I'd get a chance to ask this question, this way.

———

A big, big applause met the end of "Rainy Day People." Putting his guitar down, Gord came over and sat down, right next to me.

Here we go.

With a nudge from Laurie, I began. "Well, I've got the best seat in the house, obviously." I was pretty happy I came out with that first. "I'm just really thrilled to be here," I added. "First, I gotta say hello to Rick and Terry over there, they've been with Gord forever, as you all know . . ."

I didn't let the big applause find its own way out. I jumped in too quickly. I was nervous to get the first question over with, nervous because it was a question I hadn't planned to ask, a question I worried might risk too much self-aggrandizement in its set-up.

"Coming from a band, together a long time and staying together and being friends is a huge part of songwriting – it's like, 'If we're any good at all, it's because of that, probably.'" Internally, I reminded myself of my tendency to talk the way a frog hops. I stumbled along toward the actual question: "How important is your relationship with these guys – the long-time members of your long-time band – to your confidence, your development, your songwriting?"

Lightfoot, twinkly-eyed, said, "And they know the songs."

"That helps," I said over everyone's laughter.

"Yeah, they do, they know the songs," repeated Gordon. He talked about rehearsing and preparing for the upcoming tour, how he doesn't work much on the vocal. "I'm lucky that way," he said.

—

Then Laurie asked me to play my first song. I remember distinctly thinking, *Why do I have to play anything?*

I breathed in and out. In the audience, seemingly for the first time all night, there was silence. I thought it was the sound of everyone thinking, "Oh, God." I was feeling vulnerable; maybe there was one nervous laugh somewhere. I started.

"This is 'Morning Moon'!"

I squeaked out, "For the McGarrigle Sisters."

—

Of course, I hacked and stumbled and didn't care. I wasn't nervous. I was emotional. The next chord found itself at the moment the last one was forgotten. A funny pilot once said – and I don't like my pilots funny – "Don't worry, folks, I'll get you there on time, I'll drive it like I stole it."

Lightfoot was watching me intently, his chin a foot away from my fretboard. I didn't know whether to laugh or cry. I didn't care if I made mistakes. I couldn't stop smiling, I was feeling grand and silly at once. To want to stop and want never to stop. It was almost too much.

The song ended.

"That was a wrestling match. That was a wrestling match, Gord," I said as I sat back down between Lightfoot and Laurie. "But I won."

"The energy persisted," he said.

"That's my thing."

—

Just then, there seemed to be a pause in the show, long enough for me to sweep everything from the table: "I love being here with you. It's making me crazy," I blurted like a kid. "And you too, Laurie." Everybody was laughing and then I went for it.

"Can I read an email?" I said, to everyone and no one. "My brother sent me this email when he found out I was doing this." I could sense people were unsure. I was unsure. But I plunged into it:

> Dan Doran and I were driving in his mom's red Pinto when we heard "The Wreck of the Edmund Fitzgerald" for the first time. Without saying a word, Dan turned the car around and headed for Highway 33 so we could drive along the lake listening to the song.
>
> Neither one of us spoke during the entire song – we made it all the way to Bath before it ended. We looked at each other and Dan said, "Holy Fuck. What was that?"
>
> We picked up some beer, smoked some grass, and drove the backroads willing the song to come back on the radio for another listen.

"My brother said that," I added.

Big laughs and applause from the audience, who I think felt like I did. I pointed at Gord Lightfoot and said over the roar, "That's you, man!" Then I pointed to my seat. "And I'm here!"

I expressed my best feelings, at that moment, perfectly. We were off.

—

After that, Lightfoot talked about "Edmund Fitzgerald," but more about the song technically. Maybe he wasn't so into talking about the song's connectivity. Maybe not so into talking about it with me. My elevator went to the basement.

"Nobody would believe that that would become a popular song," Gord said, turning on a stairway light for me.

He gave me props for playing solo, without accompaniment. "Naked."

I thanked him with a quick joke – "And made even harder with these boxing gloves I'm wearing!" The audience laughed. Self-effacing to the point of obsequiousness for the people out there in radio land, the people driving home from the cottage. Doing the dishes in Vancouver.

—

After a while, we switched gears, and the topic turned to Canadian identity in song, about creating identity through music.

Lightfoot talked about the "Canadian Railroad Trilogy" in detail. He was commissioned to write the song. "We need a song like this," he was told.

"You go to the library, get the book, and it gives you ideas," Gord explained. "I used a form that was used by Bob Gibson, a major figure in the folk revival. It came out as a song, six minutes and fifteen seconds." I marvelled at how and why he remembered this.

"I played it for the guy at his desk," he continued. "The guy, Bob Jarvis, said, 'Gordon, I am impressed.' Next thing, I'm in studio with a twenty-one-piece orchestra and Rob Collier, the arranger. I was standing out there with my twelve-string."

Lightfoot explained: "I could've said no. I could've said, 'I can't write something specifically, never worked on commission, I can't do it.' That's what came out of it – probably as Canadian a song as you can find."

Then, as if suddenly aware that he was venturing into something misty, Gord settled back into more familiar ground. "[The song] goes over well, easy to handle, consistent . . ."

———

Laurie changed the subject: "Songwriting, it's a Job?"

Lightfoot said, "You wanna handle that one, Gord?"

Going after something like word association, I rapid-fired a question at Gordon: "Writer's block?"

"Alcohol," he deadpanned, fast as a whip. This just about lifted the roof.

"Superstition?" I continued.

"I won't play on Friday the 13th," Lightfoot said.

———

I wanted to get back to the subject of writer's block, and more specifically the solutions to the problem. As a way to perhaps entice Lightfoot to offer up one of his tricks for me and song-writers everywhere, I broke into what I meant by the question.

I've for a long time felt that problems with a song or any piece of writing that has bogged down or stopped can usually be solved by some practical solution, not a mystical one. The answer lies not in lighting incense nor in the Gauloise-strewn garret. The answer lies in the practical thing, the thing in front of you; the word or the line you feel is untouchable, sacred, the ringer, the ace, the right bauer, the whole-rest-of-the-song-can-go-to-hell-but-this-line-stays line.

Yeah. Take that line and, at least for the time being, set it aside. This act of bravery, or at least willingness, can and usually does open the song up and get things flowing again. The song may not end up being about what you thought it was about – but then they rarely are. You must serve the song, and that sometimes – no, often – means ruthlessness is required.

Or at least that's how I meant it to go. On the night, I fucked this explanation up and said, "Take that *song* and set it aside," thus confusing and killing the point I was trying to make, and missing the chance to extract Lightfoot's secret. He just politely smiled, his head nodding "Okay," his eyes saying, "Huh?"

———

Laurie came to the rescue: "How has your songwriting changed over the years?"

Lightfoot said he didn't write anything worthy until Dylan showed up, how it was then possible to be real with your writing. He added, not surprisingly, that Dylan was a big influence.

Laurie liked the phrase "to be real with your writing" and repeated it and asked if that resonated with me.

I was caught in another of the many reveries the night created, and felt like I was answering a different question than the one that was asked. "Of course," I said, "Gord is the master of austerity and economy . . ."

Lightfoot continued, talking about how you just write more, develop content, make it better. He then returned to a constant theme of his, one that seems to help explain for him a lot about why he does it.

"The contract," he said. "You sign a contract. You have to do it, pay bills," and then he added, more emphatically, "you *have* to do it."

———

Laurie decided to open things up and take questions from the audience. She read one from someone who wrote, "Which of your songs are you most proud of writing?"

Lightfoot said what everyone was thinking: "Oh, I guess, 'If You Could Read My Mind.'" What followed was that special kind of applause that only happens when a great expectation is met.

The question reared on me and with nowhere to go but funny, I said, "'Jumpin' Jack Flash'?" Stupid. I tried to comply: "Probably with the boys in The Hip, 'Bobcaygeon.'" The crowd let me feel their approval; they had an expectation for me, too.

Laurie asked, "Do you have a different approach now, as opposed to when you began?"

"It's changing all the time," I said, "and I'm glad for that. I do it every day. And yet, I can never remember the approach I used the last time. I was thinking about the line in *101 Dalmatians* – 'First the lyric, dear, then the mel-o-dy.' And I've tried that, too. I've learned on the job. I started playing guitar at twenty, which is old age for guitar players. I've been playing catch-up ever since, but I just try and make a friend of the thing."

Laurie asked Lightfoot if there was anything with more relevance today than when he first wrote it.

Lightfoot struggle-struggle-struggled, and squeezed out a smiling "Perhaps."

Laurie turned to me: "Gord, whose shoes would you be in if you could?"

With nothing at the ready, I looked down and saw, delivered to me by the conversation elves, the most spectacular pair of shoes I'd maybe ever seen on the feet of the man beside me. "Lightfoot's shoes," I said, pointing. The place exploded. Everyone in the room had noticed them from the get-go, white, shiny, beautiful. "They're really something," I said. "I really want those shoes."

———

Laurie turned to me, "You're going to play a song that is brand new . . . a song that no one's heard before, right?" She wanted me to explain the song's origins.

I explained how my friend Mike Clattenburg had emailed me from Newfoundland to tell me about this new TV thing he was working on. He said that he thought I'd like it, that it was "hard Canadian and dope." The term "hard Canadian" stuck with me. It doesn't happen often, but I know it when it does. I thought to myself at that moment, "I'm gonna write a song called, 'The Hard Canadian.'" I think I did most of the heavy lifting in a hotel room in Detroit looking out my window at the Ambassador Bridge way off in the distance. I had decided to play the song on this night for Gord Lightfoot, probably to show the one thing I might have going for myself: potential.

Though I knew the title would be a red flag for some, I was pretty confident in my story. I knew I hadn't written a jingle, or something to play at a nationalistic perfection celebration. One wants to avoid playing one's music for those with nothing to learn. And perhaps this is who the Hard Canadian is: someone no one believes. I get it all from Saul Bellow. He wrote in *Humboldt's Gift* that John Keats apparently once said to Robbie Burns that "a luxurious imagination deadens its delicacy in vulgarity and in the attainable." I liked that very much.

I played the song and ended with a mistake. Over the cheering crowd I replayed the ending. "Here's the ending – I know you like endings, Gord."

———

I realized again that I wasn't making mistakes because I was nervous. It was because I was emotional. I was cruising along playing this brand-new song for one of the lights of my songwriting life, playing well, reasonably deftly, remembering everything, and it was really working, and then I remember thinking about the magnitude of it all. I started tearing up inside. I was having a real emotional response. Besides, I defy anyone to run the fretboard properly with Gordon Lightfoot perched on the end of your headstock.

———

Laurie asked Lightfoot to play a song, and he went over to the microphone and began "If You Could Read My Mind."

This is a song I will always want to hear. It always stops me in my tracks wherever I am: a grocery store line-up, at the dentist's office. It's this line that does it, of course: "I never thought I could act this way and I've got to say that I just don't get it / I don't know where we went wrong but the feeling's gone and I just can't get it back."

That is the line. A songwriter can live three lifetimes and never come up with a line as simple and effective as that, as sad and vulnerable and genuine, as plain-spoken and heartbreaking and respectful. This is the dream we all dream – as long as we don't have to live it.

What followed was an almost frightening applause, people saying thank you for this song of a thousand listens.

After Gordon had finished and was making his way over to where we were sitting, Laurie said, "Now Gordon's rolling his eyes. What's wrong?"

Gordon replied, a little exasperated, "It's all in a day's work. That is the easiest song to sing. I play it over and over again and it always feels good. It always feels good. You know it's going to go over like gangbusters. I really work hard on communication with my audience. I try and get the stuff that feels good to me and good to them."

Laurie turned to me: "What about you, Gord? I remember interviewing you once and you said to me the same thing, about the audience – that you'd rip your heart out and hand it to them if you could."

Silence.

I paused for dramatic effect and let those words settle in the audience. I swallowed for effect and then tentatively offered the only thing I could. "Ahem . . . I did?"

Laurie, smiling: "You did."

"I mean, maybe my kidney . . ." The audience laughed and I got out of answering for another crazy pronouncement of my youth. But then, realizing that the question was asked for a reason, I dug deeper.

"You don't want to leave anything on the stage," I explained. "You want to throw it all out there, get it off the stage, the kick drum, all of it. Coming up in Kingston, I love the blues – Kingston was a blues town." I referenced the once-legendary Prince George Hotel, where all the guys came through. "I snuck in when I was sixteen and saw John Lee Hooker," I recalled.

"That's where [The Hip] came together," I continued. "Blues is about a work ethic. Otis Redding, James Brown, Howling Wolf, Johnny Cash (well, he's not really the blues – but then he is, too), guys that really sweat, guys that give it all. I just give it all. 'Cause I don't know how to do anything else."

"Happy Birthday, Gord!" a woman from above, in the balcony, interjected in a sing-songy voice. "I know your birthday's coming up!" she added.

"Thanks, Mum," I responded. "You probably should know when it is."

———

Laurie then asked, "Can a song be too personal?" She said it twice.

Lightfoot thought about it, then said, "No, I don't think so." He talked about moments, the ones he'd like to forget, the experiences he cherishes. He admitted for all songwriters that our personal lives are woven into a lot of our songs. "My life has been actually quite complicated in that regard," he said. There was knowing laughter from the audience.

"Are there songs you don't like to sing anymore?" Laurie asked.

Gordon talked about when he used to sing "The Last Time I Saw Her": "I'd always think about my first wife – a very fine woman, classy Swedish lady," he explained. "We had two children together. She's gone now, she died three years ago." His voice trailed off a bit. "When I sing that song, I think about her and it's kind of sad." Silence. "But the show must go on." No knowing laughter this time.

Laurie broke the silence. "What about you, Gord? Are there songs that are too personal?"

I tore my stare away from Gordon's face. "'Fiddler's Green' is a song we just did for the Help Haiti Show," I said. "I just thought this song was the appropriate choice for that night. My

sister lost her second son, Charles, when he was a baby and –"
I was starting to crack. It's a very hard song to sing and nearly
impossible to talk about. I tried to pull out of it, remembering
to myself how when I was at Charles's funeral a relative came
up to me and said I should write a song about it. I switched
gears: "You get this a lot, like say you're at a Sunday gathering
and someone drops a tray of drinks and someone says, 'You
should write a song about that' – no, YOU should write a song
about that!"

I didn't get back to my story of Charles.

⸺

Gordon rescued me from a near-collapse and took things quickly
away. "You can write a song about anything," he said, talking
about the time he was holed up in a room with nothing to say
and a contract demanding that he come up with something, so
he wrote a song called "Walls."

"Let's hear another song from Mr. Downie," Laurie said.

I started to say what I had come there to say. "I don't know
if I'll get another opportunity to say this so I'm gonna say it right
now. When I might not get the chance, I like to do a just-in-case
hug. I'm not gonna hug you, Gord. I'm gonna say this thanks to
you. Until tonight I didn't know you except from the radio. I'm
the ten-year-old kid listening to 'Sundown' – that song was like a
secret from you to me, and it blew my mind that a song could be
a secret and so mysterious and so dangerous."

"It was a dangerous time," Gordon said with his impeccable timing.

"Exactly! Well, anyway," I pushed awkwardly forward. I
wasn't going to let even Gordon Lightfoot stand in the way of
what I wanted to say. I looked right at him. "From then until

today, I've looked to your austerity and your economy every time I put pen to paper." The audience went silent. I continued, "I must also thank your long-time members of your long-time band, because that's instructive to me, too." A huge and respectful applause arose, the kind that is only reserved for long-time bandmates. I was on top of the applause now, riding it. "I just gotta say thank you. You've been a great teacher, and I could never write enough songs to properly repay you or honour you. But I will try."

—

At this moment, to give gravity to my words, I did what I've always done: I tried to punctuate my point with a song. I dropped into "Bobcaygeon" on my old Martin gut-string. This guitar plays itself. "Bobcaygeon" is a simple song with a crazy detour in the middle. It begins with a man leaving the country in the morning to go to work in the city for the afternoon and evening, and then driving back to the country at sun-up, arriving at the same porch he left twenty-four hours earlier. The narrator is describing, the entire time, just what is happening. Little else. It is a song that unfolds chronologically, in real time. It uses simple, everyday language. The crazy detour goes like this: "That night in Toronto, with its checkerboard floors / riding on horseback keeping order restored / 'til the men they couldn't hang, stepped to the mic and sang / and their voices rang with that Aryan twang." That is the weird shift, the surprise. The singer, the narrator, is a cop.

I finished the song. I said thanks and waved to the good people.

Laurie said in a whisper, "It's so unusual not to be singing along. I had to be so quiet."

"It's restraint, right?" I said.

"That's a great song," Laurie said.

"Thanks," I said. "I'll pass it on to the boys."

———

Gordon stepped in, incredulous, almost. "To be able to use the name 'Bobcaygeon' in a song! I mean, it has to be done! Well done!" Everyone laughed.

"And 'constellation'!" I added.

Then Gordon said, "I like the way you say the word 'Canadian.' It's subtle. Like writing lyrics, everything has to match or roll smoothly."

I was thinking, *I love how Gordon says "like."*

"It's like making a bed, isn't it?" I offered.

"Paying the bills," Gordon added.

"Smooooothing it out." (A riff too far.)

———

Laurie set up Lightfoot's last song. "Gordon, your last song is 'Let It Ride.' Why?"

Gordon called it "a spunky little tune and fun to play." He mentioned that he is now, of course, aware that Randy Bachman did another song with the same title, and then added, "But I didn't know anything about that."

Gordon and Rick and Terry played "Let it Ride," from 1986's *East Of Midnight*. This song wants to be "Que sera, sera / whatever will be will be." But it isn't. "I will not stand corrected, I have not harmed anyone," the lyrics say. "I just let it ride. Ride ride ride." But there's a sense that the singer of this song can't just let it ride: "Even when I'm sleeping, I can't seem to unwind,

I just let it ride. . . . The mouths I feed are many and they all say
'thanks a lot.' They just let it ride. . . . Proud of every tear I've
ever cried. Just let it ride."

It is a strange song. Many of Gord's songs are a little bit
strange. And I mean that in the best way. I once read John
Gardner's *On Becoming A Novelist,* where he describes the "quality of strangeness." Gardner quotes Coleridge: "There can be no
great art without a certain strangeness." Gardner explains,
"There come moments in every great novel when we are startled
by some development that is at once perfectly fitting and completely unexpected." To my ear, many of Gordon's songs have
this, which, more than any other thing, might explain their wide
appeal. If you listen closely, Gordon's songs seem to be saying
more than one thing at once. They are paradoxes. They can't be
pinned down. They are deceptive, alluring, contradictory. They
are not what they seem.

———

There was one question that kept wanting me to ask it, that kept
tapping its stick incessantly on the rink of my mind, demanding
the puck. It was a question for Gord Lightfoot, sitting insistent
on my mind's shoulder: *To forgive yourself in public?*

To forgive ourselves in public? Is that why we write songs, Gordon?

That line is one of the only reasons to watch the 2009 Rob
Marshall film, *Nine.* I wrote it down. It's what his long-suffering
wife, played by Marion Cotillard, says across a screening room
to Daniel Day Lewis's old and vainglorious Italian film director,
Guido Contini, just before she leaves him for good. "You think
to create is just to forgive yourself in public."

On this night with Gord Lightfoot, I wanted to ask this
question: *Is this why we create?* I wanted to, but the time never

seemed right. Like it would be unfair to make him – or anybody – try and answer that. It was a question I was never able to ease into. There was one moment, maybe, when I might have, but then it was gone. I marvelled, at the time, at my maturity, how far I'd come.

Besides, I guess we were having too good a time. I just let it ride.

MIGUEL SYJUCO

Visitation

It's just after dawn when we set out for the prison. The streets of our gated subdivision are shiny with last night's rain. We pass quiet houses. Maids and gardeners are out front sweeping driveways, clipping hedges, disembarking from the backs of pickup trucks just returned from market. A houseboy, plastic bag at the ready, watches a fat Dalmatian take a shit on the sidewalk. At the guardhouse, cars line up to exit the subdivision and enter the city. We inch forward. From where we are, the sun catches, glitters, in the glass shards cemented atop the high walls that are there to keep people out. The guards salute as we pass.

Today is the day I'm visiting Paco in prison. In the more than eleven years that he's been there, I've never been to see him. I don't know what's kept me. Or maybe I do, but have up to now been too ashamed to admit it.

My brother Marty and his American boyfriend, Michael, ride in the car with me; for years now they've been working on a documentary film on Paco. They've told me: no wearing flip-flops or shorts, because that's what the inmates wear, and in case there's an incident the guards need to be able to distinguish visitors from prisoners. On the way, we pass by a service centre to buy thirty pieces of KFC chicken for Paco and his boys. Michael and Marty go to Starbucks next door for coffees. I watch the café's security guard, his blue uniform freshly pressed, fight boredom by washing the storefront windows. He squeegees left to right, carefully twisting downwards, then right to left, to avoid making streaks. Beside him, amongst the umbrellas in an umbrella rack, rests his shotgun.

The New Bilibid Prison is a walled complex on the outskirts of Manila. From where we are, the sun strikes the razor wire fixed atop the high walls to keep people in. We drive through an open gate guarded by a huge sculpture of the previous warden's face. It's fifteen feet high and ten feet wide, a poor man's Mount Rushmore rendered in concrete and cheap paint. The face is a garish white, the lips an unnatural red, the hair and eyebrows inexplicably green. Entering the grounds of the Bilibid prison is misleading – there are rolling lawns amidst the encroaching tropical foliage, and humble but well-kept houses line the roads. "These are where the guards live," Michael tells me, "and the wives of the inmates." We pass a small lake surrounded by manicured lawns fenced in by rusted barbed wire. A statue of a blindfolded Lady Justice stands in the middle of the lake.

The prison, built by the Americans during their colonial occupation of the Philippines, looks like a castle barbican. Marty drops us off at the entrance; he has filming to do outside. In the entry room, female clerks sit at windowed counters like those at a movie theatre box office. "On weekends," Michael says, "this place is packed." We line up and deposit our IDs with the women. High on a wall, a sign lists prohibited items. Among them: cameras; yeast (so prisoners can't brew moonshine); knives (of course); pail handles (so they can't fashion shivs); petroleum jelly; tin foil (used to make pipes for crystal meth). Tickets in hand, we stand in another line to enter.

Michael explains to me how the place is run. The prison walls contain twelve thousand prisoners in the space of four hectares. It is a makeshift city run by gangs, like something out of a bad sci-fi movie – *Escape from New York* comes to mind. Within, provincial and cultural affiliations have their own groupings – the Cebuano gang, the Ilonggo gang, the Tagalog gang, the Chinese Mafia, the political prisoners, the Manila City Jail gang, the Muslim gang. The few times guards venture in, it's to conduct periodic raids. The rest of the time, the prisoners rule themselves, meting out their own justice, their own order. Two things keep visitors like us from being harmed: protection by the gang of the inmate being visited, and the fact that harming a visitor would result in across-the-board suspension of visiting privileges. "It's what all the prisoners live for," Michael tells me, seeing worry in my face. "They need visitors for contact, for money, for the businesses the prisoners run on the inside. If a prisoner disrespected a visitor, then visiting privileges would be suspended. The other prisoners would probably kill the inmate who was responsible for that."

At the end of the queue, guards frisk us, search our bags, dig deep into the KFC bucket to make sure nothing's hidden. On a desk is a box filled with confiscated items, none of them evidently dangerous. A radio plays a power ballad, Jon Bon Jovi singing: "Ohhh, we're halfway there! Ohhaohh, living on a prayer. Take my hand, we'll make it I swear . . ." We walk down a dim corridor, its humming fluorescent bulbs giving off more sound than light. Three guards open a metal door and sunlight pours in, blinding us. Michael and I step through, blinking. The sound of the guards locking the door echoes behind us.

In a huge open square, scores of inmates mill about. They watch us brazenly. We catch sight of Paco amidst a group of a dozen men, his fair mestizo skin making him stand out. One of Paco's boys holds an umbrella for him, shading him from the already searing sun. A couple of men open two umbrellas for us.

Others take our bags. They surround us like bodyguards. Paco and I hug. I've known him since we were thirteen years old.

"Long time no see," he says. "The last time I saw you was . . . when was that? I think in the lobby of my apartment building."

"Yeah," I reply, "my girlfriend used to live there." I'd seen Paco that evening, in Manila, while the kidnapping, rape, and murder were being done in Cebu, on a different island six hundred kilometres to the south. I'd been waiting for the elevator, to go up to visit my girl; when the doors opened, Paco came out, on his way to meet some twenty of his friends and classmates at a bar down the road. They took pictures of their celebration. When Paco returned to the apartment building later that evening, his name was written in the logbook by the security guard on duty. The following morning, Paco came over to our house to do his laundry. He could not have been in Cebu that night, where the judge ruled that he was, committing what the judge decided he had committed. That was a decade ago.

Paco and his men lead us down a broad avenue. "We have to take this road," Paco says. "This is the allied side." I ask him what that means. "The other side belongs to our enemy gang. The Happy-Go-Luckies." A play on the word *Ilonggo*; the rival gang is from Iloilo province. "If we go to that side, we have to bring a lot of boys. For protection." A long building runs along our right. To our left, against a high wall, are stalls selling fruit, fish, chunks of meat, food prepared by the inmates' wives who live outside. Here and there are makeshift bench presses made of modified office chairs and thin mattresses; the barbells are made from coffee or powdered milk tins that have been filled with cement and set on either side of a metal bar. Paco points to that long building to our right. "That's death row," he says. "I was

there for two years before the President abolished the death penalty." I asked him what death row was like. "It was okay," he
says. "I was friends with its mayor, so he took care of me."

It's surreal walking beside Paco. He was nineteen when I
last saw him, before he was sent to jail. He's now thirty-one. He
doesn't seem much different than when I knew him. Maybe because he's been a constant part of my life. When I visit my
brother and sister-in-law in San Francisco for Christmas, Paco
calls his sis to wish her season's greetings. Throughout the year,
she keeps us abreast of what's new with her brother. Marty and
Michael's documentary-in-progress ensures I've seen Paco age
through the years, heard his voice, so much so that it feels as if
only weeks have passed – not a decade – since I spent time with
him. When I knew him in high school, he was a cocksure
toughie. Now, he's quiet and humble. He speaks matter-of-factly,
with nothing more to prove to himself.

We pass more stalls selling more goods – sachets of shampoo, cigarettes, candy, pirated DVDs. One stall rents out VHS tapes.
The whole place reminds me of the way Cebu was when it was
a small community, before it became a big city, before Paco and
I grew up and left for Manila in the early nineties. I tell Paco this.
"Yeah," he says, "the only thing we can't get here is ice. Or ice
cream. That's why when Michael brings ice cream in a cooler,
it's real special." Paco smiles at Michael. From a small house
nearby we hear someone singing karaoke. The guy sings: ". . .
And more, much more than this, I did it my way." His voice is
quite terrible.

"Last count," Paco says, "that song's killed one hundred
forty-seven people." I wait for Paco to elaborate. When he
doesn't, I ask him: "Is it because if someone sings it badly, he's
killed?" I'm joking, awkwardly. "No," he says. "That's the most
popular song in here. What happens is that during evenings in

the karaoke bar, people are drinking, people are drunk, and one
table requests that song. But the next table has also requested
that song. So when the song comes up, they fight over it. And
sometimes someone gets killed."

We enter the building of Paco's gang. His is the *Batang Cebu*
gang (Children of Cebu). Michael explains to me that in the past
few years the building has changed – before, the corridors were
crumbling concrete, pitch dark, and you had to feel your way forward to get to Paco's room. Now, the walls are painted, the floor
is tiled, there is a huge fish tank in the entry corridor. Colourful
fish swim peacefully. In the main hallway are framed paintings of
beach landscapes, of pastoral scenes. The place looks like a low-
priced island resort with aspirations to bigger things. At the end
of the hall, we enter a room and climb a staircase so steep it's
almost a ladder. At the top is Paco's small area. The place is
homey – in the decade that he's been here, he's somehow managed to collect items to make himself relatively comfortable. Two
electric fans rotate and circulate the air. There is a small kitchen,
complete with a chef's knife and tongs hanging on the wall, and
a round dining table with a plastic floral tablecloth. The living
room has a wooden armchair and a cot. On one wall is a console
with a TV, an old stereo, shelves made of mismatched wood on
which are rows of pirated DVDs, and framed pictures of Paco's
family. A souvenir street sign hangs on the wall, declaring PARKING
FOR SPANIARDS ONLY. Set inside one wall are two fish tanks, each
containing big tropical fish lit up by fish-tank lights. Against the
wall near the living room is a window that would overlook the
corridor from where we came, but Paco has closed it off and
painted a convincing trompe l'oeil: a sun-drenched farm scene
with a mango tree, dusty fields, and rolling hills in the distance
beneath a cumulus-clouded sky; there are even venetian blinds
over the window, to complete its verisimilitude.

Browsing his shelves, I ask Paco what sort of DVDs he likes to watch. "*Sopranos*," he says. "*Prison Break*." He says this without any irony whatsoever.

"What do you want to drink?" Paco says. A cellular phone, plugged into the wall and charging by the TV, rings. He answers it and talks to whoever it is, casually, as if they could be making plans for a night on the town that evening. Paco hangs up. We sit at the dining table and he pushes us to eat the fried chicken we brought. I try to beg off, because we bought it for him and his friends. Paco shouts out and a man scurries into the room, takes our drink order, and leaves. We sit and shoot the shit at the dining table; meanwhile, men come in and out, unpacking the chicken, preparing rice. One of them retrieves from its hiding place the video camera that Marty and Michael had arranged to be brought in months ago (by paying a priest to smuggle it). Michael accepts it and excitedly scans the footage that Paco and his friends have taken so far. The scene in the room is little different from that of a *merienda* in many traditional Filipino households, only for this afternoon snack the maids aren't maids; they're inmates in orange "Bilibid Maximum Security Prison" T-shirts. They call Paco "Boss."

As we wait for lunch, Paco tells me about his moonshine business. The liquor here used to be horrible but he'd asked his sister to send him a brewing book. She'd bought him an *A to Z of Wine and Spirit Making*. Paco had studied it and learned to make superior moonshine using a pressure cooker and copper tubing. The moonshine he and his gang made became the best in Bilibid and sold well. "So well we were able to fix this building, fix my room, and buy weapons," Paco says. I ask him how they never got caught brewing. "We only brew at night. During the day, we take it all apart. If anyone looks, they'll only find a pressure cooker, which we keep rice in. The copper tubing is hidden in the plumbing." Paco shouts out and another of his men scurries in. Paco tells him to get me a sample of the moonshine. The guy leaves and returns with some in a shot glass. I try it. It's smooth and delicious.

When one of the men comes in to set the table, a dog sneaks into the room. Paco smiles. "Hello, Kaldereta!" he says, petting it on the head. (*Kaldereta* is a Filipino stew, usually made with goat, but sometimes with dog.) Paco shows me the dog's right ear. A tattoo says "*Batang Cebu*." "You see," Paco says, "he's just like all of us in the gang. We have our tattoos on our right arm. He has it on his right ear."

Paco tells me about his crew, about how he's now an adviser – one of the top members of the gang – and how they wanted him to be the mayor of the gang but he refused. Too much responsibility, too much danger, he explains. He tells me about the Happy-Gos and how they used to be allies, "but one day, they invited our leader to their place to talk, and they cut his head off." I ask him why they did that. "As a sign of distrust," he says.

His men serve lunch. Because Paco knows Michael is vegetarian, there is a dish of stir-fried vegetables. A tall man enters the room and takes a seat with me, Paco, and Michael. This is Elmer, the mayor of the *Batang Cebu* gang. He is quiet and polite. When he speaks, his English is perfect, his views sharp and worldly. (I find out later he's in prison for massive tax fraud; he was an accountant. Here, in prison, he's respected for his education.) We eat some of the chicken with the rice. The sodas we drink are somehow ice cold. We talk about Paco's case, all the theories about why he was framed. While taking apart a chicken wing with his fingers, he tells us how over the years his anger has swelled and festered, turning his mind to dark thoughts. He recounts how a friend suggested paying 30,000 pesos ($600) to rub out the police informant who had fingered Paco in court, and how he considered it briefly. "But what good would it do?" Paco says. "And besides, maybe one day the truth will come out of him." He picks up a drumstick and bites into it. He tells us about a list he made of all the people who testified falsely against him – the crooked informants, the mercenary lawyers. With so much time on his hands, Paco slowly compiled their names and addresses, then the names of their wives and children. When that list was complete, he made a vow that when he got out he'd kill them one by one. Paco doesn't make eye contact with us and instead shakes his head as he speaks. Hearing him say such things is so out of character for the Paco that we know. He says that it was on his birthday a few years ago when he was struck by an epiphany. He took the list from its hiding place and tore it up. He says that despite his anger, he knew "it was just wrong," that he refused to "enter prison innocent and come out of it a killer." And how ever since that birthday, things have been better in his head and in his heart.

Later, when Paco goes to the bathroom, Michael tells me about the times they'd be sitting there talking and some kids would enter the room to ask Paco for their allowance. Or how some inmate would ask for Paco's time for advice on a certain problem. Michael explains that Paco is respected by his community, and together with Elmer the mayor they take care of their gang members. They make sure they all have enough to eat, that they receive protection from other gangs, that they get medicine when they are sick, that their kids get allowances for food and books to go to school. Elmer nods in agreement.

When Paco returns, I ask to use the bathroom, and he leads me through a door I'd not noticed. It's his bedroom, with a well-made bed and an electric fan at its foot. Along one wall is a massage table, one of those with a hole for your face when you're on your stomach. Paco's bathroom is clean. He proudly shows me his shower – a large plastic canister on a shelf high on a wall, with a massage showerhead cut in half and puttied into a hole in the canister. "Look," he points, "it's near the ceiling. During the day the roof gets very hot, so in the morning I take a nice warm shower."

Later, lunch finished, Elmer excuses himself. He says he has to attend to some business. Paco, Michael, and I adjourn to the living room to chat. Paco shouts out, and men come in and clear the plates. They take their turn at the table and eat the leftovers. I sit with Michael and Paco on the couch in front of the TV. We smoke cigarettes.

Paco tells us more stories. About the recent riots because of overcrowding. About the Justice Minister whose rule used to be draconian, but who is now old and weak after a kidney transplant. About how the minister got a kidney from his own driver. About how Paco had one day entered a friend's room, only to find the friend hung by the neck, clearly dead. And how he quickly took the chair that had been used to reach the noose "because it was made of good wood."

Paco tells us about the last gang war, when their rivals wanted to take over their building. A fierce fight ensued and he'd had to send his men to dig up their guns and ammo, only to discover the firearms no longer worked. They'd become moist in the ground during the rainy season. He tells us how the *Batang Cebu* won anyway, "because we had more knives. Even though they had lots of soap." Soap? "Yeah," he says. "You get the soap, especially the old one, because it becomes hard like a stone, and you wrap a shirt around it, like a whip. And if you hit someone over the head maybe ten or twelve times, they'll be dead." And how do the gangs get their knives? "They get an electric fan and remove the plastic fan blades and attach sandpaper to the motor. With it, they can sharpen anything." How are these things hidden from the guards? "Because the guards usually conduct surprise raids at night, what happens is all the old inmates sleep in the hallways in the evenings. When the guards come, their way is blocked by sleeping people. Many of the inmates are in their sixties and seventies, and they wake up and stand slowly. So by the time the guards get past them and come down the corridor, they've lost the element of surprise."

Paco and I talk about what he's going to do when he gets out. I tell him he should come to Montreal and I'll show him an amazing time. Michael says Paco should spend a year travelling the world. "No," Paco says, "I need to work right away. I need to start a new life as soon as I can."

Time passes quickly and soon we realize we have to go. Michael tells Paco that he and Marty are going to Cebu to get footage for their documentary. "Oh," Paco says, smiling, "I'll go with you guys. We'll go to the beach. Come pick me up tomorrow morning." Paco laughs, Michael and I smile. I ask Paco if one day he'd like me to write his story, so that we can tell the world the truth. He smiles and nods as if he has been waiting a long time for me to offer.

Outside the *Batang Cebu* building, Paco squints in the sunlight. He bids us goodbye and sends us away with a dozen of his guys, who hold umbrellas over our heads. I turn around and see Paco going back into the building. As we walk, Michael tells me that Paco never really leaves that area because it's dangerous. He'd only come to pick us up that morning because I was a special guest. Surrounded by his men, we take another route on the way out. There are more stalls selling goods, handicrafts made by the prisoners – ships inside rum bottles, frog statues made of toothpicks. We pass an area – a "Kiddie Park," the sign says – with concrete slides and a swing set and flowers, for the inmates' kids when they visit. We pass chapels and prayer rooms – Seventh Day Adventists, Baptists, Catholics, Muslims. We pass the Maximum Tennis Club, built by a congressman who was convicted of raping an eleven-year-old girl, but who, despite his sentence, ran for congress from his jail cell and won, because his family holds their district tightly. We pass tattooed men on the side of the road having their hair cut by other tattooed men. We pass the Inmates' Diabetic Association and the Islamic League of Bilibid. I turn around and realize that our escort has swelled into some twenty-five gang members. Michael tells me this is nothing – on the times he's visited and asked to see the other areas of the rival gang, Paco brought him in "with the entire *Batang Cebu* gang, probably about fifty or sixty of them. I felt like I was at the front of a parade, with all the rival gangs watching us carefully."

Our escorts bring us back to the square by the entrance. We join the hordes of women and children leaving husbands and fathers behind. Inching our way into the bottleneck to get out, I watch a young mother carrying her infant. She's holding above them a colourful umbrella. It gets caught in the rusty barbed wire that lines the top of the narrow passageway. The fabric tears when she pulls at it. We step through the metal doorway and back into the visitors' room to retrieve our IDs. Bon Jovi is on the radio again, singing another sad song.

ABOUT THE CONTRIBUTORS

—

Caroline Forbes

DIANA ATHILL was born in 1917. She worked for the BBC throughout the Second World War and then helped André Deutsch establish the publishing company that bore his name. Athill's distinguished career as an editor is the subject of her acclaimed memoir *Stet*, which is published by Granta Books, as are five other volumes of memoirs – *Instead of a Letter*, *After a Funeral*, *Yesterday Morning*, *Make Believe*, and *Somewhere Towards the End* – and a novel, *Don't Look at Me Like That*. *Somewhere Towards the End* won the 2008 Costa Book Award and the 2009 National Book Critics Circle Award.

TASH AW's debut novel, *The Harmony Silk Factory*, was the winner of the Whitbread Award and a Commonwealth Writers' Prize for Best First Novel, as well as being longlisted for the Man Booker Prize and the Guardian First Book Award. His second novel, *Map of the Invisible World*, set in post-Independence Malaysia and Indonesia, was published to critical acclaim in 2009 and has been translated into twenty-three languages. Malaysian by birth, he now lives in London, England.

David Franco

DAVID BEZMOZGIS is a writer and film-maker. His first book, *Natasha and Other Stories*, was published in 2004. His novel, *The Free World*, will be published in 2011. In 2009, David's feature film, *Victoria Day*, premiered at the Sundance Film Festival. David's work has appeared in numerous publications including *The New Yorker*, *Harper's*, *Zoetrope: All-Story*, and *The Walrus*, and his stories have twice been included in *The Best American Short Stories* (2005, 2006). David has been a Guggenheim Fellow, a MacDowell Fellow, a Sundance Institute Screenwriting Fellow, and a Dorothy and Lewis B. Cullman Fellow at the New York Public Library. Born in Riga, Latvia, David immigrated to Toronto with his parents in 1980.

JARED BLAND is the managing editor of *The Walrus*, and sits on the board of directors of PEN Canada. His writing has appeared in *The Walrus*, the *Globe and Mail*, and *Toronto Life*. He lives in Toronto.

Bryan McBurney

JOSEPH BOYDEN is a Canadian with Irish, Scottish, and Métis roots. His first novel, *Three Day Road*, won the Rogers Writers' Trust Fiction Prize and the McNally Robinson Aboriginal Book of the Year Award, and was shortlisted for the Governor General's Award for Fiction. His second novel, *Through Black Spruce*, won the Scotiabank Giller Prize. He is also the author of *Born with a Tooth*, a collection of stories that was shortlisted for the Upper Canada Writer's Craft Award. He divides his time between Northern Ontario and Louisiana, where he teaches writing at the University of New Orleans.

DAVID CHARIANDY lives in Vancouver and teaches at Simon Fraser University. His first novel, *Soucouyant* (Arsenal Pulp Press, 2007), won the *ForeWord Magazine* Book of the Year Award for Literary Fiction. *Soucouyant* was also shortlisted for the Governor General's Award, the Commonwealth Writers' Prize for Best First Book (Canada and the Caribbean), the Amazon.ca/ Books in Canada First Novel Award, the Ethel Wilson Fiction Prize, the Toronto Book Award, and the ReLit Award, as well as longlisted for the Scotiabank Giller Prize and the International IMPAC Dublin Award. His second novel, *Brother*, is forthcoming from McClelland & Stewart.

DENISE CHONG's contribution draws from the story she tells in her most recent book, *Egg on Mao*, on the life and fate of Lu Decheng, and an exploration of the "human" side of human rights in China. As with her other books, Chong, a two-time Governor General's Award finalist, once again takes a deeply personal story and places it in its complex social context. Her previous book, *The Girl in the Picture*, was groundbreaking in its depiction of life in war-torn South Vietnam. Her family memoir, *The Concubine's Children*, a longtime national bestseller, was one of the first book-length narratives of life in the early Chinatowns of Canada.

KAREN CONNELLY is the author of nine books of fiction, non-fiction, and poetry. Her latest book, the memoir *Burmese Lessons: A Love Story*, has received critical acclaim in the U.S. and Canada, and was shortlisted for the B.C. National Award for Canadian Non-Fiction, Canada's most prestigious literary non-fiction prize. She is also the author of *The Lizard Cage*, an internationally acclaimed novel about Burma/Myanmar, which won Britain's Orange Broadband Prize for New Novelists in 2007. She has won the Governor General's Award for Non-Fiction as well as the Pat Lowther Award for poetry. Her forthcoming book, *oh canada crack my heart*, is her first new collection of poems in more than a decade. She lives in Toronto with her family and also has a home in Greece.

ALAIN DE BOTTON is the author of eleven books, including *How Proust Can Change Your Life*, *Essays in Love*, *The Architecture of Happiness*, *The Pleasures and Sorrows of Work*, and, most recently, *A Week at the Airport*. He lives in London, England, where he started two organizations, The School of Life (www.theschooloflife.com) and Living Architecture (www.living-architecture.co.uk).

Born in Dublin in 1969, **EMMA DONOGHUE** did a PhD in English at Cambridge before settling in 1998 in London, Ontario, where she lives with her partner and two small children. She writes literary history as well as drama for the stage and radio, but is best known for her fiction, which includes historical titles

(*Slammerkin*, *Life Mask*, *The Woman Who Gave Birth to Rabbits*, and the Scotiabank Giller Prize–longlisted *The Sealed Letter*) as well as contemporary ones (*Stirfry*, *Hood*, *Touchy Subjects*, *Landing*, and *Room*, a finalist for the Man Booker Prize and winner of the Rogers Writers' Trust Fiction Prize). For more information, visit www.emmadonoghue.com.

Gordon Hawkins

The Canadian writer **GORD DOWNIE** (1964–) worked as a paper boy, a pizza maker, and in a tobacco field, and has written a book of poetry and hundreds of songs with and without the Tragically Hip, including his latest solo release, *The Grand Bounce* (2010). Downie has been acclaimed as "one of the coolest customers in Canadian music, right up there with Leonard Cohen and Neil Young" (*Toronto Star*) and "a totally sweet genius" (*Scott Pilgrim Vs. the World*).

Will Ormshaw

MARINA ENDICOTT's novel *Good to a Fault* was a finalist for the 2008 Scotiabank Giller Prize, won the Commonwealth Writers' Prize for Best Book (Canada and the Caribbean), and was a Canada Reads selection in 2010. Her new novel, *The Belle Auroras*, about a sister act touring the prairies in early vaudeville, is forthcoming from Doubleday. In 1992 she went with Peter Ormshaw, a poet and journalist, on his first posting with the RCMP to Mayerthorpe, Alberta. Her long poem "The Policeman's Wife, Some Letters," about the murder of four Mounties in Mayerthorpe in 2005, was shortlisted for the CBC Literary Awards.

STACEY MAY FOWLES is a writer and magazine professional living in Toronto. Her first novel, *Be Good*, was published by Tightrope Books in 2007. In 2008, she released an illustrated novel, *Fear of Fighting*, and staged a theatrical adaptation of it with Nightwood Theatre. It was later selected as a *National Post* "Canada Also Reads" pick for 2010. Her writing has appeared in various magazines and journals, and has been widely anthologized. Most recently, she co-edited the anthology *She's Shameless: Women write about growing up, rocking out and fighting back.*

RAWI HAGE was born in Beirut and lived through nine years of the Lebanese civil war. He is a writer and a visual artist. His first novel, *De Niro's Game*, was a finalist for numerous prestigious national and international awards, and won the International IMPAC Dublin Literary Award. His second novel, *Cockroach*, won the Quebec Writers' Federation Award and was shortlisted for numerous prestigious awards including the Scotiabank Giller Prize, the Governor General's Award, the Rogers Writers' Trust Fiction Prize, and the Prix des libraires du Québec. Rawi Hage resides in Montreal, Canada.

ELIZABETH HAY's new novel will be published in 2011. Her previous book, *Late Nights on Air*, won the Scotiabank Giller Prize. She lives in Ottawa.

Mary Haggard

STEVEN HEIGHTON's most recent books are the novel *Every Lost Country* and a poetry collection, *Patient Frame*. His previous novel, *Afterlands*, has been published in six countries, was a *New York Times Book Review* Editors' Choice, was chosen a "Best of the Year" title by ten publications in Canada, the U.S., and the U.K., and has been optioned for film. His poems and stories have appeared in the *London Review of Books*, *Poetry*, *Tin House*, *The Walrus*, *Europe*, *Poetry London*, *Brick*, and *Best English Stories*. Heighton has won a number of awards – including four National Magazine Award golds – and has been shortlisted for the Governor General's Award, the Trillium Book Award, a Pushcart Prize, and Britain's W.H. Smith Award. He lives in Kingston, Ontario.

Mia Cunningham

LEE HENDERSON is the author of the award-winning short story collection *The Broken Record Technique* and the novel *The Man Game*, which was shortlisted for the Rogers Writers' Trust Fiction Prize and the Ethel Wilson Fiction Prize. He is a contributing editor to the art magazines *Border Crossings* and *Contemporary*, and he has published fiction and art criticism in numerous periodicals. His fiction has twice been featured in the *Journey Prize Stories*. He lives in Vancouver.

Beth Gwinn

GUY GAVRIEL KAY is the author of eleven novels, most recently *Under Heaven*, and a book of poetry. Kay was principal writer and associate producer for the CBC-TV series *The Scales of Justice*. He has written reviews and social and political commentary for the

National Post, the *Globe and Mail*, and *The Guardian*. Translations of his fiction exceed twenty languages, and Kay has appeared at literary events around the world. He has been shortlisted for and won numerous literary awards and is the recipient of the International Goliardos Prize for his contributions to the literature of the fantastic.

Claire McNamee

MARK KINGWELL is a professor of philosophy at the University of Toronto and a contributing editor of *Harper's Magazine*. He is the author of fifteen books of political and cultural theory, including the national bestsellers *Better Living* (1998), *The World We Want* (2000), *Concrete Reveries* (2008), and *Glenn Gould* (2009). In order to secure financing for their continued indulgence, he has also written about his various enthusiasms, including fly fishing, baseball, idling, and cocktails. He is currently at work on a book about twenty-first-century democracy.

MARTHA KUWEE KUMSA is a member of PEN Canada's Writers in Exile Network. She worked as a journalist in Ethiopia but fled her country after a decade of imprisonment and torture. She was released from prison and came to Canada with the help of PEN and Amnesty International. She is now a Canadian citizen and teaches social work at Wilfrid Laurier University.

Phillip Chin

ANNABEL LYON is the author of *The Golden Mean*, a novel about the friendship between the ancient philosopher Aristotle and his student, the young Alexander the Great. *The Golden Mean* was shortlisted for the Scotiabank Giller Prize, the Governor General's Award for Fiction, the Commonwealth Writers' Prize (Canada and the Caribbean), the Amazon.ca First Novel Award, and the Ethel Wilson Fiction Prize. It won the Rogers Writers' Trust Fiction Prize.

David Kaufman

LINDEN MacINTYRE was born in St. Lawrence, Newfoundland, and grew up in Cape Breton; his father was an itinerant hardrock miner, his mother a school teacher. He has worked as a journalist since 1964 in newspapers, radio, and television. Since 1990, he has been co-host of the investigative television program *the fifth estate* on CBC Television. He is author of four books: *The Long Stretch* (1999), a novel; *Who Killed Ty Conn* (with Theresa Burke, 2000); *Causeway: A Passage From Innocence* (2006), a memoir; and the novel *The Bishop's Man*, the 2009 winner of the Scotiabank Giller Prize for fiction.

Jason Bomers

PASHA MALLA is the author of *The Withdrawal Method* and *All our grandfathers are ghosts*. His first novel, *People Park*, will be released in 2012.

Barbara Stoneham

LISA MOORE is the author of two collections of short stories, *Open* and *Degrees of Nakedness*, and two novels, *Alligator* and *February*. *February* was longlisted for the Man Booker Prize, *Alligator* and *Open* were shortlisted for the Giller Prize, and *Alligator* won the Commonwealth Writers' Prize (Canada and the Caribbean). Lisa also selected and introduced *The Penguin Anthology of Short Stories by Canadian Women* and, with Dede Crane, she co-edited an anthology of birth stories called *Great Expectations: 24 True Stories about Birth by Canadian Writers*.

Derek Shapton

ALICE MUNRO is the author of fourteen books of short fiction, most recently *The View from Castle Rock* and *Too Much Happiness*. During her distinguished career, she has been the recipient of numerous prizes, including the Man Booker International Prize, the W.H. Smith Book Award, the National Book Critics Circle Award, the PEN/Malamud Award, the Rea Award for the Short Story, and the Giller Prize. Her stories have appeared in such publications as *The New Yorker*, *The Atlantic Monthly*, *Saturday Night*, and *The Paris Review*. Alice Munro divides her time between Clinton, Ontario, and Comox, British Columbia.

John Morstad

STEPHANIE NOLEN is the South Asia correspondent for the *Globe and Mail*. She has reported from more than forty countries, and is a five-time NNA winner and a three-time winner of the Amnesty International Media Award. Her journalism has been cited for "creative brilliance, humanitarian compassion, personal courage, and the relentless pursuit of truth." Her bestselling book *28 Stories of AIDS in Africa* has been published in fourteen countries and six languages; it won the 2007 PEN "Courage" Award and was nominated for the 2007 Governor General's Award for Non-Fiction. She is also the author of *Promised the Moon: The Untold Story of the First Women in the Space Race* (2002) and *Shakespeare's Face* (2002). She lives in New Delhi with her partner and two young children.

HEATHER O'NEILL is the author of the bestselling novel *Lullabies for Little Criminals*, which won the CBC's Canada Reads competition in 2007 and the Hugh MacLennan Prize for Fiction. It was also shortlisted for the Governor General's Award and the Orange Prize, among other prizes. She lives in Montreal.

RICHARD POPLAK is an award-winning journalist and author, most recently, of *The Sheikh's Batmobile: In Pursuit of American Pop Culture in the Muslim World* and of the journalistic graphic novel *Kenk: A Graphic Portrait*. He is currently collaborating on a book comparing waning white colonialism in Africa with the growing Chinese advance on that continent. He splits his time between Toronto and Johannesburg.

SETH is the cartoonist behind the annual comic book *Palookaville*. His novels, which have been translated into eight languages, include *It's a Good Life if You Don't Weaken*, *Wimbledon Green*, *George Sprott (1894–1975)*, and *Clyde Fans Book One*. He is the designer of the twenty-five-volume series *The Complete Peanuts* and the ongoing John Stanley Library. His work often appears inside and on the cover of such publications as *The New Yorker* and *The Walrus*. Seth lives alongside a railroad bridge in Guelph, Ontario, with his wife and two cats.

MOEZ SURANI's poetry and short fiction have appeared internationally in journals and anthologies. He is the author of the poetry collection *Reticent Bodies*.

MIGUEL SYJUCO is a writer from Manila currently living in Montreal. His multi-award-winning, internationally bestselling novel, *Ilustrado*, was recently published in Canada by Hamish Hamilton.

Rawi Hage

MADELEINE THIEN is the author of two books of fiction. Her most recent book, *Certainty*, was a finalist for the Kiriyama Prize and won the Amazon.ca/Books in Canada First Novel Award. In 2010, she received the Ovid Festival Prize, awarded each year to an international writer of promise. Her work has been published around the world and translated into sixteen languages. A new novel, *Dogs at the Perimeter*, is forthcoming in 2011.

MICHAEL WINTER is the author of *The Big Why*, which was shortlisted for the Trillium Book Award and the Thomas Raddall Atlantic Fiction Award, and longlisted for the International IMPAC Dublin Literary Award; *The Architects Are Here*, which was longlisted for the Scotiabank Giller Prize; and, most recently, *The Death of Donna Whalen*, which was shortlisted for the Rogers Writers' Trust Fiction Prize. His first novel, *This All Happened*, won the Winterset Award. He is also the recipient of The Writers' Trust Notable Author Award. He divides his time between Toronto and St. John's.

EDITOR'S ACKNOWLEDGEMENTS

—

As always with a project such as this, there are many people whose contributions should be recognized. To begin, I must thank the writers who gamely contributed and patiently worked with me during the editorial process. Some I'd never met, and some I knew quite well; it was a pleasure and an honour to work with each of them. Special thanks must also go to Seth, for his brilliant cover design and illustration. I'm deeply grateful for the support of McClelland & Stewart, especially the generosity and encouragement of Doug Pepper, the leadership and inspiration of Ellen Seligman, and the enthusiasm and editorial expertise of Anita Chong.

I'm indebted to my fellow PEN Canada board members, as well as PEN staff Katie Addleman and Brendan de Caires, whose hard work on behalf of the organization makes a difference every day. At *The Walrus*, I benefit from the guidance and wisdom of John Macfarlane and Shelley Ambrose. Their gracious flexibility allowed me to take on this project in addition to my work at the magazine. I must also thank Paul Kim, Brian Morgan, and Jennifer Spinner in the magazine's art department, whose friendship and design expertise were essential to this project. My debt to my mother, Susan Clarke, my father, Geoffrey Bland,

and my brother, Nick Bland, is immeasurable. I'm fortunate, as well, to have the support of a group of friends, colleagues, and collaborators who led the way and urged me on: Pamela Capraru, Stephen Dalrymple, Stacey May Fowles, Dave Gilbert, Rick and Linda Groen, Adam Hammond, Lee Henderson, Steven Heighton, Amy Hick, Jen Hick, Richard Poplak, Sean Rogers, and Fern Silverman. Special thanks to Nick Mount, who taught me how to think.

And finally, this is for Danielle Groen, for all things, always.

J.B.

ACKNOWLEDGEMENTS

—

Sincere thanks to Random House of Canada and Friesens Corporation for their generous support of this anthology.

—

The lines on page 34 are from an unpublished poem by Peter Ormshaw. Reprinted courtesy of the author.

The lines by Jan Zwicky on page 37 are from her poem "Passing Sangudo," from *Songs for Relinquishing the Earth* by Jan Zwicky, published by Brick Books. Copyright © 1998 by Jan Zwicky. Reprinted with permission of the author and the publisher.

"How," from Marina Endicott's long poem "The Policeman's Wife, Some Letters," is reprinted courtesy of the author.

The quotation from Plutarch on page 59 is from *Plutarch's Lives: Complete and Unabridged in One Volume*, Dryden translation, revised by Arthur Hugh Clough, published by Modern Library.

The quotations from Roméo Dallaire on pages 59–60 are from *Shake Hands With the Devil: The Failure of Humanity in Rwanda* by Roméo Dallaire, published by Vintage Canada.

The quotations from Wade Davis on pages 136–37 are from *The Wayfinders: Why Ancient Wisdom Matters in the Modern World* by Wade Davis, published by House of Anansi Press as part of the CBC Massey Lectures series.

The quotations from Mark Abley on pages 138–39 are from *Spoken Here: Travels Among Threatened Languages*, published by Vintage Canada.

The excerpts on pages 140–41 are from *Language Death* by David Crystal, published by Cambridge University Press.

The quotations from *The Sorrow of War* by Bao Ninh are from the English-language edition edited by Frank Palmos, translated from the Vietnamese by Phan Thanh Hao, and published by Vintage Books.

The quotation from Hannah Arendt on page 154 is from *Men in Dark Times*, published by Mariner Books.

The excerpt on pages 160–61 is from *The Death of Donna Whalen* by Michael Winter, published by Hamish Hamilton Canada.

The review by Jonathan Lear referenced on pages 165–66 was of *On Bullshit* by Harry G. Frankfurt. Lear's review appeared in the March 25, 2005 issue of *The New Republic*.

The quotation from Marianne Hirsch on pages 192–93 is from "The Generation of Postmemory," published in *Poetics Today* 29, no.1 (2008): 104.

ACKNOWLEDGEMENTS

The satirical piece described on page 221 is "Subject: Our Marketing Plan" by Ellis Weiner, which appeared in the "Shouts & Murmurs" section of the October 19, 2009 issue of *The New Yorker*.

The extracts from the correspondence between Gustave Flaubert and Ivan Turgenev on pages 242–43 are from *Flaubert and Turgenev, A Friendship in Letters: The Complete Correspondence*, edited and translated by Barbara Beaumont, published by W.W. Norton & Co, Inc.

The lyrics by Gordon Lightfoot on page 269 are from "Rainy Day People" © 1975 by Gordon Lightfoot, from the album *Cold on the Shoulder*; on page 278, "If You Could Read My Mind" © 1969 by Gordon Lightfoot, from the album *If You Could Read My Mind*; and on pages 283–84, "Let It Ride" © 1986 by Gordon Lightfoot, from the album *East Of Midnight*.

The lyrics from "Bobcaygeon" on page 282 appear courtesy of Gord Downie. From the album *Phantom Power*. Lyrics by Gord Downie. Music by the Tragically Hip. Copyright © Little Smoke Music.

The lyric on page 288 is from Bon Jovi's "Livin' on a Prayer," from the album *Slippery When Wet*. Written by Jon Bon Jovi and Richie Sambora with Desmond Child.

MEMBERSHIP IN PEN CANADA

PEN Canada is a non-profit, non-partisan literary organization that fights censorship, promotes international exchange and understanding, and works to defend freedom of expression at home and abroad, and on behalf of writers whose voices have been silenced.

Membership in PEN Canada is open to everyone. There are three categories of membership: writer members, associate members, and associate student members. Criteria for the category of writer member are set out on PEN Canada's website (www.pencanada.ca). All other members are termed associate members. For writer members and associate members, the annual fee is $75/year; for associate student members, $25/year. All members have the same rights with one exception: only writer members may vote at the Annual General Meeting.

Benefits of PEN Canada Membership

All members receive:
- A charitable receipt for the full amount of membership fees or donation
- Acknowledgement in PEN Canada's Annual Report
- Eligibility for all PEN Canada members – writer members and associate members – for insurance – health, auto and home – through the Writers' Coalition of Canada
- Notice of our annual general meeting
- Notice of all PEN Canada events
- A monthly e-lert of news and upcoming campaigns and events

- A quarterly member e-newsletter
- The Annual Report
- Opportunities to serve on PEN Canada's committees
- Opportunities to participate in Rapid Action Network appeals

How to Support PEN

We urge every reader of this book to think seriously about joining Ten for PEN: a new monthly giving program and a simple way to make a real difference and help advance PEN's vital work against censorship and on behalf of persecuted writers and freedom of expression at home and abroad. Ten for PEN is an easier, more convenient, more effective way to start or renew your membership. By giving only $10 a month through this method of sustained support, you will avoid receiving annual membership renewal reminders and you will help reduce PEN's administrative costs.

For current members we urge you to convert your annual membership to Ten for PEN today.

Please call us or email us to indicate your wish to join, or to get more information. Thank you so much for your support of PEN Canada.

PEN Canada
24 Ryerson Avenue, Suite 301
Toronto, ON M5T 2P3
Phone: (416) 703-8448 Fax: (416) 703-3870
email: queries@pencanada.ca
www.pencanada.ca